ORIGEN AND THE EMERGENCE OF DIVINE SIMPLICITY BEFORE NICAEA

ORIGEN AND THE EMERGENCE OF DIVINE SIMPLICITY BEFORE NICAEA

PUI HIM IP

Foreword by Rowan Williams

University of Notre Dame Press

Notre Dame, Indiana

Notre Dame, Indiana 46556
undpress.nd.edu

Published in the United States of America

Paperback edition published in 2024

Library of Congress Control Number: 2022935752

ISBN: 978-0-268-20361-0 (Hardback)
ISBN: 978-0-268-20362-7 (Paperback)
ISBN: 978-0-268-20363-4 (WebPDF)
ISBN: 978-0-268-20360-3 (Epub)

For Natasha

CONTENTS

FOREWORD

Analysing how the earliest Christian writers set out to define and refine their concepts is an exercise that has been repeatedly reworked over the past two centuries. The once popular model of a Babylonian captivity imposed on the simple gospel by "Hellenistic" habits of mind has almost entirely disappeared from serious scholarship. A growing sophistication in our understanding of what happened to Greek philosophy in the first centuries of the Christian era prompted some more careful study of how the themes and vocabulary of that philosophy were digested and adapted, often in startlingly innovative ways, by Christian thinkers. The notion that patristic theologians, Greek and Latin alike, were either derivative or inept readers of philosophical texts has been very properly challenged, and the intellectual respectability and interest of Christian variations on their themes has been brought out (we might think here of Richard Sorabji's work on cosmology, for example).

But the present study, by one of the most promising theological scholars of his generation, takes this a stage further. When we encounter a discussion in patristic literature of a topic we might categorize as metaphysical, we should beware of rushing to the conclusion that it is merely a Christian contribution to an ongoing philosophical debate. Patristic theologians undertake the labor of conceptual clarification with two main and related aims in mind: to provide a toolkit for reading the authoritative text of Scripture and to do so in such a way as to make sure that Scripture is read in a way congruent with the basic logic of how the infinite God must be spoken of if we are to avoid idolatrous and trivializing accounts of divine life and agency. Faced with a treatment of some apparently philosophical problem, we need to ask, "Exactly what *exegetical* pitfalls is this meant to help us avoid?" And because speaking nonidolatrously of God is fundamental to our spiritual well-being, we need equally to be alert to what specific ethical and spiritual temptations have to be circumvented and what turns of phrase give unacceptable room to such temptations.

This book offers an exemplary close reading of language about divine "simplicity"—the metaphysical assumption that the divine life cannot involve any sort of plurality or divisibility. That this is in some tension with claims about Trinitarian doctrine is a familiar issue, and there have been some sound studies of how this is dealt with in the post-Nicene period. But when pre-Nicene writers discuss divine simplicity, they have in mind a set of errors that must be avoided, hermeneutical dead ends that need to be ruled out—and ruled out not only because of conceptual incoherence but because of their effect on the coherence of the life of prayer and discipleship. As Pui Him Ip shows, Trinitarian language is itself, in the thought of the greatest of pre-Nicene thinkers, Origen of Alexandria, bound up with precisely this concern to provide a defensible way through some of the complications around simplicity and plurality. Unless we understand the very particular questions he is asking, we shall just repeat the mistakes of later Greek (and modern) theologians in writing off Origen's Trinitarian scheme as an unhappy and inconsistent mélange of proper theological reflection and dubious "Middle Platonic" tropes. The argument of these pages urges, among much else, a more imaginative and generous reading of the great Alexandrian without suggesting that post-Nicene theology needs rewriting.

This is a study of admirable clarity and freshness, raising very substantial questions around method in patristic studies, the history of our histories of early Christian thinking, and the range of constraints that shape an agreed Christian "grammar" for speaking of the God of Jesus Christ. It will surely be recognized as a really significant contribution to its subject, necessary reading for serious students both of patristics and of the wider history of Christian thought.

Rowan Williams
Cardiff, August 2021

ACKNOWLEDGEMENTS

No intellectual project comes to its fruition without the help of others. First and foremost, I am truly indebted to my doctoral supervisor, Rowan Williams, for seeing the potential of the project in the first place. As a supervisor and theological mentor, Rowan taught me how to pursue scholarship that combines philosophical rigor, historical sensitivity, and theological humility. His enduring support and encouragement kept me going in times of darkness. Gregory's description of his experience studying with Origen captures well my years in Cambridge learning the craft and discipline of theology under Rowan with fellow supervisees: Οὗτος παράδεισος ἀληθῶς τρυφῆς, αὕτη ἀληθὴς εὐφροσύνη καὶ τρυφή, ἥν ἐτρυφήσαμεν (*Paner.* 16. 184).

A special note of thanks must go to Christian Hengstermann and Isidoros Katsos, who organized the intensive Origen reading seminars in the Divinity Faculty at Cambridge during the 2016–17 academic year. These seminars provided the perfect laboratory for developing and experimenting with presenting the arguments in this book (always accompanied by earthly goods such as Coca-Cola, sweets, and pizzas). Christian and Isidoros: This book would not be possible without your friendship. My attention to Platonism (chapters 1 and 2) and the "metaphysical-ethical synthesis" (chapter 5) bear the marks of your intellect.

A great number of people have contributed to my research. Samuel Fernández introduced me to Antonio Orbe and Manlio Simonetti, whose works on the polemical context of Origen's Trinitarian theology inspired me to build the argument that now forms chapters 6 and 7. I must also thank Stephen Waers, whose expertise on Monarchianism has been a constant help. Stephen read through drafts of chapters 6 and 7 carefully, offering detailed comments and suggestions that saved me from many errors. In my first-year examination, Janet Soskice and Sarah Coakley pushed me to clarify the philosophical meaning of simplicity, a concern that inspired the early chapters. In the *viva*, Ian McFarland helped me pluck up the courage to confront the problems in the structure of the original dissertation. Lewis Ayres graciously offered support and advice at every stage of research despite not having any formal obligation to do so. I especially thank him for the suggestion that I include a chapter on Middle Platonism, which has improved the overall structure of the book. Conversations with Michel Réne Barnes, Andrew Radde-Gallwitz, and John Behr at the Colloquium on Divine Simplicity in 2015 at Wheaton College led to my decision to focus on ante-Nicene developments in the book. I thank George Kalantzis for kindly giving me the opportunity to attend the colloquium and Ryan and Jenni Clevenger for their hospitality during my stay.

This book would not have seen the light of day without the generous support of various institutions. A substantial portion of the manuscript was revised during 2018–19, while I was departmental lecturer in patristics at Oxford. I owe Carol Harrison, Graham Ward, and Brian Young for the opportunity to work on the initial revision of the manuscript in such an intellectually stimulating environment. A special note of thanks goes to Mark Edwards, who took time to answer my questions, comment on various drafts, and share his encyclopedic knowledge of patristic scholarship. His concern with holding doctrinal analysis together with rigorous historical scholarship modeled the way I seek to do historical theology in this project (see the introduction). Ilaria Ramelli offered invaluable comments during her stay at Christ Church when I was revising the Origen chapters. The final revisions were carried out during the 2019–20 academic year, when I started my current position at the Faraday Institute for Science and Religion. I am indebted to Robert White, Denis Alexander, Keith Fox, and Hugh Rollinson for offering me a stable environment back in Cambridge to complete the revisions.

As with any projects of this scale, this book would be impossible without the generous engagement and guidance of many people over the years. Johannes Hoff far-sightedly set me down the path toward patristics when I was immersed in modern Trinitarian theology. Ruth Görnandt explained the complexity of the critique of metaphysics in German Protestant theology. Hugh Burling, Jonathan Carter, Ryan Mullins, and David Torrance helped me appreciate contemporary philosophers' worries about divine simplicity. On patristics, over the years I have learned a great deal from Hans Boersma,

Alfons Fürst, Thomas Graumann, Theo Kobusch, Giulio Maspero, Xavier Morales, Joseph O'Leary, Marcin Podbielski, Richard Price, Giovanni Hermanin de Reichenfeld, Luke Steven, Jonathan Teubner, and Anna Zhykova. In Oxford I have valued interactions with the patristics graduate community, especially Nicole Chen, Joseph Hamilton, Harry Lines, Michael Murray, Jenny Rallens, John Whitty, and Andrew Wong. In Cambridge I have enjoyed stimulating conversations with Alex Abecina, Barnabas and Silvianne Aspray, Johannes Börjesson, Ragnar Misje-Bergem, Rozelle Bosch, Yin-An Chen, Daniel de Haan, Victor Emma-Adamah, Andrew Fellows, Sam Fornecker, Yong-Hua Ge, Ryan Haecker, Emily Kempson, Simone Kotva, Vika Lebzyak, Nathan Lyons, Philip McCosker, Philip Moller, Julian Perlmutter, Daniel Soars, Jon Thompson, Daniel Tolan, and Mohammad Saleh Zarepour. Philip Pattenden and Neil Wright were miracle workers who taught me Greek and Latin, respectively. To all of you, I am grateful for your kindness and generosity.

I am indebted to Stephen Little at the University of Notre Dame Press, who first approached me about this project. Stephen's enthusiasm, encouragement, and professional support have made the process of publication a truly enjoyable one. I thank Eli Bortz for bringing this project to completion after Stephen moved to a different role. Barnabas Aspray, Jordan Barrett, Christian Hengstermann, Jonathan Platter, Jonatan Simons, Mark S. Smith, and Stephen Waers commented on various drafts. Vito Limone and Sotiris Mitralexis generously reviewed Greek-related matters in the manuscript. Of course, all mistakes remain my sole responsibility.

Without love, every effort becomes futile, as St. Paul reminds us. It is difficult to know where to begin when it comes to my parents, Wallace Pun Ming Ip and Yvonne Yee Chu Yeung. Without their courageous decision to relocate the family from Hong Kong to England, I would never have written this book. I am grateful for the sacrifices they made over the years. My sister Winnie Wing Yin Ip has been a long-suffering and willing listener. Over the years, she has had to put up with my (not infrequent) incomprehensible attempts to explain academic theology to her. To my family: Thank you for your selfless love, which has sustained and nourished me over the years.

Above all, thank you, Natasha, my wife and friend. You have made all this possible. This book is literally and figuratively the fruit of the sacrifices you gifted me in the past ten years. We have learned to suffer together, laugh together, grow together, pray together, and persevere together. Your unwavering simplicity in your devotion to love has inspired and enabled my contemplation of the simplicity of God. This book is a testament to the power of the truth you held onto throughout these years: ἡ ἀγάπη οὐδέποτε πίπτει (1 Cor. 13:8). It is to you I dedicate this book.

Pui Him Ip
Cambridge, September 2021

NOTE TO THE READER

This note concerns how I have used the English words "God" and "god" throughout this book as well as the translations of Scripture I have used.

ON THE USE OF "GOD" VS. "god"

This book concerns how ancient (mostly Platonic) philosophers and early Chrisians understood the nature of divinity. Not all the authors examined in this book held a monotheistic theology. In light of this, I have used the capitalized term "God" whenever it is obvious that a supreme divine first principle was in view. This is obviously the case whenever I am discussing Judeo-Christian theologians (Philo of Alexandria, Irenaeus, Tertullian, and so on). But I have also used the capitalized "God" to speak of the "primal God" (ὁ πρῶτος θεός) in the Middle Platonist philosopher Alcinous. Even though I do not wish to imply that Alcinous was a monotheist, I think it justified to use the capitalized "God" in this case since Alcinous clearly identified the primal God as the highest simple first principle in his metaphysical system. I have lowercased all uses of "god" when discussing Plato, both when he speaks of "god" in the singular and when he uses the article since it is clear that whenever Plato is speaking of *theos* in *The Republic*, he is referring to one of the classical deities in ancient mythology. This convention follows from the fact that in this book I am not committed to interpreting Plato as proposing a monotheistic theology. For a similar reason, I have used the lowercase "god" when speaking of Epicurean and Stoic theology.

Origen poses an additional challenge as he clearly differentiated between *ho theos* with the definite article (= God the Father) and *theos* without the article (= all other deities who participate in *ho theos* for their divinity). I have consistently translated *ho theos* as "The God." Whenever Origen is speaking of the divine Logos and wisdom, Jesus Christ the Son of God, I have used the capitalized "God" whenever it makes sense to indicate that Origen differentiates the divinity of Jesus Christ from the divinity of those deified through participation in Jesus Christ (e.g., the Holy Spirit, angels, and the rest of humanity). But this convention breaks down whenever I am discussing Origen in places where he is attempting to accentuate the continuity between the divinity of Jesus Christ and the divinity of the rest of the gods (*theoi*, cf. Ps. 81:1 LXX). In these cases, I have used the lowercase "god" to refer to all *theoi* without the article since the ambiguity between when *theos* should be capitalized and when it should not is telling about Origen's own Trinitarian theology. He intentionally leaves this ambiguity in many places and uses other qualifiers instead to differentiate between Jesus Christ as *theos* and other beings (e.g., human beings, heavenly bodies, and so on) as *theoi*.

ON THE TRANSLATIONS OF SCRIPTURE USED

I have made use of existing English translations of primary sources whenever possible. When no existing English translation is available, I have suppled my own. Each English translation of Scripture is taken from the standard translation of the particular primary source discussed (e.g., in the case of Philo, Irenaeus, Hippolytus, Novatian, Tertullian, and Origen). This is because, very often, these authors put forward exegetical arguments that make sense only in the light of a particular version of Scripture (e.g., a Greek or Latin text of the Hebrew Bible, a variant reading of one manuscript, and so on). This explains why, whenever I cite Scripture in this book, I use the translations of the Scriptural citations contained in the primary sources rather than modern translations of the Bible.

ABBREVIATIONS

SERIES

ACW	Ancient Christian Writers
CCSL	Corpus Christianorum Series Latina
FoC	Fathers of the Church
GCS	Die griechischen christlichen Schriftsteller
LCL	Loeb Classical Library
LXX	Septuagint
PG	Patrologiae Cursus Completus, Series Graeca
SC	Sources chrétiennes

PRIMARY SOURCES

Full information for editions of primary sources can be found in the bibliography.

Apol. (Eunomius)	Eunomius of Cyzicus, *Apologia* (*Apology*)
Apol. (Pamphilus)	Pamphilus, *Apologia pro Origene* (*Apology for Origen*).
APrax.	Tertullian, *Adversus Praxean Liber* (*Against Praxeas*)
CAr.	Athanasius of Alexandria, *Orationes contra Arianos* (*Orations against the Arians*)
CCels.	Origen of Alexandria, *Contra Celsum* (*Against Celsus*)
Civ. Dei	Augustine of Hippo, *De civitate dei* (*The City of God*)

CM	Eusebius of Caesarea, *Contra Marcellum* (*Against Marcellus*)
CN	Hippolytus, *Contra Noetum* (*Against Noetus*)
ComEp	Origen of Alexandria, *Commentarii in Ephesios* (*Commentaries on Ephesians*)
ComJn	Origen of Alexandria, *Commetarii in Iohannem* (*Commentaries on John*)
ComMt	Origen of Alexandria, *Commentarii in Matthaeum* (*Commentaries on Matthew*)
ComRm	Origen of Alexandria, *Commentarii in Epistulam ad Romanos* (*Commentaries on the Epistle of Romans*)
ComTt	Origen of Alexandria, *Commentarius in Titum* (*Commentary on the Epistle of Titus*; see Pamphilus)
CRuf.	Jerome, *Contra Rufinum* (*Against Rufinus*)
DE	Eusebius of Caesarea, *Demonstratio evangelica* (*Demonstration of the Gospel*)
Decr.	Athanasius of Alexandria, *De decretis Nicaenae synodi* (*On the Decrees of Nicaea*)
Deus	Philo of Alexandria, *Quod Deus Sit Immutabilis* (*On the Unchangeability of God*)
Dial.	Justin Martyr, *Dialogus cum Tryphone* (*Dialogue with Trypho*)
DialHe	Origen of Alexandria, *Dialogue with Heraclides*
Did.	Alcinous, *Didaskalikos* (*The Handbook of Platonism*)
ET	Eusebius of Caesarea, *De ecclesiastica theologia* (*Ecclesiastical Theology*)
Eun. (Basil)	Basil of Caesarea, *Contra Eunomium* (*Against Eunomius*)
Eun. (Gregory)	Gregory of Nyssa, *Contra Eunomium II* (*Against Eunomius II*)
Gig.	Philo of Alexandria, *De Gigantibus* (*On the Giants*)
Haer.	Irenaeus of Lyons, *Adversus haereses* (*Against Heresies*)

HE	Eusebius of Caesarea, *Historia ecclesiastica* (*Ecclesiastical History*)
Hom1S	Origen of Alexandria, *Homilia in I. Sam.* (*Homily on 1 Samuel*)
HomEz	Origen of Alexandria, *Homiliae in Ezechielem* (*Homilies on Ezekiel*)
HomJe	Origen of Alexandria, *Homiliae in Ieremiam* (*Homilies on Jeremiah*)
HomLv	Origen of Alexandria, *Homiliae in Leviticum* (*Homilies on Leviticus*)
Leg. All.	Philo of Alexandria, *Legum Allegoriae* (*Allegories of the Laws*)
Met.	Aristotle, *Metaphysica* (*Metaphysics*)
Orat.	Tatian, *Oratio ad Graecos* (*Oration against the Greeks*)
Pan.	Epiphanius of Salamis, *Panarion*
Paner.	Gregory Thaumaturgus (?), *Oratio panegyrica in Origenem* (*The Panegyric to Origen*)
PArch	Origen of Alexandria, *Peri Archōn* (*On First Principles*)
Parm.	Plato, *Parmenides*
PEuch	Origen of Alexandria, *Peri Euchēs* (*On Prayer*)
Phae.	Plato, *Phaedo*
Phil.	Gregory Thaumaturgus, *Epistola ad Philagrium* (*To Philagrius*)
Philoc.	Origen of Alexandria, *Philocalia*
Phys.	Aristotle, *Physica* (*Physics*)
Ref.	(Pseudo-) Hippolytus, *Refutatio omnium haeresium* (*Against All Heresies*)
Rep.	Plato, *Republic*
SelGn	Origen of Alexandria, *Selecta in Genesim* (*Fragments on Genesis*)
Somn.	Philo of Alexandria, *De Somniis* (*On Dreams*)
Str.	Clement of Alexandria, *Stromata* (*Miscellaneous*)
Syn.	Athanasius of Alexandria, *De synodis* (*On the Councils of Ariminium and Seleucia*)

Tim.	Plato, *Timaeus*
Trin. (Augustine)	Augustine of Hippo, *De Trinitate* (*On the Trinity*)
Trin. (Hilary)	Hilary of Poitiers, *De Trinitate* (*On the Trinity*)
Trin. (Novatian)	Novatian of Rome, *De Trinitate* (*On the Trinity*)
Urk.	*Urkunden* (see under Collections of Multiple Authors in bibliography)

Introduction

In Search of Doctrinal History

God is simple, without parts and composition. For centuries, Christian theology spoke of the one God in terms of divine simplicity. Speaking of God as simple is not to discount the mystery of Father, Son, and Holy Spirit as one God; as St. Augustine famously put it, "And this Trinity is one; and none the less simple, because a Trinity."[1] But the doctrine of divine simplicity has received severe interrogation and criticism in modern theology. By ruling out multiplicity in God, is divine simplicity compatible with the scriptural depiction of God's diverse acts in the history of salvation? Furthermore, if God is simple, how is it possible to affirm with Augustine the proper distinctions between the Father, the Son, and the Holy Spirit? This book retrieves the intelligibility of divine simplicity by tracing the doctrine's historical emergence and developments before Nicaea. This focus derives from the underlying conviction that there is something distinctive and illuminating about ante-Nicene sources that have hitherto been neglected. For it is common today to approach divine simplicity either in medieval scholastic (primarily Aristotelian-Thomistic) or fourth-century "pro-Nicene" (especially Augustinian) terms because these formulations are often regarded as representative of "orthodoxy." My burden in this book is to show that ante-Nicene sources of divine simplicity, though they might be perceived as presenting a "pre-orthodox" understanding, actually better clarify why the doctrine was never considered incompatible with Trinitarian theology. For a close examination of these sources reveals why later patristic authors (1) did not regard divine simplicity as reducible to "modalism" and (2) frequently discussed divine simplicity in the context of the Son's generation from the Father. This book will chart this neglected history in order to substantiate the point that ante-Nicene developments help us make sense of why there was no awareness of conflict between divine simplicity and Trinitarian theology among early Christians.

The stress on the "ante-Nicene" in the title of this book reflects not only a delineation of scope but also a historiographical orientation. In tracing the life of the idea of divine simplicity before Nicaea, I intend to open a conversation about how we narrate the development of patristic Trinitarian theology. As will be evident in due course, the argument of this book calls into question how we describe the transition from ante-Nicene to fourth-century developments that led to the formation of "pro-Nicene" Trinitarian theology. One way to narrate this transition is to study ante-Nicene developments *retrospectively*, that is, to read the sources as anticipating later fourth-century developments. But instead of looking back at ante-Nicene developments through fourth-century spectacles, may we gain new insights by looking forward to the fourth century through ante-Nicene developments? In this book I analyze key ante-Nicene doctrinal episodes in their own contexts with the view of exploring an alternative, forward-looking (what I have called *prospective*) historiography, making sense of later fourth-century developments through the lens of doctrinal categories prominent in the late second and third centuries. The historiographical orientation underlying this book is that allowing ante-Nicene theological language to remain in the contexts of these categories before Nicaea promises to deepen our understanding of fourth-century developments. For we can gain insights into the meaning of later "orthodoxy" from considering the shift from the doctrinal landscape of the third century to the one found in the early fourth century. In the epilogue I shall spell out in greater detail how the recovery of divine simplicity as a principle for safeguarding *both* the unity and the distinction between Father and Son—one distinctive feature of the ante-Nicene "pre-orthodox" understanding uncovered in this book—offers a new lens through which to make sense of the emergence of rival visions of the Trinity after Origen.

THE CRISIS OF DIVINE SIMPLICITY IN MODERN THEOLOGY

The doctrine of divine simplicity has been the subject of intense debate in modern systematic and philosophical theology.[2] The problematization of the doctrine has its origin in the classics of modern Protestant systematic theology.[3] In this context, the doctrine has been understood as the basic idea that there are no distinctions in God. As early as Isaak August Dorner (1809–84), we already find the judgment that "all distinctions in God are expunged as objective existences" due to Augustine's doctrine of divine simplicity in *Trin.* VI.7.[4] If divine simplicity allows no internal distinctions in God, then everything in God is identical to everything else. Along this line, many consider divine simplicity as a notion of divine unity in which "all difference becomes swallowed up," as Dorner puts it.[5] The great German Protestant theologian Wolfhart Pannenberg (1928–2014), commenting on Augustine again, finds in the Bishop of Hippo's affirmation of divine simplicity an attempt to define the unity of the divine substance "in such a way as to rule out any idea of substantial distinction."[6] More recently, Robert Jenson (1930–2017) rehearses the same point that divine simplicity in Augustine expresses nothing but the view "that no sort of self-differentiation can really be true of him [i.e., God]."[7] Thus a consensus emerges from the classics of modern Protestant systematic theology: divine simplicity as found in classical Christian theology constitutes a purely metaphysical notion of the divine nature that rules out all distinctions in God.

Interpreted thus, divine simplicity seems to generate many grave theological conclusions. Most embarrassingly, the doctrine appears to be in conflict with the doctrine of the Trinity, as Dorner sums up well: "The contrast between . . . simplicity of the divine essence, which excludes all distinctions from God, and the doctrine of the Trinity, which it is still hoped to retain, needs simple mention."[8] If God is utterly simple, ruling out all distinctions in God, how could there be any distinctions between the Father, the Son, and the Holy Spirit? Pannenberg argues that Augustine was committed to divine simplicity "even at the cost of making the differentiation of the three persons in God an impenetrable secret."[9] What Pannenberg is hinting at is that Augustine's commitment to divine simplicity ultimately led to a lack of clarity regarding whether we can really speak of the three divine persons as *distinct*. In line with Pannenberg's judgment, Jenson argues that Augustine's theology fails to affirm the Trinitarian distinctions because of his commitment to divine simplicity: "Moreover, he [Augustine] did not notice that Nicaea asserts eventful differentiation in God. The reason he did not is apparent: . . . unquestioning commitment to the axiom of his antecedent Platonic theology, that God is metaphysically 'simple,' that no sort of self-differentiation can really be true of him."[10] For the giants of Protestant systematic theology, Augustine's statement in *Civ. Dei* XI.10 appears less as a profound proclamation of the mystery of the divine life and more as a sign of the problematic tension that had gone unnoticed. Modern philosophical theologians, like their systematic counterparts, also suspect that classical Trinitarian theology is ultimately unable to uphold the distinctions between the divine persons due to the commitment to divine simplicity and hence in danger of falling into the heretical view of "modalism."[11] This potential incompatibility between simplicity and Trinity has received a precise formulation from philosophers in recent years. They argue that divine simplicity leads to a *logical* incompatibility with upholding distinctions between divine persons.[12] If the lack of distinctions in God leads to various "identities" being posited, then we are left with the following logic:

1. All that is distinct in God must be identical to the same reality due to divine simplicity.
2. God the Father, the Son, and the Holy Spirit are distinct.
3. (a) The Father, the Son, and the Holy Spirit must be identical to each other, and (b) each divine person must be identical to the Godhead as a whole.

If this is correct, then it is difficult to see how divine simplicity would not simply dissolve the proper distinctions between the divine persons.[13] The sentiment underlying contemporary philosophical analyses is summed up well by G. C. Stead (1913–2008). On the basis of his pioneering work on the history of the doctrine, Stead concludes that the classical affirmation of divine simplicity seems to lead inevitably to an understanding of God that is "totally unrelated to the Trinity of Persons in which we believe it [divine simplicity] is deployed."[14]

DOCTRINAL HISTORY AS A MEDIUM FOR DOCTRINAL CLARIFICATION

The foregoing reception history illustrates the problematic status of divine simplicity in modern systematic and philosophical theology. This has divided contemporary scholarship into two camps, those wishing to defend the doctrine and those wishing to highlight the unpalatable theological and philosophical consequences following from the doctrine.[15] My starting point in this book is that the contemporary debate has been too reliant upon pure doctrinal analysis. Rigorous analysis of the language of simplicity no doubt yields fruitful metaphysical and theological insights. Yet doctrinal analysis alone can never entirely establish the intelligibility of certain points that have been woven into the fabric of classical Christian theology.[16] In a perceptive reading of John Henry Newman's *The Arians of the Fourth Century*, Rowan Williams remarks that for Newman, it is not possible to grasp the meaning of the Nicene Trinitarian doctrine simply by analyzing and expounding on the *Symbolum Nicaenum*, as in the tradition of Bishop Bull's *Defensio*.[17] Rather, the meaning of doctrine must be grasped in light of the history of theological concepts and vocabularies or, in Williams's terms, how doctrinal language forms an *ecology*—a complex web of theological terms and contexts that give meaning to one another.[18] Doctrinal history is thus "no less a necessary task for the theologian," for "a sound dogmatic theology depends on honest doctrinal history."[19] My argument in this book seeks to inject a similar impetus to the contemporary debate on divine simplicity by establishing that the doctrine has a history dating from *even before Nicaea* and this history is essential for a sound analysis of the doctrine that avoids distortion and oversimplification. My overarching claim is that developments of divine simplicity before Nicaea have resulted in a distinctive "doctrinal ecology" that grants intelligibility to the doctrine and its involvement in Trinitarian discourse in the first place.[20] It is by renarrating and reimagining the formative contexts surrounding divine simplicity that we can make sense of the intelligibility of the doctrine and its significance for Trinitarian reflections for Christian theology today. Only in this light, I argue, can analysis of divine simplicity proceed in a sure-footed way.

Two issues discussed in this book suffice to illustrate my point. First, as the above reception history has shown, modern discussions of divine simplicity have relied on a definition that seems to entail the deprivation of all multiplicity in God. Divine simplicity, understood as the absence of parts or composition in God, implies that multiple terms ("divine attributes") applied to God must be identical to each other (the "identity thesis"). This assumption makes some sense when one analyzes the concept of simplicity on its own. But this is ultimately an oversimplification when viewed in light of developments within the Platonic tradition. What cannot be gleaned simply from rigorous philosophical analyses apart from doctrinal history is that divine simplicity emerged in the patristic period carrying over the background of *The Republic* and the Platonic theory of forms. This background offers conceptual clarification on a couple of important points. First and foremost, it is the absence of *contrary* qualities in God that is affirmed by divine simplicity. Moreover, this insight on the definition of divine simplicity can be grasped only if one situates the doctrine in light of the Platonic concern with safeguarding God's goodness, the initial context in which the doctrine emerged in Book 2 of *The Republic*. The insistence on divine simplicity, then, is fundamentally bound up with what one might call the *ethical* simplicity of God—the sense in which God is pure goodness and self-consistent.[21] When interpreted this way, it will certainly be less difficult to imagine how divine simplicity could accommodate the plurality of acts, characteristics, and thoughts in God so long as these do not bring about internal conflicts within God that would render him untrustworthy.

The second example relates to the frequently rehearsed worry that divine simplicity seems to be making a claim that is logically equivalent to "modalism" and so cannot be compatible with Trinitarian theology.[22] For a philosopher like Hasker, it seems incomprehensible that a great mind such as Augustine would fail to see this elementary issue.[23] This perception is understandable when one operates with a methodology in which the meaning of doctrine is examined purely on the basis of logical analysis. However, such an approach leads to an oversimplistic account of the relationship between divine simplicity and Trinitarian theology. As I shall highlight in chapters 3–7, divine simplicity emerged as a central part of early Christian Trinitarian language (strictly speaking, Father-Son language) through specific ante-Nicene polemical contexts. An analysis that lacks sensitivity to these contexts would lead to a distorted picture. For divine simplicity could not possibly be identified with Monarchianism in the patristic period because the origin of the latter in the late second and early third centuries was mainly connected with the issue of *prosopological* exegesis, concerned primarily with identifying the number of speakers required to make sense of the Scriptural narrative.[24] Later patristic theologians identified and defined the Monarchian position primarily as the approach to interpret the narrative of Scripture that assumed only one divine "subject" acting and speaking, whereas divine simplicity was understood primarily as a "grammar of theology" that safeguards God from unworthy theological language that attributes self-inconsistencies or possibilities of dissolution to him. Hence there was no danger, in the minds of early Christian writers, of conflating divine simplicity with Monarchianism. This differentiation, though, is not available from the perspective of pure logical analysis apart from a *historical* account of Monarchianism and divine simplicity.

These examples illustrate the need of deeper engagements with the ante-Nicene developments charted in this book for advancing current debates on divine simplicity. My aim is not to replace doctrinal analysis by doctrinal history. Rather, I seek to highlight key aspects of how divine simplicity emerged before Nicaea that have hitherto been neglected and yet would be indispensable to strengthening the rigor of theological and philosophical engagements with the doctrine today. This book is my attempt to engage with issues arising from contemporary doctrinal analysis through the medium of doctrinal history. As such, I aspire for it to stand in the tradition represented by the works of Newman and Williams, taking the elucidation of the history of doctrine as a task that possesses a strictly *theological* contribution, namely, clarification of the meaning of doctrinal language.

THE PATRISTIC DOCTRINE OF DIVINE SIMPLICITY: *STATUS QUAESTIONIS*

This book both draws upon and moves beyond scholarship that has previously shaped the doctrinal history of divine simplicity. The origin and development of divine simplicity have been extensively investigated in light of the Greek philosophical tradition by the pioneering works of Stead and the magisterial survey presented in an article by Pannenberg.[25] The narratives offered by Stead and Pannenberg are animated by the claim that the doctrine of divine simplicity in early Christian thought was the legacy of the problems arising in Platonic-Aristotelian philosophy. As a result, both Stead and Pannenberg seek to narrate how the Christian doctrine of divine simplicity emerged as a series of attempts to wrestle with the legacy of Platonic-Aristotelian philosophy in the context of Christian theology. This classical approach to the doctrinal history of divine simplicity in light of the developments in Greek philosophy will not be abandoned in this book. Like Stead and Pannenberg, I am committed to the assumption that the emergence of divine simplicity in ante-Nicene Christian sources will not be intelligible apart from the developments in the Greek philosophical tradition. But I offer chapters 1 and 2 as an attempt to revise the picture offered by Stead and Pannenberg by rethinking the developments in light of *The Republic*. For Stead and Pannenberg, divine simplicity is a purely metaphysical doctrine that has little room for making sense of any multiplicity attributed to the Christian God, not least that necessary for any notion of a Triune God or divine freedom. However, as will be evident in chapters 1 and 2, my argument is that if Plato's discussion in *The Republic* is given a more central role and the developments of divine simplicity within Platonism read in light of it, one will be led to rather different conclusions. In particular, one will be forced to place a stronger emphasis on divine simplicity as an *ethical* idea, chiefly concerning God's perfect goodness, communicated through a sense of perfect self-consistency. In the present study, then, I in no way seek to minimize the role of developments in Greek philosophy in narrating the emergence of divine simplicity in early Christian thought. I seek rather to provide a more nuanced account of the philosophical developments that will in fact lead to a different interpretation of the significance of divine simplicity for ancient writers, including ante-Nicene theologians.

More recent scholarship has stressed the need to move on from the kind of analysis and narrative exemplified in the classical accounts of Stead and Pannenberg. By focusing so much on identifying divine simplicity as a remnant of non-Christian philosophical theology, these accounts offer very little about what actually motivated the early Christians to introduce divine simplicity into their discourse about God and, further, how they appropriated the idea for their own theological, polemical, and ecclesiastical agendas. Lewis Ayres and Andrew Radde-Gallwitz have advanced an alternative approach in which they seek to attend to how divine simplicity functions in early Christian sources.[26] They propose to pay much closer attention to the immediate contexts of the patristic sources in order to determine the role divine simplicity played in these contexts.[27] It is by determining the function of divine simplicity as a "grammatical rule"—a rule that regulates theological speech—that one can gain a fuller picture of the intelligibility of divine simplicity in early Christian thought. The result is a much richer doctrinal history of divine simplicity in the patristic period. It is my aim in this book to add to this emerging picture from Ayres and Radde-Gallwitz's work. The bulk of this book, chapters 3–7, follows this new approach by attending to divine simplicity's "grammatical" function in ante-Nicene sources. While Radde-Gallwitz has already spelled out how divine simplicity serves as a "grammatical rule" in the ante-Nicene period in relation to theological epistemology, this book offers a complementary narrative by further clarifying how divine simplicity also assumes a "grammatical" role in the context of ante-Nicene Trinitarian theology—specifically on the question of the Father-Son relation. This book will thus further fill out the picture painted by Ayres and Radde-Gallwitz on the patristic developments of divine simplicity.

Ayres and Radde-Gallwitz have successfully mapped out the way divine simplicity functions in the post-Nicene context in both anti- and pro-Nicene theological trajectories. But the narrative of this book will raise a significant issue that remains unaddressed by their works. This is the question concerning the transition from ante- to post-Nicene understandings of divine simplicity. As Ayres and Radde-Gallwitz note, there are divergent theological accounts of divine simplicity across the patristic period.[28] But, most notably in the fourth century, divergent accounts in turn led to radically incompatible theological visions of the Trinity. How are we to make sense of this puzzling phenomenon? While in this book I do not pretend to resolve this puzzle, the ante-Nicene developments set out in chapters 3–7 nonetheless are intended to offer fresh ideas to this end. The decisive insight is that before Nicaea, divine simplicity seems to have assumed two roles in relation to the Father-Son relation. It was possible for ante-Nicene theologians to utilize simplicity as a tool to frame both the distinction and the unity between the Father and the Son. In the epilogue, I shall return to how this observation might open up new possibilities for narrating the development of patristic Trinitarian theology in the fourth century.

NEITHER "NICENE" NOR "SUBORDINATIONIST": THE INTELLIGIBILITY OF ORIGEN'S TRINITARIAN THEOLOGY

Origen of Alexandria (c. 185–c. 253), arguably the most important Christian thinker before Nicaea, occupies a central place in my argument. This choice is intentional. Origen offers a unique vantage point for grasping the doctrinal ecology before Nicaea for three reasons. First, Origen offers the richest and most sophisticated presentation of divine simplicity in the ante-Nicene period, as we shall see in chapter 5. His understanding of the doctrine thoroughly integrates the Platonic developments mapped out in the early chapters of this book, in particular uncovering the intelligibility of the close connection between the ethical and metaphysical senses of simplicity. Hence Origen provides an excellent portrait of divine simplicity in ante-Nicene Christian thought, highlighting how philosophical ideas were interwoven with Scriptural exegesis on this theme. Second, Origen's works were explicitly engaged with the two most significant doctrinal contexts that shaped ante-Nicene Trinitarian thought: Valentinianism and Monarchianism, as will be evident in chapters 3 and 4. Given Origen's involvement in these disputes, his writings are especially illuminating for spelling out the unique role played by divine simplicity in the formation of Trinitarian reflections before Nicaea. And finally, Origen provides the most natural reference point for measuring the transition from ante-Nicene to Nicene and post-Nicene Trinitarian discourse. As Christoph Markschies has observed, Origen remains "the systematic point of departure for the severe Trinitarian conflicts of the fourth century."[29] This is because Origen sets out a discussion of all the key theological issues that in one way or another became controversial later on: the doctrine of three hypostases,[30] the unity of will between the Father and the Son,[31] the image of God Christology,[32] subordination,[33] eternal generation,[34] and *homoousios*.[35] As a result, focusing on Origen will enable this study to further facilitate comparisons between ante- and post-Nicene understandings of divine simplicity, especially in the context of Trinitarian theology. In light of these considerations, Origen provides an excellent focus for appreciating the ante-Nicene developments concerning divine simplicity and its role in the formation of early Christian Trinitarian discourse.

More than any other theologian in the ante-Nicene period, Origen invites retrospective analysis. This is partly inevitable due to the close proximity between Origen's thought and the central issues that consumed the fourth-century controversies.[36] However, this proximity is a double-edged sword, as it has far too often led to Origen being considered largely in relation to questions and categories that gained centrality only in the fourth century. In one of the most comprehensive studies of Origen's Trinitarian thought in recent years, Christoph Bruns argues that Origen has yet to reach "systematically coherent and conceptually unambiguous solution with regard to the ontological status of the Son as the divine Logos."[37] According to Bruns, these shortcomings were due to the theological immaturity of Origen's age, but overall, while there are inconsistencies and terminological uncertainties in Origen's Trinitarian theology, the great Alexandrian master's thinking corresponds in substance to the whole of what was to come in the Nicene teaching. Bruns concludes that Origen should be regarded as a forefather of the Nicene faith, as was first suggested by Athanasius (*Decr.* 27) and more recently by Ilaria Ramelli.[38] But as Mark Edwards aptly puts it: "A historian trained in any other discipline will want to know why Origen should be subjected to any judgement, even a charitable one, according to standards that were only defined a century after his death (if even then)?"[39] Such a retrospective perspective is found not only among scholars who wish to demonstrate Origen's continuity with later Trinitarian orthodoxy. For much has also been written on the claim that Origen's theology provides a kind of precursor to "Arianism."[40] Less often, though, is Origen's Trinitarian theology studied in light of his own ante-Nicene context.[41] Given that we know Origen himself articulated the key doctrinal boundaries between "orthodoxy" and "heresy" he was working with, it seems natural to approach Origen's Trinitarian thinking in light of his own contexts.[42] This approach characterizes my reading of Origen's Trinitarian theology in chapters 6 and 7. In these chapters I read Origen primarily in light of his third-century context. In doing so, I am committed to the claim that Origen's Trinitarian thought was perfectly *intelligible* within his own doctrinal context, providing that we interpret his theological language within the doctrinal ecology in which it belongs. I reconsider two main strands of Origen's thought—the distinction and unity between the Father and the Son—by contextualizing these ideas in relation to Monarchianism and the Valentinian account of emission. It is through such a reading of Origen that I proceed in this book to uncover the distinctive roles divine simplicity played in shaping Trinitarian reflections *before Nicaea.*

THE STRUCTURE OF THE ARGUMENT

In this book I set out to examine the origin of the doctrine of divine simplicity and how it first emerged as a major part of theological speech in early Christian reflections. I propose to do so by narrating the developments before Nicaea that played a crucial role in establishing the doctrine's prominence in early Christian theology, especially in the context of Trinitarian reflection. The book begins by laying the philosophical groundwork. Chapters 1 and 2 retrieve a richer philosophical understanding of divine simplicity, engaging with the developments within Platonism and tracing the roots of the idea in Plato's *Republic.* Though Aristotelian developments are clearly important, I focus on Platonism because viewing divine simplicity in light of *The Republic* and the Platonic theory of forms offers new clarity on one thorny issue that has puzzled contemporary philosophers and theologians, namely, the kind of multiplicity supposed to be absent in a simple God. My goal in the early chapters is thus to establish the lesser-known Platonic background for understanding the origin of divine simplicity in early Christian thought, complementing the heavy focus in recent discussions on the Aristotelian formulation of the doctrine found in Thomas Aquinas and the scholastics.

The rest of my narrative (chapters 3 to 7) charts the emergence of divine simplicity in early Christian theology. In chapters 3 and 4 my focus shifts to the significance of divine simplicity in ante-Nicene Trinitarian discourse. The burden of these chapters is to show that historically, divine simplicity was integral in shaping how early Christians approached speaking of the Father-Son relation, a crucial element in the formation of Trinitarian theology. Supposing that God is simple, what is the consequence for our understanding of the Father-Son relation emerging out of Scripture? Early Christian thought on this issue was clarified, as I shall argue, through responding to the ideas of Valentinian emission and Monarchian identification of Father and Son, respectively. What emerged from this engagement was a problematic that brought divine simplicity to bear on early Christian language of the Father-Son relation: can one maintain an anti-Monarchian distinction between Father and Son while holding onto an anti-Valentinian account of generation compatible with divine simplicity? As I shall argue, the possibility of going beyond the binary of Valentinian emission and Monarchian identification of Father and Son makes the search for a via media an intelligible option in the ante-Nicene period. This via media was most fully worked out by Origen.

In the final three chapters the narrative focus is on the figure of Origen. As a Christian philosopher, Origen drank deeply from the wells of Platonic philosophy.[43] It is therefore unsurprising that divine simplicity is a central idea in the Alexandrian's doctrine of God, thoroughly integrating the Platonic developments mapped out in chapters 1 and 2. But as a churchman and exegete, Origen was directly responding to the two doctrinal issues that shaped ante-Nicene Trinitarian thought charted in chapters 3 and 4, namely, Valentinian emissions and Monarchianism. Chapters 5–7 together therefore present how Origen's understanding of divine simplicity and the way this doctrine shapes his account of the Father-Son relation consummate the Platonic-philosophical and ante-Nicene doctrinal developments charted in the earlier chapters of the book.

CHAPTER 1

The *Locus Classicus* of Divine Simplicity

What does it mean for God to be simple? And why *must* God be simple? The reasoning underlying the patristic affirmation of divine simplicity is a puzzling one. G. C. Stead laments that while lengthy treatments have been written on the use of ἁπλοῦς—the Greek term for simplicity—to denote a moral virtue, little is found that explains the difficult and complex doctrine of *divine* simplicity.[1] According to Stead, divine simplicity was an idea adopted by early Christians from Greek philosophy in a vague fashion. A set of interrelated terms (ἁπλοῦς, ἀμερής, ἀξύνθετον) were used to express the idea of divine simplicity without sufficient clarity as to the distinctive meaning of each term.[2] This is problematic, Stead contends, because the terms commonly associated with divine simplicity were used in different philosophical contexts in antiquity.[3] The interconnection between the terms commonly entangled with divine simplicity by early Christian authors—unity (*unicus*), priority (*primus*), immutability (*immutabilitas*), constancy (*constans*), goodness (*bonus*), and truth (*verus*)—calls for a systematic study in its own right given the complexity of the matter. The lack of systematic clarity on this issue in early Christian thought thus led Stead to conclude that the patristic understanding of divine simplicity remains "largely intuitive."

METAPHYSICAL AND ETHICAL SIMPLICITY

The difficulty with divine simplicity goes further still. In antiquity, the term "simple" possessed many senses.[4] It is therefore unclear which meaning is of prime importance when it comes to *God's* simplicity. As Stead has already alluded to, there are broadly two distinctive senses of simplicity. First, "simple" can be understood in an ethical sense. One who is simple is one who is morally pure. The ethical sense is concerned with the constancy of a virtuous agent who, in contrast with the evil-doer, is always perfectly self-consistent and hence trustworthy. Second, "simple" can be understood in a metaphysical sense. Something is metaphysically simple if it is ontologically basic. Consequently, a simple reality possesses a sense of constancy that exempts it from suffering any change. One way to gain clarity about divine simplicity is to judge, with Stead, that the simplicity of God, compared to moral simplicity, belongs to "another realm of discourse."[5] On this assumption, God's simplicity is primarily concerned with the metaphysical sense and not the ethical sense. Hence, while the ethical sense of simplicity is relatively clear, the lack of metaphysical precision surrounding the idea of *divine* simplicity in early Christian thought warrants Stead's judgment that the doctrine remained vague in the patristic period. But in reality, it is far from clear that divine simplicity was merely a metaphysical idea for the ancients, as we shall see.

While the doctrine of divine simplicity cannot be reduced to a matter of how words are applied to God, Stead's classical studies highlight genuine difficulties with approaching the meaning of the doctrine in antiquity. Further clarity, then, is therefore necessary for making sense of divine simplicity when it first emerged in early Christian thought. In particular, two issues are pertinent for this task. First, how did various ideas (unity, immutability, indivisibility, etc.) become connected to divine simplicity? Is it correct to follow Stead's judgment that the interconnection between these ideas lacked clarity in antiquity? Second, is there a sharp disjunction between metaphysical and ethical simplicity in the case of the divine? Is it right to consider, with Stead, that divine simplicity belongs to a different domain of discourse than ethical simplicity? The aim of this chapter is to establish a baseline meaning of divine simplicity that will serve as the foundation for the rest of the study. Here I offer a fresh attempt to clarify these issues through examining a hitherto underused resource in the study of divine simplicity in antiquity, that is, Plato's *Republic* 380d–383c. My central thesis is that *Rep.* 380d–383c should be regarded as the *locus classicus* of the idea of divine simplicity in antiquity. In other words, I shall argue that this text supplies a starting point in light of which one can make sense of subsequent developments on the theme of divine simplicity. The two parts of this chapter will consider both the context and the content of this passage in order to substantiate this claim. From this consideration, clarity will emerge regarding the two fundamental issues highlighted by Stead concerning the meaning of divine simplicity in antiquity.

THE *LOCUS CLASSICUS*: PLATO'S *REPUBLIC*, BOOK 2

The Wider Context of *Rep.* 380d–383c

Rep. 380d–383c, to my knowledge, is the earliest direct discussion of *divine* simplicity in Greek philosophy.[6] Plato's discussion on this theme is situated within the central topic of Book 2, namely, the education of the guardians of the state. In *Rep.* 377e, Socrates begins an argument about the role of traditional fables about the gods in the state's educational program for the guardians. According to Socrates, not all traditional stories told about the gods, such as those found in Hesiod or Homer, are appropriate for the guardians to receive in their youth.[7] Any traditional poet who "images badly in his speech the true nature of gods and heroes" (εἰκάζῃ τις κακῶς τῷ λόγῳ περὶ θεῶν τε καὶ ἡρώων οἷοί εἰσιν) is to be blamed. By presenting tales about some deity suffering at the hand of his son or gods warring with other gods, traditional fables could lead to a malformed understanding of justice and injustice in the guardians. In light of this, Socrates suggests that there is a need in the ideal state to lay down the "patterns for theological speech" (οἱ τύποι περὶ θεολογίας) according to which poets must compose their myths about the gods. For Socrates, the principle of composition is that a god must always be described as he is.[8] *Rep.* 379b–383c, then, sets out two laws (νόμοι) that unpack this principle in detail.

The first law of theological speech aims to safeguard divine goodness. The premise of this law is that a god is good (ἀγαθός) and must be spoken of as such.[9] Consequently, a god is not to be portrayed as "the cause of all things." Since goodness cannot lead to anything harmful, a good god cannot be the cause (αἴτιον) of evil. One must conclude that a god should be regarded not as the cause of all things (πάντων αἴτιος) but as the cause of only good things (τἀγαθά). This law has practical implication for assessing theological literature. When one encounters poets who wish to associate evil deeds with the gods in their stories, Socrates suggests two possible responses. Either one forbids them to say that the evil deeds are the work of the gods or to devise some interpretation of the events according to which the gods' actions were righteous and good and the people suffering apparent evil deeds at the hands of the gods were in fact "benefited by their chastisement."[10] The first law of theological speech, then, would require poets to present the gods as good, identifying the divine as the cause of only good things.

Starting from *Rep.* 380d, Socrates then turns to propose a second law that aims to safeguard the simplicity of the gods. He asks:

> Do you think that god is a wizard and capable of manifesting himself by design, now in one aspect, now in another, at one time himself changing and altering his shape into many forms and at another deceiving us and causing us to believe such things about him; or that he is simple [ἁπλοῦν] and less likely than anything else to depart from his own form?[11]

In this passage, Socrates offers two contrasting pictures of a god. On the first account, the god is depicted as capable of appearing in multiple forms (πολλὰς μορφάς). This picture portrays a god who is changeable from one form to another, like a sorcerer who changes himself to deceive others. Socrates probably had in mind stories such as those about Thetis transforming herself in the *Odyssey* or Hera disguised as a priestess in Aeschylus's stories.[12] In contrast, on Socrates' preferred account, a god should be portrayed as simple (ἁπλοῦν) and "least of all likely to step out of his own form (τῆς ἑαυτοῦ ἰδέας)."[13] It is, then, in the context of putting forth an alternative theology to the one found in traditional Greek mythologies, that divine simplicity acquires its role alongside divine goodness as one of two laws that regulate the pattern for theological speech in the ideal state.[14]

The wider context, therefore, suggests that the primary role assigned to divine simplicity in *Rep.* 380d–383c is that of a normative "pattern for theological speech." This observation lends considerable weight to my earlier suggestion that *Rep.* 380d–383c should be treated as a paradigmatic background to the doctrine of divine simplicity in antiquity. For it is precisely as a "pattern for theological speech" that we find the language of divine simplicity employed in early Christian thought, a point firmly established by recent scholarship.[15] According to Lewis Ayres, divine simplicity is best understood as a strategy or principle commonly used by patristic authors to shape "the basic contours . . . of appropriate patterns of theological speech."[16] Divine simplicity, for the early Christians, concerns the "grammar" for talking about God as "a set of rules or principles intrinsic to theological discourse, whether or not they are formally articulated."[17] Patristic writers constantly draw on divine simplicity as a rule to eliminate theologically untenable positions on a range of topics.[18] Even though they might be "loose and inconsistent" in terms of their definitions of simplicity, nevertheless there are consistent patterns of how they use the doctrine to shape theological discourse about God.[19] Andrew Radde-Gallwitz extends Ayres's analysis further by suggesting that divine simplicity is employed by patristic writers as a grammatical rule similar to logical rules such as the law of noncontradiction.[20] Just as human discourse is governed by the rule of noncontradiction such that we may not attribute two contradictory claims or statements to a subject, so theological discourse about God is governed by grammatical rules such as divine simplicity in addition to the usual logical rules.[21] Thus, divine simplicity is not merely a first-order claim about the absence of parts or composition in God but also provides a "second-order rule for speaking about God."[22] The conclusions reached by recent scholarship, however, follow naturally if Plato's discussion in *The Republic* is taken as the *locus classicus* of divine simplicity in antiquity. The first law of theological speech, that God can be assigned only as the source of goodness, is undoubtedly a central pillar that regulates early Christian theological discourse. One should then expect the second law to be assimilated by Christian authors as well. Moreover, it is not difficult to imagine that divine simplicity, set out in the context of a philosophical critique of traditional myths, passes through to later well-educated writers (including early Christians) through their Graeco-Roman education.[23] In light of the wider context of *Rep.* 380d–383c, there are then good reasons for regarding this text as a foundational background for the intelligibility of divine simplicity in antiquity.

Analysis of *Rep.* 380d–383c

Rep. 380d reveals three contrasting accounts of deities at the heart of Socrates' understanding of divine simplicity. First, he contrasts a god who possesses multiple forms with a god who is single in form. Second, he contrasts a god who can change into multiple forms with a god who is incapable of such changes. Third, he contrasts a god who deceives with a god who is truthful. In this text, then, Socrates interweaves three themes with divine simplicity that expand the meaning of the doctrine: unity, immutability, and truthfulness. Conversely, with reference to these themes, the opposite of simplicity can also be defined through multiplicity, mutability, and deceitfulness. As Socrates' argument for divine simplicity unfolds, these themes are interconnected closely so as to form a constellation of ideas.

The case Socrates offers for divine simplicity rests on a two-part argument: if a god is truly capable of appearing in multiple forms, as suggested by some of the fables of the poets, then either (a) a god is able to do so through some form of change, or (b) a god is doing so only deceptively while remaining single in form by nature. In *Rep.* 380e–381e, Socrates refutes the possibility of a, and in *Rep.* 381e–383a, he refutes the possibility of b. In both cases, he seeks to show that both possibilities will lead to absurdities, leading him to conclude that it is not right to depict a god as appearing in multiple nonconsistent appearances that will lead to deception about the divine. In the first part of the argument, Socrates refutes the possibility of change in a god by considering the nature of a perfect being. He argues that a god cannot appear in multiple forms, taking different forms at different times, because a god cannot change. If a god changes from one form to another, then either he is changed by another or he changes himself. The first option is rejected with the following argument:

1. The best things are least liable to be altered or changed (ἀλλοιοῦταί τε καὶ κινεῖται) by another (380e).
2. A god (and divinity in general) is in the best condition in every way (ὁ θεός γε καὶ τὰ τοῦ θεοῦ πάντῃ ἄριστα ἔχει) (381b).
3. A god is not liable to be altered or changed by another.

Socrates' argument relies on the idea that what is most perfect admits the least change by external causes. The standard of perfection invoked here is one of permanence: what is perfect should also be permanent, because if something lacks permanence, then its state is hardly in the best condition since it is subjected to corruption. Having rejected the possibility of a god's being changed by another, he turns to reject the second option, namely, that a god would change himself:

4. If a god changes himself, then either he becomes (a) better and more beautiful or (b) worse and uglier (381b).
5. Premise 4a is absurd since a god is perfect and lacking in nothing (381c).
6. Premise 4b is absurd since no one would deliberately make themself worse (381c).
7. A god would not wish to change himself.

This second argument further clarifies what it means for a god to be perfect, as asserted previously in the second premise of the first argument. According to Socrates, if a god is perfect, then it is inconceivable that he could change himself *for the better* since it is impossible for a god to be better than he is. Furthermore, if a god is perfect, then it seems obviously absurd that such a perfect being would make himself worse than he is, that is, less perfect. It follows, then, that a perfect god also would not change himself. With the two sets of considerations taken together, the conclusion of Socrates' argument is that a god cannot be changed by another, nor would he change himself, since both conclusions are absurd when applied to a god, the most perfect being.

It is worth noting that Socrates' argument clarifies the precise sense of immutability underlying a god's simplicity that is entailed by the god's perfection. The key observation is that the second step above (premises 4–7) defends only the claim that a god *would not* change himself. It does not seek to establish the claim that a god *could not* change himself. This is because premise 6 does not state that a god *could* not deliberately make himself worse but rather relies on the intuition, without further elaboration, that no one *would wish* to deliberately make themself worse.[24] Hence it is crucial to note this distinction and observe that given Socrates' commitment to premise 6, his doctrine of divine immutability entails two rather precise claims: (a) a god *cannot* be changed by another, and (b) a god *would* not change himself. Due to divine immutability in this sense, it is impossible for a god to appear in multiple forms, now appearing in one form, then later in another.[25]

Having established divine immutability, Socrates then turns to the second part of his argument for divine simplicity. Given that a god is immutable, is it possible that he could still appear in multiple forms but through an act of deception? In other words, could a god deceptively appear in multiple forms even though in reality he is single in form? Socrates refutes this possibility with the following argument:

1. If a god deceives us regarding his form, then he is willing to be false.
2. True falsehood—possessing falsehood in one's soul—is abhorred by all gods and humans (382a–c).
3. Falsehood merely in words could in no way be useful to a god (382c–d).
4. The divine is in every way free from falsehoods.

This argument ultimately rests on the implicit assumption that divine perfection also consists of *ethical* immutability. This is the idea that if a god is morally perfect, he would not choose to deceive anyone regarding his true nature. A god is immutable, then, also in the sense that he will not present himself in a form that deviates from what is consistent with his nature. From this assumption, Socrates argues that both true falsehood (ἀληθῶς ψεῦδος) and falsehood in words (τὸ ἐν τοῖς λόγοις ψεῦδος) cannot be found in a god. First, a god, being a perfectly moral being, despises true falsehood. The idea of true falsehood refers to the case in which there is true ignorance in the soul of either the deceiver or the deceived.[26] While Socrates does not spell this out explicitly, the thought seems to be that a god cannot act (e.g., appear in multiple forms) to produce true ignorance in the deceived since he is a perfectly moral being who despises any falsehood. The further thought that a god could deceive others because of ignorance about his own nature is obviously absurd. It is then absurd to hold that a god would deceive either due to true falsehood in someone or due to true falsehood in himself. Second, it is also not possible that a god would choose to deceive anyone for a cause serviceable to him. While in the case of human beings there are instances in which it might be serviceable to deceive another, it would be absurd to imagine that any of these instances would ever occur in the case of gods. As Socrates explains:

> But what of the falsehood in words, when and for whom is it serviceable so as not to merit abhorrence? Will it not be against enemies? And when any of those whom we call friends owing to madness or folly attempt to do some wrong, does it not then become useful to avert the evil—as a medicine? And also in the fables of which we were just now speaking owing to our ignorance of the truth about antiquity, we liken the false to the true as far as we may and so make it edifying. . . . Tell me, then, on which of these grounds falsehood would be serviceable to god. Would he because of his ignorance of antiquity make false likenesses of it? . . . Would it be through fear of his enemies that he would lie? Would it be because of the folly or madness of his friends? . . . Then there is no motive for god to deceive.[27]

In other words, the grounds for regarding falsehoods as useful in the case of human beings, when applied to a god, would lead to absurd conclusions. Based on the impossibility of attributing true falsehood or falsehood in words to a god, Socrates concludes that it is absurd to believe that a god can appear in multiple forms through deception.

Drawing together the two parts of the argument, Socrates summarizes the second law concerning divine simplicity as a pattern for theological speech: "God is altogether simple and true in deed and word, and neither changes himself nor deceives others by vision or words or the sending of signs in waking or in dreams."[28] This sentence aptly captures how the core meaning of divine simplicity is to be understood in relation to the two conclusions established by the two parts of Socrates' argument: immutability and truthfulness. Or, to put it in more striking terms, to say that a god is simple is to say that he is immutable in the *metaphysical* sense (he cannot be changed by another, nor would he change himself) and in the *ethical* sense (he does not deceive by appearing in ways inconsistent with his nature).

Plato's *Republic* and the Intelligibility of Divine Simplicity

Rep. 380d–383c clarifies two fundamental questions concerning the meaning of divine simplicity in antiquity I mentioned at the beginning of this chapter. First, this text shines a great light on the assumption commonly made by ancient writers that a god's simplicity is intrinsically connected to his unity, immutability, constancy, goodness, and truthfulness. It does so by unveiling the supposed link between the different ideas. Divine simplicity is linked to divine unity because God's self-consistency implies that he would not appear in multiple forms in a deceptive manner. The first part of Socrates' argument shows how divine simplicity is grounded in divine immutability. The second part of Socrates' argument highlights that divine simplicity is also grounded in a god's constancy, which underlies his truthfulness. Moreover, in *The Republic* a god's simplicity is set out alongside his goodness as one of the two indispensable laws that regulate the pattern for theological speech in the ideal state. *Rep.* 380d–383c, therefore, addresses Stead's puzzlement by putting forth a framework that accounts for why it was intelligible and considered coherent in antiquity to set out the idea of divine simplicity through this specific constellation of ideas.

Second, in this passage the core meaning of divine simplicity surfaces. Divine simplicity, it turns out, is deeply grounded in a god's perfect self-consistency and truthfulness. This meaning is set out apart from any considerations of the commonly supposed metaphysical qualifications for a god's simplicity, namely, noncomposition and partlessness. Contrary to Stead's judgment, then, divine simplicity did not originate in antiquity as an idea that belongs to "another realm of discourse" from that of ethical simplicity. If anything, ethical simplicity seems to be the more primary sense attributed to a god in *Rep.* 380d–383c.[29] In this passage, a god's simplicity is largely understood in terms of perfect self-consistency. The term ἁπλοῦς is applied to a god on this basis. But of course, divine self-consistency, what I have called a god's ethical immutability, is understood in relation to the constellation of ideas I mentioned above. A god is self-consistent in that he is one without appearing in multiple forms. A god is so because he is immutable in that he could not be changed and would not change himself. A god is also one and immutable because he is truthful and hence free from deceit. A god who is simple is first and foremost a god who is true in word and deed. It is then apparent that self-consistency, expanded in relation to this constellation of ideas, is what is denoted by the term ἁπλοῦς in this passage. *Rep.* 380d–383c thus challenges the assumption that divine simplicity is primarily a metaphysical idea belonging to another realm of discourse than that of ethical simplicity. Rather, it seems that divine simplicity originated as a synthesis of metaphysical and ethical considerations.

This chapter has put forward the case that *Rep.* 380d–383c should be regarded as the *locus classicus* of divine simplicity in antiquity. If this is correct, then we find in *The Republic* a basic framework that foregrounds the intelligibility of the doctrine for the ancients, accounting for both divine simplicity's role as a second-order rule of speech in theological discourse and its basic meaning. Admittedly, though, the notion of ethical simplicity that emerged from this passage is surprising in the light of what philosophers and theologians commonly understand to be the doctrine of divine simplicity. It is not yet clear, in particular, how Plato's discussion in *The Republic* can account for the metaphysical dimensions (a god's partlessness, noncomposition, incorporeality, etc.) commonly recognized as the primary content of the doctrine. *Rep.* 380d–383c, then, cannot be the full story.

One further problem, moreover, needs highlighting. As Gerhard van Riel has argued, it is questionable whether Plato's gods can be identified as metaphysical first principles.[30] On this issue, Plato scholars are divided in their opinions. Some hold that this identification is indeed latent in Plato's works.[31] Others hold that evidence does not point toward this identification.[32] If van Riel is correct, that Plato's gods are souls that are dissoluble, composite beings subjected to fate imposed by the metaphysical order at large, then Plato's theology is a long way from putting forward a metaphysical first principle of all things, a notion that was central for the early Christians. Is the doctrine of divine simplicity found in *The Republic* at all relevant to understanding the Christian God who is the supreme metaphysical principle of all things?

While it is hardly likely that the "divine" in *Rep.* 380d–383c is already identified as a metaphysical first principle by Plato, this possibility is latent in his discussion of forms in the same work. In *Rep.* 475e–480a, in the context of describing the nature of the true philosophers, Plato sets out an important discussion on the nature of forms. In order to clarify the nature of the true philosophers, this passage put forward a fundamental distinction. Readers are invited to reflect on the nature of forms. For instance, we consider the fair and honorable (καλός) as the opposite of the base and ugly (αἰσχρός). As opposites, then, the fair and the ugly are two, and consequently, each is one. This conclusion can be generalized, Socrates observes, to all the forms that have an opposite. The good (ἀγαθός) is opposite to the bad (κακός), thus forming a pair in which each is one. Similarly, the just (δίκαιος) is opposed the unjust (ἄδικος), hence forming another pair in which each is one. The conclusion is that "in itself each [form] is one," but that "by virtue of their communion with actions and bodies and with one another they present themselves everywhere, each as a multiplicity of aspects."[33] Each form, then, is fundamentally one. But each appears in multiple forms as a result of its appearance in the form of actions, bodies, and combinations with other forms. With this distinction in mind, the "lovers of spectacles and the arts" and "men of action," who are attached to the sense-perceptible appearances of things, cannot be true philosophers as they are unable to understand the true nature of the forms in themselves. The true philosophers, on the contrary, possess true knowledge of the beautiful and the good because they contemplate the beautiful and the good in and by themselves. But what essentially distinguishes the forms from particulars? According to Socrates, the form of Beauty, in contrast to many beautiful things, is "always remaining the same and unchanged" (ἀεὶ κατὰ ταὐτὰ ὡσαύτως ὄντα).[34] This implies the impossibility for the form of Beauty to appear in its contrary state, that is, to be ugly. Particular beautiful things, however, will always be capable of appearing in the contrary state. For instance, a beautiful flower will become ugly when it wilts. A just person might appear unjust due to circumstances or a change of character. In other words, as Constance Meinwald put it succinctly, "changing the context will typically reveal beautiful things to be ugly in some way, at some time, in some respect, etc."[35] Particular things, then, are subjected to the possibility of changing from their current state to their contrary state, whereas a form, "always remaining the same and unchanged," will never be found in its contrary state.

This passage uncovers a close connection between the essential character of the forms and the description of divine simplicity already latent in *The Republic*. For the language of god's simplicity in *Rep.* 380d–383c amounts to the claim that the divine is "always remaining the same"—one, immutable, free from contraries—which is also the language used by Plato for the forms.[36] This connection opens up the possibility, in the context of later Platonism, to identify the simple divinity as the source of all there is in *The Republic*, that is, the form of the Good.[37] This connection provides a path to make sense of later developments of divine simplicity in ancient philosophy in which metaphysical qualifications of the doctrine will be emphasized. As will become clear in the next chapter, later writers in the Middle Platonic period seized upon this possible connection and hence the possibility of identifying the simple divinity as this highest form, the supreme first principle of all things ("God" with a capital G). This development in the Middle Platonic period turned out to be crucial in shaping the metaphysical aspects of divine simplicity integral to the ante-Nicene Christian understanding. And so it is to Middle Platonic sources that we must now turn in search of the missing metaphysics.

CHAPTER 2

From the Simple God to the Simple First Principle

In an essay on the genealogy of the "philosophical concept of God" in early Christian theology, Wolfhart Pannenberg argues that divine simplicity emerged primarily in the context of reflections on the first origin of all there is, the ἀρχή of all things. For early Christians, "Everything composite can also be divided again, and consequently is mutable."[1] The ultimate origin, however, cannot be composite. This is because every composite has a "ground" of its composition outside of itself and so is preceded by this ground. Hence, a composite cannot be the ultimate cause and origin of all things since whatever grounds the composite would constitute a more fundamental reality than the composite itself. Therefore, the ultimate origin must be simple. On this account, the identification of God as the ἀρχή constitutes the source for the emergence of divine simplicity in early Christian theology. Pannenberg's genealogy accentuates the problem I highlighted at the end of the previously chapter. In the *locus classicus*, *The Republic*, we encounter primarily the ethical sense of simplicity: a divine being is simple in the sense of self-consistency and trustworthiness. Nevertheless, divine simplicity did not emerge in early Christian theology with this as its obvious primary sense. Rather, metaphysical qualifications were central in early Christian expressions of divine simplicity. How do we account for the rise of these further qualifications? The aim of this chapter is to address this issue by documenting the crucial development in the Middle Platonic period that will account for the transition from the *locus classicus* of divine simplicity to the form of the doctrine in early Christian theology.[2]

Pannenberg, like G. C. Stead, contrasts divine simplicity with the idea of faithfulness and trustworthiness ("ethical simplicity").[3] But the picture is more complex. Pannenberg is no doubt correct in suggesting that divine simplicity is reliant on metaphysical reflections concerning the nature of the first principle (ἀρχή). But these considerations are only intelligible when understood in light of their connections with the core idea found in *The Republic*, as I shall endeavor to show. In other words, these reflections should be treated as development from the *locus classicus* rather than as the *locus classicus* itself. What I have undertaken in this chapter is an exercise of mapping out the intelligibility of this connection. My central thesis is that between *The Republic* and early Christian theology, there became available in the Middle Platonic period a coherent way to synthesize the simple deity and the simple first principle.[4] In this period, the simple deity of *The Republic* is often explicitly identified as the supreme first principle of all things. This identification, then, is responsible for the further metaphysical qualifications of divine simplicity that anticipate the early Christian form of the doctrine. To unfold this argument, I will rely on two sources in this period, the Middle Platonist Alcinous (c. mid–second century CE) and the Jewish philosopher Philo of Alexandria (c. 20–15 BCE to 45–50 CE). Examining these two sources will allow me to spell out the developments responsible for the transition from the simple deity in Plato's *Republic* to the God who is identified as the simple ἀρχή of all things in early Christian theology.

DIVINE SIMPLICITY IN ALCINOUS'S *DIDASKALIKOS*

Alcinous's *Didaskalikos* bears a title that translates literally as "instruction manual."[5] Such a manual could have been written for beginners, but it is more likely that it was written to serve as a reminder for those who have had some preliminary instructions in the doctrines of Platonism. The manual sets out a basic presentation of Platonism according to the tripartite division of philosophy: logic, physics, and ethics.[6] Theology is situated as a discussion of one of the three first principles in physics. It is in chapter 10 of the *Didaskalikos* that we find Alcinous's theology. While the theology presented in this chapter is unique and hardly presents a "representative" Middle Platonic position, nevertheless, the *Didaskalikos* sheds significant light on the transition from the simple deity in Plato's *Republic* to the simple God in early Christian theology.[7] For Alcinous illustrates how, by this period, the doctrine of divine simplicity has acquired further metaphysical dimensions. He develops the doctrine further by integrating insights from other Platonic dialogues as well as adopting Aristotelian considerations wherein a deity is explicitly identified as the supreme intellect, the unmoved mover, and the highest first principle.[8]

God as Intellect

At the beginning of *Did.* 10, Alcinous introduces a deity as a first principle (ἀρχή) through what he calls a process of induction (ἐπαγωγή).[9] According to him, even though Plato indicates that such a principle is "more or less beyond description (ἄρρητον)," nonetheless, it is possible to arrive at some notions of the divine. The process for determining the nature of the divine is sketched out as follows:

1. If there are intelligibles (νοητά), then these neither are sense-perceptibles (αἰσθητά) nor participate in what is sense-perceptible (μετούσια τῶν αἰσθητῶν).
2. Rather, intelligibles participate in "certain primary objects of intellection" (πρώτων τινῶν νοητῶν).
3. Thus primary objects of intellection in an absolute sense (πρῶτα νοητὰ ἁπλᾶ) must exist.
4. Given that we accept that there are intelligibles (e.g., for Platonists, forms exist), there must be primary objects of intellection.

As John Dillon has noted, the argument probably boils down to this: "If there are objects of intellection at all (and we accept that there are),[10] there must be primary objects of intellection (and therefore an intellect to cognize them)."[11] But what is the nature of the intellect that is appropriate to cognize these primary objects of intellection? Such an intellect cannot be a human intellect. This is because, as Alcinous qualifies in *Did.* 10,164.13–18, human intellects cannot apprehend the intelligibles in a "pure and uncontaminated mode." Whenever human intellects are attempting to apprehend the intelligibles, they still retain sensible images through their imaginations such that notions of size, shape, or color accompany their apprehension of intelligibles. In other words, human intellects struggle to shrug off sense-perceptible notions in order to arrive at a pure conception of the intelligible. What is required, however, is a *divine* intellect that is free from sense-perception and thus is able to apprehend the intelligibles (forms) in a pure and uncontaminated mode. This, then, is the conclusion of Alcinous's argument: inferring from the existence of primary objects of intellection, which Platonists affirm to exist, a first principle in the form of a purely intellectual deity must exist. Given the pure intellectual nature of this deity, this conclusion explains with Plato's predication in *Tim.* 28c, namely, that human modes of intellection that are "contaminated" will find it difficult to comprehend the nature of divinity. So, despite difficulties, Alcinous concludes that Platonist philosophers can grasp at least that there exists a divine first principle that is purely intellectual.

Alcinous, however, goes further to identify a supreme intellect as the primal God (ὁ πρῶτος θεός). In an argument from a "hierarchy of value," as Dillon aptly calls it, Alcinous moves through a series of comparisons to establish this conclusion.[12] Intellect is superior to soul. But intellect ἐν ἐνέργειαν ("actualized intellect") is superior to intellect ἐν δυνάμει ("potential intellect") since the former "cognises everything simultaneously and eternally" (πάντα νοῶν καὶ ἅμα καὶ ἀεί). But then the cause (ὁ αἴτιος) of actualized intellect is finer still. So whatever existed prior to the cause of actualized intellect would be the primal God.[13] This primal God is also said to move other intellects without itself being moved and must be "everlastingly engaged in thinking of itself and its own thoughts."[14] The nature of the primal God, therefore, is best identified as the most perfect, most supreme, and most primordial intellect.[15] Alcinous, then, not only identifies the divine as a first principle that is purely intellectual in nature; he also identifies a primal God as the highest and most perfect principle.

The identification of divinity as purely intellectual was most notably developed by Aristotle in *Metaphysics* Λ. What we have seen is that this idea also finds an important place in Alcinous's theology.[16] Through the two arguments, the primal God, as the highest first principle, is described by Alcinous as the supreme intellect. In what follows, I will show that Alcinous further spells out the simplicity of the primal God, which I will refer to simply as "God" with a capital "G," with further metaphysical qualifications that go beyond the doctrine of divine simplicity in *The Republic.* I shall suggest that it is the identification of God as the supreme first principle by Alcinous that led to these further qualifications of divine simplicity.

Divine Partlessness and Its Implications

In *The Republic*, the simple deity is single in form. But the sense of oneness connected with the simplicity of God is developed much further by Alcinous.[17] As a systematizer of Platonism,[18] he actualizes the potential latent in *The Republic* to identify a simple deity as the supreme first principle that unifies all intelligible forms. This enables Alcinous to further qualify the sense of oneness associated with the simple God. In *Did.* 10, 164.31–165.4, he lists a number of attributes that qualify the sense of perfection worthy of God, writing: "The primary god, then, is eternal, ineffable, 'self-perfect' (that is, deficient in no respect), 'ever-perfect' (that is, always perfect), and 'all-perfect' (that is, perfect in all aspects); divinity, essentiality, truth, commensurability, good." In a remarkably dense sentence in the middle of enumerating the divine attributes, Alcinous expresses concern for safeguarding God's oneness in the face of the appearance of multiple divine attributes: Λέγω δὲ οὐχ ὡς χωρίζων ταῦτα, ἀλλ' ὡς κατὰ πάντα ἑνὸς νοουμένου (But I do not say these things as though one is separated from another, but as though one thing is conceived according to all of them).[19] *Prima facie*, what Alcinous seems to propose here is what has sometimes been called the "identity thesis," the idea that since multiple divine attributes are one in God, they are to be conceived as identical with one another, with each attribute identical to God.[20] But I suggest that the meaning of this sentence will become clear if we take Alcinous to be developing a possibility latent in *The Republic*, since in that work, as I have indicated previously, we find a close connection between the description of the simple deity and the essential characteristic of a form. Both are described as unchangeable and one in the sense of lacking the possibility of appearing in a state contrary to itself. If we take the simple deity to be the absolute standard of goodness, beauty, truth, and being, applying the essential characteristic of a form, then it follows naturally that the simple deity must be perfectly one without the possibility of contraries in him.[21] Interpreting the sentence in this light, Alcinous seems to be saying that while the enumeration of divine attributes might imply that God is composed of multiple attributes possessing independent existence, rather a single divinity is to be conceived from all the multiple attributes in a harmonious manner such that no contrary qualities can possibly be associated with it. This dense sentence, then, suggests that Alcinous considers God, his supreme first principle, also the highest Form that unifies the multiple divine attributes; hence, the divine attributes cannot be conceived as possessing an independent existence in which God participates in order to acquire these qualities.[22] The identification of God as the highest first principle, a possibility latent in *The Republic*, therefore, leads Alcinous to further qualify God's oneness beyond the sense in *The Republic*.

This identification of God as the highest first principle leads Alcinous to further elaborate on God's simplicity by developing a theology that synthesizes a wide range of Platonic sources. In *Did.* 10, 165.5–16, the terms he attributes to God reveal their origin in the First Hypothesis of Plato's *Parmenides*.[23] To begin, "God is not a part of anything, nor is he in the position of being a whole which has parts" (οὔτε μέρος τινός, οὔτε ὡς ὅλον ἔχον τινὰ μέρη). This description draws on the language of *Parm.* 137c–d, according to which the One (τὸ ἕν) cannot be a whole that consists of parts because this would result in the contradiction that the One is many. Further, for Alcinous, "Nor is he [God] the same as anything or different from anything; for no attribute is proper to him, in virtue of which he could be distinguished from other things" (οὔτε ὥστε ταὐτόν τινι εἶναι ἢ ἕτερον· οὐδὲν γὰρ αὐτῷ συμβέβηκε καθ' ὃ δύναται τῶν ἄλλων χωρισθῆναι). Here the language is reminiscent of *Parm.* 139c, where Plato states that the One neither "can . . . be the same with another or with itself; nor again other than itself or another." Finally, Alcinous's God "neither moves anything, nor is he himself moved" (οὔτε κινεῖ οὔτε κινεῖται). This final clause draws from the language of *Parm.* 139b, where the same conclusion is drawn regarding the One. The language about the One as part of the logical exercise in the *Parmenides* has thus been transposed by Alcinous into a theological key.[24] God, then, must also be one without parts (ἀμερής).

Alcinous defends God's partlessness through an argument in *Did.* 10, 165.34–36: "God is partless, by reason of the fact that there is nothing prior to him. For the part, and that out of which a thing is composed, exists prior to that of which it is a part." He invokes a brief example from geometry to back up this point, but Alcinous's thinking here seems to be closely related to considerations associated with Plato's argument for the soul as noncomposite (ἀξύνθετον).[25] In *Phae.* 78b–81a we find a distinction set out between composite and noncomposite things. On the one hand, every composite by nature is liable "to be decomposed, in the same way in which it was compounded" (διαιρεθῆναι ταύτῃ ᾗπερ συνετέθη). On the other hand, only a noncomposite thing (ἀξύνθετον) cannot be decomposed. Noncomposites, then, are things that "always remain the same and in the same state" (ἀεὶ κατὰ ταὐτὰ καὶ ὡσαύτως), whereas composites are those that "vary from one state to another and are never the same" (ἄλλοτ' ἄλλως καὶ μηδέποτε κατὰ ταὐτά).[26] "Composites," thus, refers to those things that lack permanence, whereas "noncomposites" refers to those things that possess permanent existence. Now in order to refute the suggestion that the soul is like a harmony (τὸ ἁρμονίαν), *Phae.* 92a–95a examines the dependence relation that exists between a composite and its parts. This consideration sheds light on the reasoning underlying Alcinous's argument for divine partlessness. According to this passage, composition entails a relative order of priority regarding the existence of the composite and its parts. A composite could not pre-exist the elements or parts from which it is constituted because it is necessary that the elements exist before a composite is formed by putting together the parts. For example, a harmony is created from the putting together of the sounds made by physical instruments. So it is a composite in that it is put together out of the sounds of the instruments. But it is clear that a harmony could not exist before the instruments because without the latter, the sounds would not exist.[27] In this manner, the existence of the parts of a composite must always precede the existence of the composite itself. Noncomposition, therefore, could express a sense of priority of existence because only noncomposites could have nothing existing prior to themselves. Further, composition, Socrates argues, implies a sense of the dependence of the composite on its parts. A composite cannot be in a different state from its parts because it cannot act or be acted upon in any different ways from the ways its parts are acting or acted upon.[28] This sense of dependence leads to a sense of contingency in a composite regarding its characteristics. A composite's characteristics are always contingent upon how its parts are put together. Consider the example of a model that consists of various parts. If it is put together well, it is a better model. If it is put together less well, it is a worse model. Thus a composite, as a whole consisting of parts, is dependent on how well its parts are put together. The logic of noncomposition in *Phaedo* thus clarifies the underlying reasoning behind Alcinous's defense of divine partlessness. Putting it in Alcinous's own terms, the point *Phaedo* establishes is that only a noncomposite is primordial (ἀρχικός). In the case of God, since he is the supreme first principle of all things, nothing can be prior to him. Now if God is a whole consisting of parts, that is, if he is composite, then he cannot be primordial. It follows that God must be without parts. Deploying reasoning perhaps similar to that found in *Phaedo*, Alcinous was able to expand on the logic of divine simplicity through a defense of divine partlessness.

Alcinous's integration of *Parmenides'* language of the One (and perhaps *Phaedo*'s reasoning on the nature of noncomposites) into his theology results in two further consequences: God is (1) motionless and (2) incorporeal. That God is motionless (ἀκίνητος) amounts to the requirement of immutability that follows from the basic sense of divine simplicity in *The Republic*. Alcinous's defense of God's motionlessness actually uses the same argument for divine immutability we examined previously when discussing *Rep.* 380e–381e.[29] God cannot be subjected to change because he cannot be changed by someone stronger, which is absurd and he would not choose to change for the better or the worse, which is absurd for a perfect being. Alcinous, then, has little problem in identifying the sense of immutability entailed by God's simplicity as also a consequence of God's partlessness. The idea that God is without a body, however, is not explicitly found in the constellation of ideas connected to divine simplicity in *The Republic*. The logic underlying the connection between God's simplicity and his incorporeality is set out clearly here by Alcinous. If God is partless, then he must also be incorporeal (ἀσώματον). Alcinous's argument is as follows:

1. Every body is composed of matter and form (ἐξ ὕλης . . . καὶ εἴδους).
2. If God has a body, then he must be composed of matter and form.
3. But if God is composed of matter and form, then he is composed of parts.

4. But God is partless, which amounts to saying he is simple and primordial.
5. God cannot have a body.

The key steps in this argument are 3 and 4. Premise 3 is not spelled out explicitly by Alcinous, but it is in essence contained in what was said earlier in *Did.* 10,165.35–36, where a part (τὸ μέρος) is explicitly identified with "that out of which a thing is composed" (τὸ ἐξ οὗ). In other words, for Alcinous, to be a composite of matter and form is to have parts. If 3 is granted, then 4 follows given Alcinous's previous argument for God's partlessness. Hence, from this argument, God's incorporeality follows naturally from divine partlessness.

In summary, building on a number of Platonic sources, the nature of Alcinous's supreme first principle, the primal God, is described as partless, noncomposite, immutable, motionless, incorporeal. What is unmistakably clear is that this ἀρχή is the simple deity of *The Republic*. This is clear from *Did.* 10,166.5–7, where we read that it is "absurd" (ἄτοπον) for God to be composed of matter and form on the ground that this would contradict the fact that God is simple (ἁπλοῦς) and primordial (ἀρχικὸς). The self-consistent and nondeceitful deity described in *The Republic* as ἁπλοῦς now becomes, for Alcinous, the supreme ἀρχή of all things. This identification is further supported by the fact that the argument for the immutability of the simple deity in *The Republic* was applied by Alcinous to his supreme first principle, the primal God. Alcinous's theology, then, showcases how, in the Middle Platonic period, the simple deity of *The Republic* has acquired further metaphysical qualifications that follow from the consideration of the nature of the ἀρχή (partlessness, noncomposition, immutability, motionlessness, incorporeality). As I have suggested, this was made possible by the potential already latent in *The Republic*, namely, the identification of the simple deity as the highest first principle that unifies all the intelligible forms. Furthermore, Alcinous's theology reveals how the simple deity of *The Republic*, now further qualified as partless, can also be conjoined with the Aristotelian idea of the divine as the most supreme intellect. Hence, Alcinous's theology also demonstrates how an organic link between divine simplicity and pure intellectuality, one that was not explicitly spelled out in *The Repubilc*, might be established. As we shall see, the idea that divine simplicity is integrally connected to God's pure intellectuality will be a recurrent theme among ante-Nicene Christian writers.

DIVINE SIMPLICITY IN PHILO OF ALEXANDRIA'S *QUOD DEUS SIT IMMUTABILIS*

No passage from Platonic philosophy to early Christian thought, however, can proceed without going through the Jewish exegete and philosopher Philo of Alexandria. This is especially so with regard to divine simplicity since this doctrine arguably forms the heart of Philo's theology.[30] Since the connections between Philo's account of divine simplicity and ante-Nicene theology are numerous, a comprehensive inquiry here will not be possible. But in what follows, I shall restrict my attention to a key work, *Quod Deus sit Immutabilis*.[31] In this work, Philo demonstrates clearly how divine simplicity could be applied as a "pattern for theological speech," as suggested by *The Republic*, in the context of the monotheistic theology set out in the biblical text. In Philo's case, of course, the monotheistic theology in question is a Jewish one. But so far in our narrative, I have been at pains to stress that the discussion of divine simplicity in Platonic sources does not necessarily suppose a monotheistic theology. Philo's *Deus* thus reveals the possibility in antiquity of an intelligible transposition of divine simplicity as a "pattern for theological speech" from Platonism to Judeo-Christian monotheistic theology. And it is not surprising that, as we shall see, in several aspects Philo anticipates in *Deus* how ante-Nicene writers draw upon divine simplicity to regulate *Christian* theological discourse.

The overall context of Philo's *Deus* 20–69 is the interpretation of Genesis 6:5–7: "The 'Lord God,' says Moses, 'seeing that the wickednesses of men were multiplied upon the earth and that every man intended evil in his heart diligently all his days, God had it in His mind that He had made man upon the earth, and He bethought Him. And God said, 'I will blot out man, whom I made, from the face of the earth.'"[32] The problem arising from this passage is that some readers, whom Philo judges to be "careless inquirers" (τινὲς τῶν ἀνεξετάστων), might arrive at the conclusion that God "repented" of creating the world when he saw the corruption of humanity and hence was filled with anger, wishing to destroy the whole race through the flood to come. In his exegesis, Philo offers two discussions of divine immutability (*Deus* 20–32, 51–69) to correct an anthropomorphic reading that implies that God changes.[33] The fundamental premise of Philo's exegesis, which gives this work its title, is summed up in *Deus* 22: "For what greater impiety could there be than to suppose that the unchangeable changes" (τί γὰρ ἂν ἀσέβημα μεῖζον γένοιτο τοῦ ὑπολαμβάνειν τὸν ἄτρεπτον τρέπεσθαι)? In what follows, I will highlight how Philo's theology here, as Dillon and Winston have remarked, is unmistakably shaped by Plato's second law of theological speech in *Rep.* 380d–383b.[34] As in *The Republic*, Philo sets out a doctrine of divine simplicity to safeguard divine self-consistency and uses it as a rule to shape his interpretation of Genesis's anthropomorphic language of God. But as a philosopher in the Middle Platonic period, Philo, like Alcinous, also identifies the simple God as the first principle of all things. In Philo the understanding of simplicity as self-consistency was conjoined with the understanding of simplicity as without composition (and hence incorporeal). The identification of God as the supreme first principle leads Philo to articulate an anti-anthropomorphic account of the theological language found in the biblical text.

Deus 20–32: Divine Simplicity as a Pattern for Biblical Interpretation

In *Deus* 20–32, Philo offers his first argument against an anthropomorphic reading of Gen. 6:5–7, which implies that God is changeable. This argument is grounded in an exploration of what we might call the state of perfection. Among humans, who generally display "vacillation of mind and judgment," perfection is found only in students of philosophy, who acquire as their reward "that they do not change with changing circumstances, but with unbending steadfastness and firm constancy take in hand all that it behoves them to do."[35] For Philo, the sense of immutability associated with perfection is mentioned by the lawgiver in the Torah. Philo interprets Deut. 5:31, "Remain immobile here with me" (σὺ δὲ αὐτοῦ στῆθι μετ' ἐμοῦ), as a divine exhortation to the philosopher to move toward the state of an immutable will that is "unbending, unwavering, and broad-based."[36] In other words, the teachings of the philosophers and the divine lawgiver both confirm that the state of perfection among humans is characterized by absolute immutability in the sense of self-constancy.

Further on, Philo elaborates what this state of perfection is like in the soul of the philosopher:

> Wonderful indeed is the soul of the Sage, how he sets it, like a lyre, to harmony not with a scale of notes low and high, but with the knowledge of moral opposites, and the practice of such of them as are better; how he does not strain it to excessive heights, nor yet relax it and weaken the concord of virtues and things naturally beautiful, but keeps it ever at an equal tension and plays it with hand or bow in melody. Such a soul is the most perfect instrument fashioned by nature, the pattern of those which are the work of our hands. And if it be well adjusted, it will produce a symphony the most beautiful in the world, one which has its consummation not in the cadences and tones of melodious sound, but in the consistencies of our life's actions.[37]

The philosopher, like a lyre, sets out his acts as though they form a perfect harmony or symphony. Philo, no doubt aware of the critique of modeling the soul as a harmony in Plato's *Phaedo*, is keen to qualify throughout that the picture of the soul as a lyre producing harmonies is not to be interpreted literally. This is simply an image that aids our understanding. The harmony of the soul, then, is a harmony not of high and low notes, but of "the knowledge of moral opposites" and their "practice." The symphony of the soul is to be found not in the "cadences" and "tones of melodious sound," but "in the consistencies of our life's actions." With this caveat in mind, Philo commends this analogy as possessing a powerful image of what God is like. If the perfection of the philosopher is best reflected in the "unbending steadfastness" and "firm constancy" of his soul, which Philo invites his readers to understand as a consequence of the perfect harmony and consistency between all acts, then God must indeed be most appropriately thought of as one who "ever holds fast to what he purposed from the first without any alteration" (μένει δὲ ἐφ' ὧν ἐξ ἀρχῆς ἐβουλεύσατο οὐδὲν αὐτῶν μετατιθείς).[38] Philo's God, then, is one who is always consistent with what he wills, never appearing to contradict his purposes. The soul of the philosopher thus serves as an analogy for the divine who is described in *The Republic* as simple and truthful.

Further parallels between Philo's God and Plato's simple deity in *The Republic* emerge when we turn to the next stage of the argument

Table 2.1. Philo's *Quod Deus sit Immutabilis* 27–28 and Plato's *Republic* 380e–381e Compared

Deus 27–28	*Republic* 380e–381e
1. God is changeable only	1. A god is changed only if
a. through instability in himself (διὰ τὴν ἐν αὐτοῖς) (*Deus* 27–28.4).	a. A god changes by himself (ὑφ' ἑαυτοῦ) (*Rep.* 381c–381e).
i. Men frequently change from one original judgment to its contradiction (27–28.3).	i. If a god changes himself, then either he becomes (a) better and more beautiful or (b) worse and uglier.
ii. God has no such internal inconsistencies (ἀψίκορος) (28.3–4).	ii. Premise a is absurd since a deity is lacking in nothing (381c).
b. God would not change through instability outside himself (διὰ τὴν ἐκτὸς) (*Deus* 28.4–29).	iii. Premise b is absurd since no one would deliberately make oneself worse (381c).
i. Men are led to a change of mind by external influences (28.4–29.1).	iv. A god would not change himself.
ii. (Hidden premise): Premise i is possible only due to the lack of certainty about the future in men.	b. A god is changed by something else (ὑπὸ ἄλλου) (*Rep.* 380e–381b).
iii. But God has perfect foreknowledge of the future (29.1–32.8).	i. The best thing is least liable to alternation or change by something else (380b). ii. Divinity is in the best condition in every way (381b).
iv. God cannot be changed by instability outside himself.	iii. A god is not liable to alternation or change by something else.

for divine immutability in *Deus* 27–28. According to Philo, there are two ways in which common men are subjected to change. This occurs through "instability whether it be in themselves or outside them" (ἢ διὰ τὴν ἐν αὐτοῖς ἢ διὰ τὴν ἐκτὸς ἀβεβαιότητα). He then turns to refute both of these possibilities for God. It is illuminating to compare side by side the structure of Philo's argument with that of Plato's (see Table 2.1).

As is clear, the individual steps and the ordering of the steps in Philo's argument differ considerably from Socrates' argument in *Rep.* 380e–381e. On the possibility that God might be changed by changing himself, Philo focuses on illustrating this in the realm of human affairs.

For humans frequently change their minds in an arbitrary way from one original judgment to its opposite. This, Philo argues, cannot be found in God. Socrates' argument in *The Republic* proceeds in a more logical manner, focusing on setting out why God would not change himself. On the possibility that God might be changed by something else, the steps of the two passages are more closely aligned. The two arguments converge in the line of thought that the divine, as the most perfect, is the least liable to change by something else. This is set out generically in *The Republic*, but Philo develops this argument in a new direction by introducing God's perfection through his foreknowledge. According to Philo, unlike human beings, since God is the creator of the whole universe, including time, God is not subject to future uncertainties. There might be an additional hidden premise that Philo introduces into his argument, namely, that humans are liable to change by something else due to their lack of foresight about future events, which in turn leads human beings to act in contradictory ways under external influences. The overall comparison shows that while there are significant differences, the overarching structure of Philo's argument remains the same as that in *Rep.* 380e–381e. Like Alcinous's argument for God's motionlessness, the overall logic of Philo's *Deus* 27–28 is also structured to establish God's immutability based on the external/internal division found in *Rep.* 380e–381e. God is immutable because, first, God cannot be changed by another, and second, God would not change himself. Thus Philo's theology is reminiscent of that in *The Republic* not only at the level of his description of God but also at the level of the surface structure of his argument for divine immutability.

Deus 20–32, then, can be read as Philo's application of the second pattern for theological speech in *The Republic* in the context of biblical interpretation. Doing so leads Philo to his basic interpretation of Gen. 6:5: Given divine simplicity, it is not possible to interpret this verse as suggesting that God "repented." For how could a perfectly self-consistent God change his mind? Just as myths and fables concerning deities in Plato's ideal state should be "filtered" through the rule of divine simplicity, the language of God in the biblical text should likewise be interpreted. In this way, Philo showcases how the simplicity of God can enter as a "grammatical rule" into the domain of biblical interpretation.

Deus 51–69: Divine Simplicity and Anti-anthropomorphism

As in the case of Alcinous, Philo's understanding of divine simplicity also goes beyond *The Republic*. This is evident in Philo's second consideration of divine immutability, set out in *Deus* 51–69, a passage concerned with the exegesis of Gen. 6:7: "I will blot out man whom I made from the face of the earth, from man to beast, from creeping things to fowls of heaven, because I was wroth in that I made him."[39] What Philo illustrates additionally in this section is how the metaphysical qualifications of divine simplicity supply a foundation for his critique of reading the anthropomorphic language of God in the Hebrew Scriptures literally. Hence Philo highlights the potential of divine simplicity for transforming the understanding of God in biblical monotheism.

Some people, on reading this passage, would take it that God, whom Philo identifies as "Being" (τὸ ὄν), feels wrath and anger. But those who read this passage rightly, Philo argues, respect that God is by nature distinct from humans. These readers, whom Philo calls lovers of the soul, are able to behold the truth that

> He [i.e., God] is not susceptible to any passion at all [ἔστι δ' οὐδενὶ ληπτὸν πάθει τὸ παράπαν]. For disquiet is peculiar to human weakness, but neither the unreasoning passions of the soul, nor the parts and members of the body in general, have any relation to God [ἀσθενείας γὰρ ἀνθρωπίνης τὸ κηραίνειν ἴδιον, θεῷ δὲ οὔτε τὰ ψυχῆς ἄλογα πάθη οὔτε τὰ σώματος μέρη καὶ μέλη συνόλως ἐστὶν οἰκεῖα].[40]

Grasping that God is not like humans, who are composed of bodily parts—since lovers of the soul are able to "converse with intelligible and incorporeal natures"—these readers will not be tempted by an anthropomorphic reading of the passage because they have learned to detach from their conception of God every idea gained from created things.[41] In their approach to God, lovers of the soul dissociate qualities (ποιότητες) that belong to created beings from God so that it is possible "to descry existence needing nothing in its unique solitariness, and free from all admixture and composition in its absolute simplicity" (μόνην καὶ καθ' ἑαυτὴν ἀπροσδεᾶ καὶ ἁπλῆν φύσιν ἰδεῖν ἀμιγῆ καὶ ἀσύγκριτον).[42] Elsewhere, Philo offers further clarification of what this absolute simplicity entails:

> God is alone, a Unity, in the sense that His nature is simple not composite, whereas each one of us and of all other created beings is made up of many things. I, for example, am many things in one. I am soul and body. To soul belong rational and irrational parts, and to body, again, different properties, warm and cold, heavy and light, dry and moist. But God is not a composite Being, consisting of many parts, nor is He mixed with aught else.[43]

The language used in this passage reflects that, like Alcinous, Philo also conceives God's simplicity with the help of familiar metaphysical considerations. God's unity is further qualified by partlessness and noncomposition. Further, this state of simplicity is taken to imply divine incorporeality. Hence, in addition to what we have seen previously in *Deus* 20–32, where God's perfect self-consistency differentiates the divine nature from that of humans, Philo is able to further differentiate God's simple mode of existence as the highest first principle from the composite mode of existence common to created beings. The superiority of lovers of the soul, then, is summed up by their ability to encounter God *as he is*, refusing to let go of God's simple nature by mingling this nature with created qualities.

If divine simplicity lies at the heart of the theology that belongs to the lovers of the soul, then the doctrine also forms the ground of Philo's robust critique of a second group of readers whom he calls lovers of the body. In contrast with lovers of the soul, lovers of the body, who read Gen. 6:7 as suggesting that God was getting angry at the actions of his people, are unable to throw off the bodily senses. As a result, lovers of the body fail to recognize that God, as a simple being, does not operate like a composite being: "And [they] do not reflect that while a being which is formed through the union of several faculties needs several parts to minister to the need of each, God being uncreated and the Author of the creation of the others needs none of the properties which belong to the creatures which He has brought into being."[44] Being uncreated, God does not need the parts or properties that are proper only to creatures. God is not like humans composed of several faculties, each of which needs a particular part that forms the whole being. In *Deus* 57–59, Philo helpfully expands on what he means through specific examples of human operations. God, unlike humans, who need sensory faculties for seeing, hearing, walking, and receiving, has no needs for the corresponding bodily parts (i.e., eyes, ears, limbs, and hands) to carry out these functions. This is because, in the case of humans, each bodily faculty is responsible for a specific sensory function. Seeing, hearing, walking, and receiving are separate senses that require separate bodily parts to carry out these functions. Whereas God is simple and incorporeal. God thus has no need for separate bodily faculties to carry out these functions. Philo offers a mixture of imaginative explanations to account for this claim. Since God is present everywhere, he needs no limbs to get around. God has no need to receive anything because, as creator, he possesses all things. Moreover, he gives gifts to creation through his minister, the Logos. Hence, God has no need for hands to receive and give. God's vision is unlike human vision because, while humans require external light from the sun or a fire to perceive anything, God himself is his own light, which has illumined his own vision before the creation of the world. So God does not need bodily eyes for sight. God, unlike humans, has no need for renewed nourishment. Anthropomorphism is a failure to recognize that all the bodily parts that are necessary for humans to perform basic functions are unnecessary for God. Since lovers of the body fail to recognize the central quality of the divine life, its simplicity, as incomprehensible in terms of the operations of human life, they were led to a faulty exegesis of biblical language.

The foregoing analysis reveals that Philo establishes divine simplicity as a pattern for theological speech to govern how Scriptural language of God, in this case Gen. 6:5–7, should be interpreted. His understanding of divine simplicity testifies to the key development in the Middle Platonic period we have already seen in Alcinous, namely, the identification of simple God as the highest first principle. Hence Philo's God is perfectly self-consistent as well as without composition and incorporeal. But Philo also witnesses a further development. In the hands of the Jewish exegete of the Hebrew Bible, God's simplicity is transposed into the domain of biblical monotheism, leading to a robust critique of anthropomorphism. Thus, in Philo the anthropomorphic language of God in the Hebrew Scriptures is criticized and filtered through the principle of divine simplicity, which states that God's life and operations cannot be understood in terms of human categories and operations. The use of divine simplicity as an anti-anthropomorphic strategy to safeguard the radical distinction between divine and human operations will be a recurrent theme in later Christian sources, making Philo a great precursor to the ante-Nicene doctrine of divine simplicity.

In the Middle Platonic period, a crucial development occurred that accounts for the transition from the doctrine of divine simplicity of *The Republic*, its *locus classicus*, to the form of the doctrine found in ante-Nicene Christian thought, a subject that will form the subject of the remaining chapters. In this chapter I have argued that this crucial development was the identification of a simple deity as the supreme first principle of all things. This possibility was already latent in Plato. Actualizing this possibility, Alcinous and Philo were able to offer in their own ways further metaphysical qualifications of divine simplicity that are familiar in later sources: God is partless, without composition, without the possibility of change through passions, and incorporeal. Without speculating further on the exact development that led to this synthesis, in this chapter I have illustrated how, by the Middle Platonic period, further metaphysical qualifications of divine simplicity have arisen in a coherent manner.[45] It will be in this form that divine simplicity is found in ante-Nicene Christian discourse.

This conclusion, however, needs to be further qualified. It is worth stressing that the development of metaphysical qualifications of divine simplicity by no means implies an abandonment of the sense in *The Republic*. These further qualifications are intelligible only when they are viewed as integrally connected to the basic intuition set out in *The Republic*. That such a close connection exists is already hinted at by Philo's analogy between the perfect state of the souls of the philosophers and God in *Deus* 24–25. The perfect human life is the imitation of the life of the one who is truly simple, that is, both metaphysically (partlessness, immutability, incorporeality) and ethically (self-consistency and truthfulness).[46] Joseph Amstutz, in his philological investigation of the meaning of simplicity in Philo, concludes that God's simplicity "for Philo is not merely a metaphysical aside, but an essential element of his spiritual teaching."[47] This is because, for Philo (e.g., *Deus* 56), only the perfect man is able and worthy to apprehend the perfect simplicity of God. This Philonic vision is possible only if metaphysical simplicity and ethical simplicity were to be conceived as two interconnected aspects of a single idea of perfection. So, when someone is defending God's metaphysical noncomposition or immutability in the early Christian era, the thought of safeguarding God's perfect constancy and trustworthiness is unlikely to be far away. We shall see this synthesis in full when we turn to Origen.

To conclude, we must return to Philo once more. In *Deus* 82–83 he draws out one further aspect of divine simplicity. It turns out that simplicity should regulate not only the language of God, whom Philo speaks of as *monas*, but also the nature of the word (Logos) produced by God's act of utterance. Commenting on Ps. 61:12 (LXX), "The Lord spake once, I have heard these two things," Philo writes:

> "Once" is like the unmixed, for the unmixed is a monad and the monad is unmixed, whereas twice is like the mixed, for the mixed is not single, since it admits both combination and separation. God then speaks in unmixed monads or unities. For His word is not a sonant impact of voice upon air, or mixed with anything else at all, but it is incorporeal and unclothed and in no way different from the monad.

According to Philo, if God is simple, a *monas*, it follows that the divine act of utterance must also be singular and unmixed as well. This is why the divine writ contrasts the "once" of God's utterance with the "twice" of human utterances to indicate this difference in the modality of speech. But if God is simple and the divine act of utterance is simple, Philo concludes that the result of this utterance, God's word (ὁ λόγος αὐτῷ), shares the nature of its originator. This follows because that which is simple utters "unmixed unities" (μονάδας . . . ἀκράτους). Since what is simple is unmixed, it is impossible for a simple God to utter something that is in any way different from himself. This observation will prove to be the starting point for divine simplicity to occupy a central place in the formation of Christian Trinitarian language in the ante-Nicene period.

CHAPTER 3

Irenaeus's Critique of Valentinian Emission and the Proto-Trinitarian Problematic

So far, I have been sketching out the philosophical meaning of divine simplicity available by the time of the early Christian era. The remaining chapters will have a narrower focus. The following two chapters will turn to early Christian sources in the late second to early third centuries and narrate what I shall denote the "ante-Nicene Trinitarian problematic." The term "Trinitarian," though, needs to be qualified when used in the present context. These chapters are chiefly concerned with how divine simplicity became central in the development of early Christian speech about the nature of the Father-Son relation. Hence the problematic that will form the heart of the following two chapters is "Trinitarian" only insofar as it is one that forms a crucial component of what might be called "fully Trinitarian" theologies.

The central question underlying the ante-Nicene Trinitarian problematic can be summed up thus: if God is simple, what is the consequence for understanding the language of the Father-Son relation emerging out of Scripture? It turns out that ante-Nicene developments on this question were shaped during two interrelated doctrinal-polemical controversies in the late second to the early third century. This chapter examines the first episode integral to the formation of the ante-Nicene problematic, the anti-Valentinian polemic of Irenaeus of Lyons in his work *Adversus Haereses*. Irenaeus is often identified as one of the earliest theologians who held the doctrine of divine simplicity.[1] Further, it is commonly stressed that Irenaeus's specific presentation of the doctrine seems to commit him to the "identity thesis" as an implication of divine simplicity. To recall, this is the claim that if God is simple, then God's attributes are identical to each other and, further, identical to God-self.[2] The presence of this thesis in Irenaeus is justified by the language found in Book 2 of *Adversus Haereses*. But what is less often emphasized is that Irenaeus's language of divine simplicity forms the heart of an argument against a specific theological idea in the second century, namely, the "Valentinian emission" (Latin: *prolatio* / Greek: προβολή).[3] The Valentinians were engaged in speculative protology, a task common in the Neo-Pythagorean philosophy of the time.[4] They sought to provide an account of the origin of multiplicity in the cosmos from a single first principle. To do so, Irenaeus reports that they conceived of creation as coming into being through orderly emissions of many entities called aeons. The aeons served as intermediaries between God and the world. These aeons were emitted in a spiritual realm called Pleroma. Based on this framework, the Valentinians imagined a mythological account of the emissions of multiple aeons in the Pleroma in order to present creation as the result of a drama in the spiritual realm. In mounting a critique of the Valentinian myth, Irenaeus brings out God's simplicity as a theological weapon against the notion of emission central to the myth. The task undertaken in this chapter, then, is to situate Irenaeus's use of divine simplicity in the central chapters of Book 2 of *Adversus Haereses*, where his critique of Valentinian emission unfolds. I shall argue that when Irenaeus's affirmation of divine simplicity is read as an integral part of his wider critique of Valentinian emission, the significance of his discussion for the development of theological speech on the Father-Son relation emerges with clarity. As we shall see, Irenaeus, in line with the ancient sources we have examined so far, establishes divine simplicity as a pattern for theological speech for his polemical discourse. In doing so, in his critique of Valentinian emission Irenaeus actually opens the possibility for divine simplicity to become an important factor that shapes theological discourse on the nature of the Son's generation from the Father.

VALENTINIAN PROTOLOGY

We must begin by setting out the target of Irenaeus's critique. Valentinian protology refers not to a single system but rather to multiple systems that were devised in an attempt to provide a mythological account of creation based on number symbolism.[5] Even within *Adversus Haereses*, where we find one of the few extant reports of Valentinian protologies, Irenaeus presents a number of variations that combine similar themes and ideas. Thus, strictly speaking, we should speak of Valentinian *protologies* in the plural. But given that my purpose here is to examine Irenaeus's critique of Valentinian emission based on divine simplicity, only one particular presentation of the Valentinian system is required. In the opening chapters of Book 1 of *Adversus Haereses*, Irenaeus presents the details of the Valentinian myth, which he criticizes in Book 2 on the basis of divine simplicity.[6] For our purposes, we shall restrict our attention to the so-called *grande notice* and the necessary details criticized by Irenaeus in Book 2.[7]

According to Irenaeus, the Valentinians proposed that in the beginning was the perfect God called First Beginning, First Father, or Profundity. This perfect God is invisible and incomprehensible, eternal and ingenerate. The First Father had existed in quiet throughout the ages along with Thought, which is also named Grace and Silence. Everything came forth from Profundity, who decided to emit a seed that would be the beginning of all things. The method for this emission, characteristic of the rest of the Valentinian account, is expressed using human sexual imagery. Profundity deposited the beginning of all things as a seed in the womb of Silence, who co-exists with him. The beginning of all things, then, came from the conjugal union of the first couple, First Father and Silence.[8]

Valentinian protology is divided into three stages. The first two stages account for the emission within the spiritual realm, the Pleroma (Fullness). The third stage accounts for the emission of everything outside the Pleroma, namely, nonspiritual realities.[9] In the first stage we have the formation, alongside First Father and Silence in the Primary Ogdoad, of the remaining six aeons: Mind, Truth, Word, Life, Man, and Church. The Primary Ogdoad is divided into the Tetrad, which the Valentinians regarded as the root of all things.[10] This Tetrad consists of First Father, Thought, Mind, and

Truth. In this Tetrad, Mind (also called Only Begotten, Father, and Beginning of all things) and Truth were generated as a result of the impregnation of Thought by the seed of Profundity. Subsequently, the second couple—Mind and Truth—combined to emit Word and Life. Word and Life, in turn, combined to emit Man and Church. So apart from Profundity and Thought, the remaining aeons in the Primary Ogdoad were generated as a result of conjugal unions in which one pair of aeons emitted another pair.

From the first Ogdoad arose a second stage of emissions of other aeons based on the conjugal unions between aeons of the second Tetrad: Word, Life, Man, and Church. Wishing to glorify the First Father, Word and Life together emitted ten other aeons, whereas Man and Church together emitted twelve aeons. Together with the Primary Ogdoad, all the emissions form the thirty aeons central to the Valentinian notion of spiritual reality, the Pleroma.

Finally, in the third stage Valentinian protology provides a myth of the Fall that leads to the creation of the rest of reality outside the Pleroma. According to this myth, only Mind, the third aeon in the Primary Ogdoad, knows the First Father. The First Father is incomprehensible to all the other aeons because Thought wished the other aeons to have the desire to seek after the First Father. As a result, the other aeons grew in their desire to know and see the First Father. Beginning from Mind and Truth, the passion to know the incomprehensible Father spread across all the aeons until it reached the last and youngest of all aeons, namely, Wisdom. Due to this passion, the material-soulish universe was created outside of the Pleroma. It was, then, the passion of Wisdom that was responsible for everything that exists besides the Pleroma. Valentinian protology, therefore, accounts for the generation of nonspiritual reality from spiritual reality through the passion arising within the latter. This point will become important for Irenaeus's critique.

This brief description of the three stages of Valentinian protology suffices for making sense of Irenaeus's critique. The key aspects criticized by Irenaeus on the basis of divine simplicity are (1) the creation of the Primary Ogdoad, (2) the subsequent emission of the aeons from the Primary Ogdoad, (3) the possibility of passion and ignorance arising in the Pleroma. I have included as figure 3.1 Joel Kalvesmaki's helpful representation of the Valentinian system summarized in Irenaeus's *grande notice* for the sake of clarity.

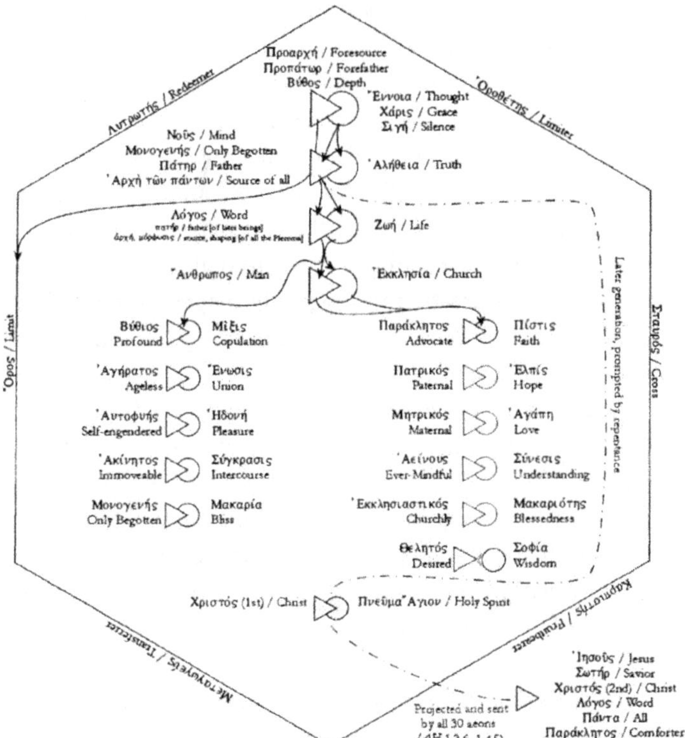

Figure 3.1. The Valentinian Pleroma, According to Irenaeus, *Against Heresies* 1.1–9. Male aeons are assigned (arbitrarily) triangles, females circles. Hollow triangles and circles represent the original thirty aeons. Arrows indicate lines of projection. The large hexagon represents Limit, who is assigned six names and is said to be hexagonal. Illustration by Joel Kalvesmaki, "Formation of the Early Christian Theology of Arithmetic Number Symbolism in the Late Second and Early Third Century," PhD dissertation, Catholic University of America, Washington, DC, 2006, 17.

DIVINE SIMPLICITY AND IRENAEUS'S ANTI-VALENTINIAN GRAMMAR OF GENERATION

Valentinian protology rests on the idea of emissions that account for the process that mediates between God and creation. In two chapters of *Adversus Haereses*, Book 2, Irenaeus criticizes the idea of emissions on the basis of divine simplicity. In unfolding his critique, he develops in passing a set of conditions that must be satisfied by any accounts of generation involving the simple God as the generator. In other words, divine simplicity is to serve as a pattern for theological speech that regulates how one should (or should not) speak about generations from God.[11] I put these conditions under the heading "principle of unity" because they stress the unity, required by God's simplicity, between the generator (the simple God) and the generated. Upon these conditions Irenaeus builds his case against Valentinian emissions as creating theologically inappropriate divisions between God and what is generated by him, leading to a materialistic and anthropomorphic notion of God.

The general shape of Irenaeus's arguments set out in *Haer.* II.13 and II.17 is the same.[12] At the heart of both arguments is the set of disjunctions presented in *Haer.* II.17.2. According to Irenaeus, there are two ways to interpret the nature of emission in the Valentinian myth. Either the aeons are emitted in a manner appropriate for a simple God or they are emitted in a way that violates God's simplicity. In *Haer.* II.17.2 Irenaeus presents the two options in more precise terms:

> So, we ask this question: how were the other aeons emitted? Did they (1) remain united to the one who emitted them, as the rays to the sun; or were they (2) [emitted] as a distinct and separated work, so that each of them would exist separately and have its own form, just as human beings have their source from human beings, and cattle have their source from cattle? Or was it by sprouting, like branches from a tree? And were they (1) of the same substance as those from whom they were emitted, or did they (2) have substance from some other substance? And were they emitted (1) at the same time so that they would be contemporary to some order, [or] that (2) some would be older and others younger? And were they (1) simple and of one form, and in every way equal and similar, just as air and light are emitted; or were they (2) composite and of different form, dissimilar to their fellow members?

> Quaeretur igitur, quemadmodum emissi sunt reliqui Aeones? (1) Vtrum uniti ei qui emiserit, quemadmodum a sole radii, an (2) efficabiliter et partiliter, uti sit unusquisque eorum separatim et suam

> figurationem habens, quemadmodum ab homine homo et a pecude pecus, aut secundum germinationem, quemadmodum ab arbore rami? Et (1) utrum eiusdem substantiae exsistebant his qui se emiserunt, an (2) ex altera quadam substantia substantiam habentes? Et (1) utrum in eodem emissi sunt, ut eiusdem temporis essent sibi, an (2) secundum ordinem quendam, ita ut antiquiores quidam ipsorum, alii uero iuueniores essent? Et (1) utrum simplices quidam et uniformes et undique sibi aequales et similes, quemadmodum spiritus et lumina emissa sunt, an (2) compositi et differentes, dissimiles membris suis?

The use of *utrum . . . an* throughout this passage confirms that Irenaeus is presenting pairs of options regarding the nature of the aeons' emissions. I have indicated the pairs presented in each sentence by 1 and 2. This structure is consistently present above, with one oddity presented by *aut secundum germinationem, quemadmodum ab arbore rami* in the middle. As I shall highlight in due course, Irenaeus does not set out an argument when he turns to this language later on except to carry forward his conclusions drawn from the metaphor of rays from the sun. This oddity notwithstanding, it is apparent that all the first options, labeled 1 above, stress the *unity* between the generator and the generated, whereas all the second options, labeled 2 above, imply *discontinuity* between the generator and the generated. In light of this structure, we can summarize the above passage by the following four pairs:

i. The generated remains one with the generator vs. the generated has a distinct separate existence from the generator.
ii. The generated is consubstantial with the generator vs. the generated is out of the substance of the generator.
iii. The generated is contemporaneous with the generator vs. the generated is from the generator with a temporal ordering.
iv. The generated and the generator are simple, single in form, and similar to one another vs. the generated and the generator are composite, different in form, and dissimilar.[13]

The idea of simplicity enters in the last pair as a contrast to composition. The series of contrasting accounts i–iii, concluding in iv, suggests that the descriptions of the first option in each of i–iii are taken to be summed up by simplicity and the descriptions of the second option in each of i–iii by composition. We may thus interpret the above passage as Irenaeus's attempt to outline contrasting interpretations of emissions. The first takes the nature of the generator and the generated to be simple; the second takes the generator and the generated to be composite. I will now examine how the disjunctions outlined in i–iii above form the heart of Irenaeus's argument against Valentinian emissions. As will become clear, Irenaeus takes inseparability, consubstantiality, and contemporaneity to be conditions required in order for any process of generation from God to be compatible with divine simplicity.[14]

Inseparability

According to Irenaeus, the Valentinians compromise divine simplicity because they conceive of the aeons as generated "distinctly and separately" (*efficabiliter et partiliter*) from the First Father after their emissions.[15] He puts forward two arguments against the possibility that the aeons are generated *efficabiliter et partiliter* from God. His first argument is straightforward: such a mode of emission resembles animal generations, a typical example of something emitted *efficabiliter et partiliter*.[16] In animal generation, the offspring comes forth from the parent having a separate existence. What Irenaeus means is that there is a non-overlap of the animal's and its offspring's spatial location. The animal offspring has a distinct existence in the sense that the spatial form of the offspring is clearly marked off from the spatial form of the parent.[17] As a result, animal generation results in the generator's having two spatially separated existences. For Irenaeus, then, the language of something generated *efficabiliter et partiliter* always brings up the kind of emission associated with animal generation. Inevitably, this language implies that both the generator and the generated possess corporeal attributes such as spatial location and size. So if the aeons were emitted from God as having separate existences, as Irenaeus thinks Valentinian emissions imply, then God is subjected to an animal-like generation characteristic of corporeal, not spiritual, substance. Given that corporeal existence is characterized by its composite nature,[18] the language of something emitted *efficabiliter et partiliter* violates divine simplicity.[19]

Irenaeus's second argument against the aeons' being generated *efficabiliter et partiliter* is more complex.[20] It is grounded in his analysis of human mental activities.[21] He suggests that the Valentinians might have imagined their emissions—specifically the ones within the Primary Ogdoad—in light of human mental activities. In the case of human beings, separate terms such as Thought, Understanding, Intention, and Word are markers of different stages of mental activates. These names do not denote something distinct from the mind itself but rather "particular activities of the mind relating to a determined object and immanent to this mind."[22] The various stages of intellectual activity eventually form the basis for generating an "uttered word" and, as such, they are "co-emitters" of a word. However, Thought, Understanding, and the like remain *within* the Mind. What Irenaeus had in mind can be summarized as follows:

1. First activity of the Mind: When Mind first fixes itself on an object, its first activity is named Thought (*ennoia*).
2. Second stage: When Thought develops and takes possession of the soul, it is called Intention (*enthymesis*).
3. Third stage: When Intention remains fixed on the same object for a long time and grants approval to the object of intellectual activity, then we have Understanding (*sensatio*).
4. Fourth stage: When Understanding has been maintained for a long time—in other words, when "Intention" has granted approval to a given object for intellectual activity for a long time—then it becomes Counsel (*consilium*).
5. Final stage: When the activity of Counsel becomes "very extensive," it becomes Thought (*cogitatio*). Thought as the result of pursuing intellectual activities for a long period could be properly called a Word (*uerbum*), "from which the uttered word is emitted (*ex quo emissibilis emittitur uerbum*)."[23]

Now Irenaeus argues that in the case of the human mind, Understanding, Intention, Thought, and the like—categories of mental activity—are differentiated due to the progressive development of intellectual activities. The different stages of mental activity acquire different names according to "continuance and development" (*secundum perseuerationem et augmentum*) of the mind, not because of a change (*non secundum immutationem*).[24] The example of the human body undergoing the aging process illustrates this point. The body constantly undergoes development in time, meaning that it is young at one stage, then becomes mature at another stage. In other words, while the body at different stages of its aging process is given different names ("young" and "old"), nonetheless it is one and the same body that is aging. By aging, our bodies do not become a different substance but remain the same. Likewise, in the case of the Mind, the various names such as Thought, Understanding, and Intention are simply referring to the same Mind in its various stages of development of its activity. So we distinguish between the mental categories not because the mind is changed into something else in each stage of its activity but because the mind's activity possesses different stages of development. While there are different names for the different stages of development in intellectual activities, these names nonetheless refer to realities that remain *within* the Mind and are not separated from it. As a result, a sense of unity remains between the Mind, on the one hand, and the various stages of intellectual activities, on the other. In Irenaeus's own words, "All these activities are one and the same thing (*Vnum autem et idem*): they have their origin in the mind and get their names because of development."[25]

This analysis reveals two errors in Valentinian emissions should these be considered as arising from an analogy with the process of human mental activities. First, the Valentinians have misunderstood how the human mind functions. If the emissions in the Primary Ogdoad are indeed imagined according to human mental activities, then the Valentinians have failed to recognize that the differentiation between Mind, Word, and Thought does not lead to a distinction *secundum substantiae demutationem*.[26] If the Valentinians have attended to how human mental activities function, then they will have discovered that the different stages of mental activities are emitted *per radium* and so are "one and the same" (*Vnum . . . et idem*).[27] As a result, the aeons could not be conceived as possessing distinct and separate existences from one another. Second, and more significantly, the Valentinians have fallen into anthropomorphism. The mind's activity unfolds and develops in different stages of development only because humans are composite, made up of soul and body:

> You do not understand that in man, who is a composite ensouled being . . . one might speak of such things, namely, of man's mind and of man's thought, and that from the mind came thought, and from the

> thought the intention, and from the intention the word. Really, according to the Greeks, the word is the directing power that develops thought; that is something else from the organ by which the word is uttered. So at times man rests and is silent; at times he speaks and acts. . . . The tongue, being fleshy, is not able to keep up with the speed of the human mind, which is spiritual; hence our word is held back within and is not instantaneously uttered as it was conceived by the mind, but piecemeal, as the tongue can minister to it.[28]

In other words, the differentiation *secundum perseuerationem et augmentum* between different activities of the human mind is simply due to the composite nature of human beings. While human mental activities in principle do not suffer delays in their development, the limitations of bodily organs nonetheless introduce these delays. Accordingly, different stages of development of human mental activity are marked off due to the introduction of these delays. God, however, does not admit such developments because his mind differs from human minds.[29] It would be absurd to think of God's mind as embodied, because this would lead to the conception of God as composite like humans. So even if one reads the Valentinians charitably and interprets their emissions as grounded in generation *secundum perseuerationem et augmentum*, their account still falls into the grave error of anthropomorphism.

It is clear, then, that both of Irenaeus's arguments are centered around the commitment to divine simplicity. In the first argument, Irenaeus highlights that spatial and corporeal generation straightforwardly violates God's simplicity. Hence a simple God cannot be involved in generation that leads to a generator-generated distinction *secundum substantiae demutationem* or *secundum corporis amissionem*. In the second argument, Irenaeus adds a further qualification: a simple God also cannot be involved in generation that results in a generator-generated distinction *secundum perseuerationem et augmentum*. This kind of distinction is present only in the case of embodied minds in composite beings. Hence, if we apply this kind of mental distinction to God, then divine simplicity is once again violated. In offering the two arguments against the possibility that the aeons are generated *efficabiliter et partiliter*, Irenaeus thus establishes the first significant condition that must be satisfied by processes of generation from God compatible with divine simplicity:

> *Irenaeus's principle of unity (negative form)*
>
> Divine simplicity implies *inseparability*: that something cannot be generated *efficabiliter et partiliter* from God. This rules out generations that result in the following distinctions between generator and the generated:
>
> 1. Animal-like: *secundum corporis amissionem* or *secundum substantiae demutationem*
> 2. Composite human mind–like: *secundum perseuerationem et augmentum*

Generation *tanquam a sole radii*: Consubstantiality

But is it possible to articulate positively the nature of processes of generation appropriate for a simple God? According to Irenaeus, this is best approached through three metaphors: rays from the sun (*a sole radii*), lights from a light (*a lumine lumina*), and branches from a tree (*ab arbore rami*). These metaphors are apt as they reveal two further conditions on the nature of the generator-generated relation that must hold for processes of generation compatible with divine simplicity. Consubstantiality concerns the nature of the generator-generated relation with respect to substance, contemporaneity with respect to time. Irenaeus discusses the three metaphors in *Haer.* II.17.4–7. But given that his discussion of the two conditions is based primarily on the metaphor of light alone set out in *Haer.* II.17.4, I shall mainly focus in this chapter on the following analysis.

What links the three metaphors for Irenaeus seems to be the fact that the generated differs from the generator only by generation (*generatione*) or size (*magnitudine*). This is to stress that no differences of substance (*substantia*) exist between the two because the generated are of the same substance as their generator.[30] For example, in the case of rays from the sun, the former are emitted from the latter.[31] The sun serves as the source of the rays; hence, the two are differentiated by generation (*generatione*). Further, the sun's brightness is much greater than the rays emitted from it; hence the two are differentiated by magnitude (*magnitudine*). What remains the same between the two, however, is brightness. Both the sun and its rays share the nature of being bright. In this way, the rays and the sun are said to be "of one form, in every way equal and similar" (*uniformes et undique sibi aequales et similes*). In other words, the sun and its emitted rays are *consubstantial*. The example of rays from the sun offers an appropriate illustration of generation involving a simple God because the sun itself resembles a simple reality. The sun does not change due to the emission of the rays, always remaining what it is without being diminished in its own brightness. Furthermore, the sun does not emit that which is contrary to its own nature, namely, darkness. So the sun is not composed of contrary parts. Immutable and free from contraries, the sun displays the key characteristics associated with simplicity. This clarifies why, for Irenaeus, the metaphor of rays from the sun serves as an apt analogy to illustrate the conditions imposed by simplicity on the process of generation involving a simple generator. If a simple God is the generator, then what God generates can neither be contrary to God's nature nor bring about a change that would diminish God's nature. For Irenaeus, this is summed up by asserting that a simple God must generate that which is *consubstantial* with himself.

Similar analysis probably also forms the basis for Irenaeus's understanding of the other two metaphors. In the case of branches from a tree, it is difficult to see how this organic metaphor could serve as an analogy for generation involving a simple God. Irenaeus never clarifies this point. In *Haer.* II.17.6 he simply glosses over the details and states that consubstantiality follows from the metaphor. In the case of lights from a light, though, Irenaeus offers a brief analysis in *Haer.* II.17.4. He imagines the exercise of lighting torches from a single source of light. Each time a torch is lit, a new light is generated. However, these lights could be recombined with the original source any time because of the similarity of nature between the two. Hence the generated light and the source share a fundamental unity such that when the two are put back together, it will cause a change in the nature of neither the generator nor the generated. Light, then, like the sun, can be considered a simple reality. Light imagery, then, illustrates the same condition of consubstantiality between the generated and the generator that must be preserved in the case in which the generator is simple.

It is generation *tanquam a sole radii*, guaranteeing consubstantiality between generator and generated, that will be compatible with divine simplicity. The consubstantiality condition collapses the Valentinians' protology should they seek to interpret their emissions *tanquam a sole radii*. As I have highlighted above, the aim of the Valentinian system is to account for the creation of the material world based on a cosmic drama in the spiritual realm (Pleroma). This myth, as we have seen, involves the ignorance of the First Father among the emitted aeons (apart from the Only Begotten). This ignorance, in turn, provokes the rise of passion in Wisdom, which led to her Fall. Now if the aeons are emitted *tanquam a sole radii*, then it will be impossible to find either ignorance of the First Father or passion in them. Given that the First Father is impassable (which Irenaeus presumes that the Valentinians affirm), he cannot generate something that is opposite in nature to himself, namely, passions. Further, it would be absurd to say that the First Father lacks knowledge of himself. But if he possesses perfect knowledge of himself, then, using similar reasoning, it will be impossible for the First Father to generate something that is ignorant of himself. Irenaeus frequently rehearses both of these arguments on the basis of the consubstantiality condition.[32] If Valentinian emissions are to be compatible with divine simplicity, then their protology will simply fall apart.

Generation *tanquam a sole radii*: Contemporaneity

Alongside consubstantiality, the light metaphor also illustrates a final condition on the nature of generation involving a simple God. According to Irenaeus, if two things are consubstantial, then in the case of one generated from the other, we cannot relate them in a temporal ordering. Returning to the example of lighting torches, Irenaeus writes:

> For a torch that is lighted later will not have a different light from that which existed earlier. Wherefore, when the lights of these torches are brought together into one, they regain their original unity, since *there results one light that existed even from the beginning.* And one cannot tell that one is younger or older by the light itself—for the whole is one light—or by the torches themselves that received the light (for these were contemporaneous in their material substance, since the matter of the torches is one and the same), but only according to the lighting, since one was lit a short while ago, but another just now.

> Neque enim quae postea accensa est facula alterum lumen habebit quam illud quod ante eam fuit. Quapropter et lumina ipsorum

> composita in unum in principalem unitionem recurrunt, *cum fiat unum lumen quod fuit et a principio.* Quod autem iuuenius est et antiquius neque in ipso lumine intellegi potest—unum enim lumen est totum—neque in ipsis quae perceperunt lumen faculis—etenim ipsae secundum substantiam materiae idem tempus habent: una enim et eadem est facularum materia, sed tantum secundum accensionem, quoniam altera quidem ante pusillum, altera autem nunc accensa est.[33]

This is a difficult passage because Irenaeus's point is subtle. Imagine if we bring back together the various torches lit from a single source. The lights will then recombine into a single light. Now what happens to the status of the various generated lights, having been recombined? Irenaeus's first point is that this recombination results in "the one light that existed even from the beginning" (*unum lumen quod fuit et a principio*). He suggests that the process of recombination enables one to recover the single source from which the lights on the torches had been generated. He then asks: What is the relative temporal status between the generated lights, now that they are recombined into one light? When the lights are recombined, can we still identify their relative temporal status so that one is earlier than another? Irenaeus's full answer is complex, but I wish to highlight one aspect of his answer: with respect to the *substance* of light, we cannot differentiate the relative temporal status among the various generated lights. Irenaeus's argument is found in the single sentence *unum enim lumen est totum.* The point is that the light that is lit later is not a different light than one that existed earlier. Rather, *qua* substance, the two are one and the same since light is a simple substance.[34] Consequently, the recombined lights as a whole make one light. Irenaeus, then, is highlighting that consubstantiality has a further implication about the relative temporal status among the lights. Given that the generated lights are consubstantial with each other, when they recombine we are left with the whole light that existed as one in the beginning. This means that after recombination, we cannot tell the relative temporal status among the different generated lights anymore because all the generated lights have no other differentiators among them apart from their previous relative temporal status (i.e., one is lit after or before another). So when the lights recombine, we simply cannot distinguish the one that was generated earlier from the one that was generated later. This suggests that consubstantiality among the different generated lights implies that *qua* lights (that is, with respect to their substance) they are co-temporal. *Qua* substance, therefore, one generated light cannot be differentiated from another temporally.[35]

The substance of the matter seems to be this: Irenaeus is suggesting that given consubstantiality, contemporaneity also follows from the simplicity of the generator. Thus, if a simple source generates something consubstantial with itself, what is generated must be co-temporal with itself. *Qua* substance, what a simple source generates cannot be differentiated from itself according to their relative temporal status. The immediate polemical value, then, becomes apparent. If two generated lights cannot maintain their relative temporal status *qua* lights assuming that they were generated *tanquam a sole radii*, then should the Valentinians conceive their emissions *tanquam a sole radii*, they will not be able to maintain the distinct ordering of their aeons *qua* spiritual substances (i.e., *qua* being part of the Pleroma). As a result, the distinct temporal ordering of the emission of aeons will be incompatible with the claim that all aeons are part of one spiritual Pleroma.[36]

In addition to consubstantiality, contemporaneity thus constitutes a further condition on the grammar of generation required by divine simplicity. If God is simple, then what he generates *qua* substance cannot possess a relative temporal ordering with respect to himself. Hence, divine simplicity serving as a pattern for theological speech leads to two further conditions on the nature of the generator-generated relation that for Irenaeus are best illustrated from the metaphor of lights from light:

Irenaeus's principle of unity (positive form)

Divine simplicity implies that something must be generated *tanquam a sole radii*. This mode of generation is characterized by the following:

1. *Consubstantiality*: What is generated is similar to, in the same form as, and equal in every way to its source, with the two differentiated only by generation and size.
2. *Contemporaneity*: *Qua* substance, what is generated does not possess a relative temporal ordering with its source.

The "Identity Thesis"

We have seen that, for Irenaeus, divine simplicity imposes certain conditions on the processes of generation that involve God as the generator. This is spelled out negatively as inseparability and positively as consubstantiality and contemporaneity. In this final section, I suggest that it is in light of these conditions that we can make sense of Irenaeus's distinctive language of God's simplicity. This exercise, which is somewhat speculative, nevertheless provides further evidence that Irenaeus sees the three conditions sketched out in this chapter as simply unfolding the implication of divine simplicity for processes of generation.

According to *Haer.* II.13.3, God is "simple and not composite, with all members of a similar nature, being entirely similar and equal to himself. He is all Mind, all Spirit, all Understanding, all Thought, all Word, all Hearing, all Eye, all Light, and the whole Source of all blessings."[37] When read in light of the inseparability condition, this statement will become intelligible. Irenaeus, in making this statement, is perhaps suggesting that one cannot conceive God's Mind, Spirit, Understanding, and the like as generated "distinctly and separately." This can be further analyzed with respect to the two ways to avoid anthropomorphism spelled out above. First, God's attributes—Mind, Word, Wisdom, and the like—cannot relate to him as a human offspring relates to her mother. The reason is straightforward: God is incorporeal and so cannot be divided in a corporeal manner. Second, God's attributes cannot relate to God-self as though they were different stages of divine mental activities. We have already examined the reason for this: God's mind is unlike the human mind in that God's activities are not restricted by the bodily organs. Human mental activities are distinguished into various stages only because they are restricted by bodily conditions. God's mental activities are totally free from these restrictions because he is not composite. Thus, *Haer.* II.13.8 affirms that "God is all sight and all hearing—for he sees in the same way that he hears, and he hears in the same way that he sees. . . . God is all Mind and all Word, and . . . as far as he is Mind, he is also Word, and . . . his Word is this Mind." Irenaeus's language here, then, simply affirms that God's mental activities cannot be distinguished into various stages due to simplicity. Taking *Haer.* II.13.3 and II.13.8 together, Irenaeus's "identity thesis" may be interpreted as expressing that (1) God is not divisible into parts like bodies and (2) the activities of the divine Mind cannot be divided into distinct stages as human mental activities can.

Irenaeus's statement can also be read in light of consubstantiality and contemporaneity. God is "identical" to his attributes in the sense that there is perfect consubstantiality between God-self and God's perfections. What this means is that God and the divine attributes are perfectly one in the manner of the sun and its rays (or light and its source). Just as rays from the sun can ever be only bright, so God's perfections can ever be only in accordance with the divine nature. We cannot conceive of God and the divine attributes as differing in nature. So by claiming that God is "identical" with the divine attributes, what Irenaeus is affirming is that none of these attributes could turn out to be contrary to the divine nature. Contemporaneity offers a further sense in which God and the divine attributes are "identical." Given divine simplicity, it is not possible to have a relative temporal ordering among God's attributes, as well as and between God and his attributes. In *Haer.* II.13.9 Irenaeus states: "Neither can anyone assert that Mind is more ancient than Life, for Mind itself is Life, or that Life is of later origin than Mind, lest he who is the Understanding of all things—that is, God—should at any time be without Life."[38] If one divine attribute were emitted later than another, and if one attribute were understood as separate and distinct from the others, then we would have to consider how and when one could be in possession of the other. For instance, how could Mind or Word have Life if Life was emitted *after* Mind or Word, as in the Valentinian account? For Irenaeus, such questions are impossible for the simple God. There is no time in which God is without his attributes because God's attributes have no relative temporal ordering, nor do God and his attributes: "As a matter of fact, Mind, Word, Life, Incorruptibility, Truth, Wisdom, Goodness, and all other perfections are heard together with God's name."[39]

If the foregoing suggestions are on the right track, then Irenaeus's distinctive language is used to affirm inseparability, consubstantiality, and contemporaneity as consequences of God's simplicity. These conditions are what Irenaeus intends to express by the "identity thesis." This observation has the advantage of clarifying how the language from the pre-Socratic philosopher Xenophanes, widely recognized as the source of Irenaeus's "identity thesis," is thoroughly integrated into Irenaeus's wider polemic against Valentinian emissions. This constitutes a final piece of evidence that inseparability, consubstantiality, and contemporaneity are, for Irenaeus, requirements that simply follow from accepting divine simplicity.

Readers with a clear memory of the previous philosophical chapters will no doubt recognize familiar themes in Irenaeus's language of divine simplicity: immutability, incorporeality, noncomposition, and so forth. Irenaeus's distinctive language of God's "identity" with the divine attributes resembles Alcinous's similar language in *Did.* 10. Most notably, Irenaeus's anti-anthropomorphism concerning the divine operations in the clothing of Xenophanes's language in *Haer.* II.13.8—"God is all sight and all hearing, for he sees in the same way that he hears, and he hears in the same way that he sees"—reminds us of similar language in Philo. Hence Irenaeus's understanding of divine simplicity displays continuities with the Middle Platonic theology examined in chapter 2.[40] My central argument, though, has been that the need to refute Valentinian emissions provides Irenaeus the opportunity to spell out the implications of divine simplicity for speaking about processes of generation involving a simple God. The result outlines a set of conditions for any process of generation deemed compatible with God's simplicity. In doing so, Irenaeus develops a set of what might be called "proto-Trinitarian" considerations regarding the nature of generation regulated by divine simplicity as the pattern for theological speech in the manner of *The Republic.*

The potential significance of Irenaeus's reflections for Trinitarian theology examined in this chapter is obvious. But to call Irenaeus's considerations "proto-Trinitarian" is perhaps forcing a Trinitarian reading onto the texts. To begin with, Irenaeus does not specifically address the generation of the Son in Book 2 of *Adversus Haereses.* In fact, he considers the question of the Son's generation as an incomprehensible mystery.[41] Irenaeus develops the principles of unity for the specific task of criticizing the Valentinian emissions of aeons. What he discusses, then, are the generations of divine attributes that appear in Valentinian protology. None of these attributes are explicitly identified as a second divine person or hypostasis by Irenaeus.[42] A degree of overlap no doubt exists between the two problems since Valentinian emissions involve key Christological titles (Word, only begotten, truth, wisdom). Irenaeus's analysis of generation *tanquam a sole radii* also brings up ideas such as consubstantiality and eternal generation, ideas crucial for later Trinitarian reflections. The path from Irenaeus's principles to theological reflections on the generation of the Son is then easily conceivable. But Irenaeus's "grammar of generation," by stressing the unity between the generator and the generated, seems to leave unclarified the status of the distinction between the generated and the generator. Like Alcinous, in no way does Irenaeus regard the divine attributes generated from the simple God as possessing distinctive reality. Irenaeus's "grammar of generation" is thus ambiguous regarding the exact status of how the generated is distinct from the generator. As formulated, Irenaeus's principles, if applied to the Son's generation, leave open the possibility that if the Son is generated from the Father, then he is identical to the Father in a crucial sense, namely, that the Son could be reunited with the Father as a single divine being, *tanquam a lumine lumina.*[43] Such a position will become the center of controversy later on. Consequently, one should hesitate to read the Irenaean reflections examined here as straightforwardly "Trinitarian." To arrive at a fuller picture of how the implication of divine simplicity for the Father-Son relation was developed in the ante-Nicene period, what I have called the ante-Nicene problematic, a second episode will need to be examined.

CHAPTER 4

Monarchianism and the Fully Trinitarian Problematic

If a simple God can generate only what is "one and the same" as himself, does this imply the dissolution of the distinction between the generator and the generated? According to Reinhard Hübner, "If one would like to defend the oneness of God (*Einzigkeit Gottes*) against the divisions of the gnostic Pleroma, then one must (as Irenaeus explicitly did) exclude any *propria figuratio* of the Logos who would have existed in himself distinctly [i.e., *efficabiliter et partiliter*] from God, in spite of the distinction between God and Logos, Father and Son, taken from Scripture."[1] If this is right, then Irenaeus's anti-Valentinian account of generation—the only one that is compatible with divine simplicity for the bishop of Lyons—will inevitably lead to a dissolution of the distinction between generator and generated. When applied to the generation of the Son from the Father, then, such an account will not be compatible with the affirmation of Father and Son as two distinct divine persons—a central thesis in a Trinitarian conception of God. But if Irenaeus's analysis of the implication of divine simplicity for processes of generation involving God is not off the mark, then it seems impossible to reconcile the affirmation of God's simplicity with a "Trinitarian" distinction between the Father and the Son. Surprisingly, Hübner's remark on Irenaeus pinpoints an issue commonly raised by modern philosophers but in a totally different guise: is divine simplicity at all compatible with Trinitarian theology?

My aim in this chapter is to clarify how discerning the state of this question in the late second to the early third centuries, which emerged during the Monarchian controversy, forms the second important episode in the formation of the "ante-Nicene problematic." The term "Monarchian controversy" refers not to a single controversy but to a series of controversies occurring in this period.[2] Geographically, these controversies spanned Asia Minor and Rome. Hence it is a significant theological controversy among Christian communities in this period. The Monarchian controversy was the major doctrinal episode that brought about sustained theological engagements in the ante-Nicene period on the nature of the distinction between Father and Son. This is because Monarchians, according to their opponents, dissolved this distinction between Father and Son. As a result, the details of this controversy will likely shed light on the key issues for ante-Nicene theologians related to the relationship between divine simplicity and the affirmation of the Father-Son distinction.

My central thesis is that the compatibility between the model of generation that follows from divine simplicity we have seen in Irenaeus and the affirmation of the "Trinitarian" distinction between Father and Son became the explicit subject of debate during the Monarchian controversy. Hübner is surely right to identify a close connection between an anti-Gnostic rejection of emissions (and hence, as we have seen, an affirmation of divine simplicity) and the question concerning the distinction between the Father and the Son. But, as I shall argue in the second part of this chapter, the first attitude does not necessarily require a dissolution of the Father-Son distinction. This inference was likely drawn by Monarchians but, as we shall see in Tertullian's *Adversus Praxean*, the intelligibility of the anti-Monarchian position rests precisely on the unwillingness to concede the point.

Before I lay out the evidence for my claim, some conceptual groundclearing on the relationship between divine simplicity and Monarchianism is necessary. This is because, as I hinted a moment ago, modern writers have frequently raised the issue concerning the compatibility between divine simplicity and the affirmation of Trinitarian distinction. Instead of raising the potential incompatibility through the recognition of the close connection between an anti-Gnostic attitude and Monarchianism—which is how the issue was raised in the ante-Nicene period, as I shall argue—modern writers are troubled by the fact that divine simplicity seems to logically entail Monarchianism. If divine simplicity implies that multiple divine attributes are identical to each other, a claim we have seen can be inferred from Alcinous and Irenaeus, then, following the same logic, divine simplicity surely also requires the three divine persons to be identical to each another, in line with Monarchianism. William Hasker, for example, voices the puzzlement that the Church Fathers seem to have missed this obvious logical connection between the two positions.[3] The prominence of this concern in modern scholarship likely has colored the current perception of the issue at stake between divine simplicity and Monarchianism among theologians and philosophers. So before I turn to sketch out the distinctive ante-Nicene formulation of the incompatibility issue, I shall devote the first part of this chapter to clearing away the modern formulation by elucidating why early Christians did not identify the same logical connection between divine simplicity and Monarchianism.[4]

DIVINE SIMPLICITY AND MONARCHIANISM: TWO DIFFERENT THEOLOGICAL QUESTIONS

It is true that divine simplicity and Monarchianism are both driven by a concern for the unity of God that leads to a form of rejection of multiplicity. In the former, God is to be identified with the divine attributes (e.g., Word, Wisdom, etc.) since, as we have seen in Alcinous and Irenaeus, the plurality of these attributes must be ultimately characterized by a unity in order to preserve God's simplicity. Monarchianism is similarly committed to a strong notion of the unity of God. According to some Monarchians, if (1) God is one, and (2) Jesus Christ is divine, then one must conclude that the divine Son of God is identical to God the Father. Both doctrines, then, in their distinctive way render the multiplicity associated with God as lacking ultimate reality. This analogy, however, is somewhat misleading if taken as a hermeneutical lens through which to view our sources because it is too general. If one begins to scratch beneath the surface, one finds that the two doctrines address different theological problems in early Christian thought. This point will emerge clearly from examining the sources of the Monarchian controversy.

Monarchianism as an Exegetical Position

The Monarchian controversy is centred on prosopological exegesis.[5] Prosopological exegesis refers to the task of identifying "who is speaking to whom" in Scripture. In Scripture we find many passages in which the answer to this question is not obvious.[6] Theologically, this problem becomes even more troublesome when a variant form of the question is posed: who in Scripture could be identified as a divine subject? In other words, how many actors or speakers in Scripture could be identified as divine? The Monarchian controversy is best understood in relation to this question.[7] For both Monarchians and anti-Monarchians agree that two crucial premises must govern Christian hermeneutics: (1) the belief in one God (monotheism) and (2) the belief that Jesus Christ is God (the divinity of Christ). It was uncontroversial to insist that Christian hermeneutics must uphold both of these premises in some ways. What was controversial at the time concerns the exact implications of these premises for reading Scripture.

The historical referent designated by the term "Monarchian" is a much-debated topic among scholars. Influenced by Adolf von Harnack, scholars traditionally differentiate between "modalist" and "dynamic" Monarchians.[8] Whether there were indeed two different kinds of Monarchianism at the time is debatable.[9] Further, the determination of different "Monarchian" groups is complicated by the fact that it is likely that different Monarchian theologies underwent internal variations and developments.[10] Some Monarchians were also patripassians who affirmed that the Father suffered in the economy of salvation, whereas others were not. There might also have been a difference between early Monarchians and Sabellians. These historical difficulties notwithstanding, a single underlying concern unifies all theologies traditionally identified as "Monarchian": monotheism.[11] In this study I shall limit my use of the term "Monarchian" to refer to a restricted group in the third century who had a tendency to identify the Father and the Son as a result of their commitment to monotheism.[12] Monarchians of this sort were deeply concerned about the implication of monotheism for Scriptural hermeneutics. They argued that if there is only one God, and if Jesus Christ is divine, then in Scripture, passages about the divine Son of God must be regarded as having the same referent as passages about God. Consequently, if we identify the Father as God himself, then it follows that the divine Son and the Father must be *identical* to each other. For Monarchians, this is the only available conclusion if one wishes to affirm monotheism and the divinity of Christ together. Hippolytus and Tertullian both testify that this move lies at the heart of Monarchianism:

> This is the way they are claiming to establish a single God. They reply to queries by saying, "Well, if I maintain that Christ is God, then he is the Father in person—if in fact he is God at all."[13]

> And in particular this one [Monarchianism] which supposes itself to possess truth unadulterated while it thinks it impossible to believe in one God unless it says that both Father and Son and Holy Spirit are one and the same. . . .[14]

Our sources, furthermore, highlight that Monarchians arrive at the identification of the Father and the Son through exegesis. According to Hippolytus, Noetus of Smyrna—perhaps the founder of Monarchianism—built an exegetical case for Monarchianism through a number of Scriptural verses.[15] The dossier of Scriptural passages used by Noetus to support his Monarchian thesis is given by Hippolytus. In Ex. 3:6 and 20:3, God pronounces to Israel, "You shall have no other gods besides me." In Isa. 44:6 we read, "I am the first, and I am the last, and in addition to me there is no one." Bar. 3:36 states, "This is our God. No other will be compared to him." What these verses have in common is a particular language for affirming monotheism: There is no other besides the one God. According to Noetus, these verses imply that God is the "one alone" (ὁ μόνος), and so there can be no other (ἕτερος) divine person or being besides him.[16] Given this interpretation, accordingly, Noetus and his followers likely argue as follows:

1. There is only one God, the Father, besides whom there is no other.

2. Jesus Christ is God.

Therefore,

3. Jesus Christ is identical to the Father.

It seems that Noetus understands 3 to be an inevitable implication of the Scriptural passages given by Hippolytus. It is unclear whether Noetus formulates his position, namely, that there is only one divine person (*prosopon*) in Scripture, in technical language. But he clearly draws the following exegetical conclusion: given that the Father must be identified with the Son as a consequence of monotheism, the whole of Scripture must be read as though there is only *one* acting and speaking divine subject in Scripture. Moreover, Noetus also affirms that patripassianism logically follows: "The Father is himself Christ; he is himself the Son; he himself was born, he himself suffered, he himself raised himself up."[17] Thus, in its original form, Monarchianism is an exegetical-hermeneutical claim about the implication of monotheism for prosopological exegesis.

The treatment of two passages in the Gospel of John further illustrates the nature of Monarchian exegesis. John 10:30 and 14:9–11 are central for all Monarchians because these passages lend themselves well to Monarchian exegesis.[18] Monarchians interpret John 10:30 as Jesus teaching that he himself is God the Father.[19] It is easy to imagine how this conclusion seems obvious in the Monarchian framework, wherein there can be only one divine subject in Scripture. Hence Monarchians take John 10:30 as key evidence for their approach that whenever the divine Son is speaking or acting, it is the *Father* who is speaking or acting. For Monarchians, this reading of John 10:30 is further supported by Jesus's response to the question posed by Philip in John 14:9–10: "Have I been with you so long, Philip, yet you do not know me? He who has seen me has seen the Father. Do you not believe that I am in the Father and the Father is in me?" Monarchians interpret these verses as suggesting that Jesus is once again teaching that the Father and the Son are identical.[20] Even though our polemical sources do not provide us with the details of the Monarchian argument, it is not difficult to imagine how the argument might have proceeded. First, if one sees the Father when one sees the Son, then one could argue that this is because the Son is the Father. Second, one could argue that in John 14:10 the preposition "in" simply indicates identity. If the Son is in the Father and the Father is in the Son, then their identities simply overlap—in other words, they are the same person. For Monarchians, John 14:9–10 provides further evidence that Monarchian exegesis makes good sense of the narrative of Scripture.

We do not know whether Monarchians systematically apply their exegetical framework to the interpretation of the whole of Scripture. But what we have examined so far suffices to characterize the basic contours of their position. First, Monarchianism is primarily driven by the desire to maintain monotheism and the divinity of Jesus Christ together. For Monarchians, the only solution is to hold that the Father is identical to the divine Son, a solution justified by Scriptural passages such as Ex. 3:6, Isa. 44:6, and Bar. 3:36–38. Second, as a result of the Son's identification with the Father, Monarchian exegesis posits only one divine subject in the drama of Scripture. Whenever Scripture mentions a divine subject acting or speaking, Monarchians interpret Scripture as referring to the same God. This approach to prosopological exegesis has numerous implications. For instance, a dialogue between two divine subjects would be impossible. Further, the Monarchian position will look for an explanation for any difficult passages in light of their presupposition that there is only one divine subject in Scripture.[21] Thus Monarchianism is best understood as an approach to prosopological exegesis, grounded in the implication of monotheism, that rules out the possibility of having more than one divine actor in Scripture.

The Exegetical Nature of Anti-Monarchian Arguments

In response, anti-Monarchians argue that the identification of only one divine subject in Scripture leads to theological problems. Hence anti-Monarchians seek to offer a more theologically coherent reading of Scripture in order to refute their opponents. Anti-Monarchians propose instead that *two* acting subjects—the Father and the Word, his Son—must be identified to make better sense of the drama of Scripture. For anti-Monarchians, in order to preserve monotheism and Jesus's divinity together, it is not necessary to follow the Monarchians to restrict our reading of Scripture to only one divine subject. Rather, anti-Monarchians argue that plurality of divine subjects is compatible with monotheism. In the case of the Father and the Son, as long as it is possible to construe the Father-Son relation as one and undivided, it is possible to maintain both a plurality of divine subjects in Scripture and monotheism together. Thus the anti-Monarchian position differs from the Monarchian position precisely on the question of how many persons (*prosopa*) could be identified as possessing divine status in Scripture. For Monarchians, there is only *one*; for anti-Monarchians, *at least two*.[22]

The key strategy found among anti-Monarchians is to show that the Monarchian position is exegetically problematic. Anti-Monarchians attempt to out-exegete their opponents by carrying out a better reading of the Scriptural text measured by the grammatical reading techniques of the time.[23] On this basis, anti-Monarchians regard Monarchian exegesis as methodologically flawed. Apart from the critique of Monarchianism in Pseudo-Hippolytus's *Refutatio omnium haeresium* based on the writer's peculiar attempt to trace the root of all heresies in philosophy, all extant anti-Monarchian critique (*Contra Noetum*, *Adversus Praxean*, and *De Trinitate*) is grounded on the same basic point, namely, that the Monarchians have failed to pay careful attention to Scripture in their exegesis. A brief examination of one of the key anti-Monarchians techniques—close grammatical observation—will confirm this point.[24]

In the first place, anti-Monarchians point to a small set of key passages in which the grammatical structure of a given passage requires a clear distinction between Father and Son. Two examples suffice to illustrate this point. First, on Gen. 1:26, "Let us make man after our image and likeness," both Tertullian and Novatian draw on the use of the plural here in support of the thesis that the Father and the Son are distinct.[25] From the Monarchian perspective, since there is only one single God, the obvious interpretation of Genesis 1 would be that there is one *prosopon* involved in the activities of creation. But if this is so, why did Scripture use the plural pronoun in this verse? Tertullian argues that this grammatical feature refers to multiple divine *prosopa* in this chapter. This is the only acceptable interpretation, since either God is deceptive in speaking in the plural when in reality the singular would have been more appropriate or, as in Jewish interpretation, God was merely speaking to the angels given that Jews do not recognize the existence of the divine Son in the Old Testament. For the Christian, Tertullian argues, both alternatives are unacceptable. Rather, in light of the gospels, the correct interpretation is that God was always with the other two divine persons, even in the act of Creation: "[In Genesis] there already was attached to him the Son, a second Person [*secunda persona*], his Word. . . . For that reason he spoke in the plural, 'Let us make' [*faciamus*], 'our' [*nostram*], and 'of us' [*nobis*]."[26] Further, Tertullian suggests that this interpretation is proven by other Scriptural passages. In Gen. 1:27, the text did not simply state that God made man in his own image. If Monarchians were correct—that there is only one person speaking—then the author would have written that man was made "in *his* own image." But in fact, in Gen. 1:27 he wrote that "in the image of God he made him." Tertullian interprets this phrase to imply that Scripture indicates that man was made in the image of the Son. On the basis of grammatical observations, then, Tertullian argues that God made man not in his own image but specifically in the image of the Son. For Tertullian, the use of the plural thus indicates that the Father and the Son were distinct from the very beginning of Scripture.

A second example is found in the anti-Monarchian treatment of the crucial passage for the Monarchians: John 10:30. This passage receives detailed treatment from Hippolytus, Tertullian, and Novatian, further illustrating how significant it was for the Monarchians.[27] All three anti-Monarchians make use of an argument based on close grammatical analysis. Hippolytus argues that the Monarchians fail to attend to the use of the plural in John 10:30: "I and the Father are (ἐσμέν) one."[28] The plural ἐσμέν is used only when there are two or more persons involved. For Hippolytus, this point is further clarified by Jesus's words in John 17, where we read that the Father and the Son are one. According to Hippolytus, since it is absurd to think that the body of Christ (i.e., the Church) *is* (ἐστίν) one "in terms of substance" (κατὰ τὴν οὐσίαν)—for this implies that the Church's unity rules out multiple distinct persons in her constitution—it is likewise absurd to think that the Father and the Son *is* one in this manner.[29] Accordingly, if the body of Christ *are* one, indicating that the Church consists of multiple persons in unity, then on the basis of John 17, we must likewise understand the unity indicated by John 10:30 as one that preserves the plurality of persons implied by the distinction between Father and Son. Consequently, we must regard the Father and the Son as *two* divine subjects in Scripture.

We find a similar argument in Tertullian. First Tertullian argues that "I and the Father" (*Ego et pater*) is an indication that they are two. Tertullian specifically highlights the use of two nominative subjects in the passage. Second, like Hippolytus, Tertullian points out that the use of the plural verb "are" (*sumus*) is another indication that Father and Son are two, since the plural is used to speak not of one but of more than one. Third, in this passage we read that Father and Son "are one [thing] (*unum*)" in the neuter, not "are one [person] (*unus*)" in the masculine. For Tertullian, this clearly indicates that the sense of unity implied by the verse is not that of one single person. For if this were the case, then the masculine *unus* would have been used:

> When he [Jesus] says that two, of the masculine gender, are one, in the neuter—which is not concerned with singularity but with unity, with similitude, with conjunction, with the love of the Father who loveth the

> son, and with the love of the Father who loveth the Son, and with the obedience of the Son who obeys the Father's will—when he says, one are I and the Father, he shows that those whom he equates and conjoins are two.[30]

For Tertullian, the grammatical features of John 10:30 suggest that, contrary to the Monarchian interpretation, this verse clearly refers to two divine persons.

Novatian's exegesis of John 10:30 recapitulates what we have seen so far in Hippolytus and Tertullian but adds further details. First, Novatian argues that when the Son said, "I and the Father," the use of the "and" signifies that the Son wishes to differentiate himself from the Father. If the Monarchian position were correct, then the Son would have said, "I, the Father, am I." However, the text reads, "I *and* the Father," which for Novatian establishes the distinction between the Father and the Son.[31] Second, like Tertullian, Novatian points out that *unum* is used, not *unus*. Novatian's explanation is as follows:

> And since He said "one" thing [*unum*], let the heretics understand that He did not say "one" person [*unus*]. For one placed in the neuter, intimates the social concord, not the personal unity. He is said to be one neuter, not one masculine, because the expression is not referred to the number, but it is declared with reference to the association of another.[32]

Third, highlighting a point made by both Hippolytus and Tertullian, Novatian argues that *sumus*, in the plural, was used, indicating that the Father and the Son are two persons: "For He would not have added 'We are' [*sumus*], if He had had it in mind that He, the only and sole Father, had become the Son."[33] Anti-Monarchian exegesis of John 10:30 thus further confirms the characteristic of anti-Monarchian arguments in general, namely, that they combat Monarchianism as an exegetical position and refute it on exegetical grounds.

The Difference between Monarchianism and Divine Simplicity

The preceding analysis confirms that the Monarchian controversy was primarily preoccupied with prosopological exegesis. The point at stake was whether the whole of Scripture is better explained according to Monarchian or anti-Monarchian exegesis. On the one hand, based on key passages like Isa. 44:6 and Bar. 3:36–38, Monarchians argue for a prosopological exegetical framework that is consistent with monotheism. On the other hand, through close grammatical observations of passages like Gen. 1:26 and John 10:30, anti-Monarchians establish a counter case against Monarchian exegesis. Historically, then, Monarchianism as a theological position has been treated as much more than part of a syllogism. Rather, Monarchianism's merit has been assessed based on how certain Scriptural passages are read and interpreted. As a historical position in the ante-Nicene period, Monarchianism is therefore best identified as the exegetical claim, motivated by monotheism, that the whole of Scripture contains references to only one divine subject.

This conclusion clarifies the intelligibility of why ante-Nicene writers did not regard divine simplicity as entailing Monarchianism. Divine simplicity, as I have argued in chapters 1 and 2, is concerned with determining descriptions of God that are worthy of the divine. For early Christians, a theology worthy of God requires that God is always self-consistent, free from internal contradictions, and that as the supreme highest principle, God is partless, free from composition, and incorporeal. Monarchianism, however, is concerned with determining how many divine persons are acting and speaking in Scripture. Monarchians argue that monotheism implies that there could be only one divine acting and speaking subject in Scripture. Consequently, the same subject must be identified in all passages involving God. It is true that both divine simplicity and Monarchianism set out some hermeneutical rules to regulate theological interpretation of Scripture. In this regard, divine simplicity and Monarchianism function as "second-order" rules for theological discourse. But as such, divine simplicity is concerned with regulating how we interpret the meaning of language for God in Scripture, whereas Monarchianism is concerned with regulating how many divine subjects could be identified in the Scriptural narrative. Thus, historically, the theological problem addressed by Monarchianism can be clearly distinguished from the one addressed by divine simplicity. It follows, then, that the Monarchian thesis can also be clearly distinguished from the doctrine of divine simplicity. This explains why, unlike modern writers, ante-Nicene theologians were hardly tempted to draw the inference from divine simplicity to Monarchianism.

FROM THE PROTO-TRINITARIAN TO THE FULLY TRINITARIAN PROBLEMATIC

If divine simplicity did not lead to Monarchianism in the ante-Nicene period, this is not to say that theologians in this period were unaware of the potential problems at the intersection of the two positions. During the Monarchian controversy, we have evidence that some Christians became aware of a potential incompatibility between divine simplicity and the characteristic anti-Monarchian stress on the distinction between Father and Son. This incompatibility, however, is of an indirect nature. What participants in the Monarchian controversy recognized was that the model of generation put forward by Irenaeus, which follows from divine simplicity, might actually be incompatible with the anti-Monarchian affirmation of the distinction between Father and Son. The logic seems to go something like this. As we have seen, anti-Monarchians argue that, contrary to Monarchianism, Father and Son are two divine subjects that cannot be identified with each other. This raises a question about the implication of the anti-Monarchian stance on the nature of the Son's generation: does the anti-Monarchian insistence on the Son's distinction from the Father necessarily imply a materialistic process of generation akin to Valentinian emissions? This worry makes sense because, as we saw in the previous chapter, it is materialistic emissions (i.e., ones that are incompatible with simplicity) that produce the generated, which has a kind of separate existence from the generator. So if the Son and the Father are two, as the anti-Monarchians insist, then surely the former must be begotten *efficabiliter et partiliter* from the latter. Divine simplicity, then, is implicated indirectly: if the anti-Monarchian position indeed implies a kind of Valentinian emission of the Son's begetting, then it seems incompatible with divine simplicity since, as Irenaeus has shown, God's simplicity is incompatible with emission as a model of generation. Hence, in this indirect manner, through the language of generation, divine simplicity might pose a problem to the anti-Monarchian position.

The key evidence that shows awareness of this theological issue during the Monarchian controversy is Tertullian's *Adversus Praxean*. In this work Tertullian recognizes and addresses the very objection that the anti-Monarchian position could lead to Valentinian emission (Latin: *prolatio* / Greek: *probolē*). Tertullian addresses the issue directly in *APrax.* 8–9. Since this section forms part of Tertullian's overall response to Monarchianism, where he addresses several critical objections to his Trinitarian position made by his critics, it is likely that the issue was raised by Monarchians as an objection to anti-Monarchian theology. The exact nature of the connection between Monarchianism and anti-Gnosticism is far from certain in Tertullian's report, but the question was surely regarded as sufficiently important for Tertullian to feel the need to draft a direct response in *APrax.* 8–9. So it is likely that, for both Monarchians and anti-Monarchians alike, the potential connection between the anti-Monarchian position and Valentinian *probolē* and, consequently, the potential incompatibility between the anti-Monarchian affirmation of the Father-Son distinction and divine simplicity, were recognized as important points at stake.

Let us now turn to Tertullian. Does the anti-Monarchian position necessarily lead to Valentinian *probolē*? Tertullian's response, as we shall see, reveals that his take on the language of generation complicates the problematic we have seen in Irenaeus. According to Tertullian, the heart of the issue concerns the interpretation of the term *probolē*. He concedes that the anti-Monarchian position must lead to some kind of *probolē* that results in the Son's being seen as a person (*persona*).[34] However, the crucial issue is whether *probolē* must be understood in a sense that causes division (*divisio*) and hence separates (*separat*) the Father and the Son in a way analogous to how Valentinian aeons are separated from the First Father.[35] If so, then the anti-Monarchian position is indeed guilty of proposing a problematic kind of *probolē* that would diminish the Father by the generation of the Son and thus violate the unity of God. But must every emission that ends up with the generated and the generator as *two* amount to Valentinian-like *probolē*? Or, to pose the question in Irenaeus's terms: must the Son be emitted *efficabiliter et partiliter* in order for him to be a distinct person from the Father? Here Tertullian is concerned with upholding an additional element not found in Irenaeus that complicates the analysis of what constitutes appropriate language of generation, namely, the distinction between Father and Son. Irenaeus seems to be silent on this question.[36] This additional element allows Tertullian to pose a more complex form of the question concerning the nature of generation than Irenaeus: how do we account for the Son's begetting such that his generation (1) does not subject God the Father to division (the anti-Valentinian condition) and (2) maintains the Father and the Son as two distinct persons (the anti-Monarchian condition)?

Tertullian, like Irenaeus, insists that God the Father must not be diminished in any way by his generation of the Son. This would inappropriately subject God to divisions. Hence Tertullian rejects the use of *probolē* in Valentinian protology because "Valentinus secludes and separates his 'projections' from their originator, and places them so far from him that an aeon is ignorant of its father."[37] But the situation is different in the anti-Monarchian position. The distinction between Father and Son need not involve a kind of *probolē* that subjects God to division. The key is to differentiate between two kinds of plurality that results from a process of generation. In developing this point, Tertullian draws on various terminological pairs. One helpful pair is division (*divisio*) and distinction (*distinctio*). For Tertullian, *distinctio* between the generator and the generated is sufficient to differentiate the anti-Monarchian position from the Valentinian position that leads to *divisio.* As Antonio Orbe has conjectured, Tertullian's solution could also be understood in terms of the differentiation between *portio* and *pars.*[38] According to Orbe, Tertullian maintains that the Son is not a part of God that is separated from the Father. Rather, the Son is a portion of God that proceeded from him. *Portio* thus results from *distinctio* that does not diminish the generator, whereas *pars* signifies the consequence of *divisio* that violates the original nature of the generator. In light of the *distinctio-divisio* and *portio-pars* distinctions, Tertullain argues that the anti-Monarchian position does not necessarily involve a Valentinian type *probolē*:

> For . . . I say that the Father is one, and the Son another . . . not however that the Son is other than the Father by diversity, but by distribution, not by division but by distinction, because the other is not identical with the Son, they even being numerically one and another. For the Father is the whole substance, while the Son is an outflow and assignment of the whole.[39]

> Enim dico alium esse patrem et alium filium . . . non tamen diversitate alium filium a patre sed distributione, nec divisione alium sed distinctione, quia non sit idem pater et filius, vel modulo alius ab alio. Pater enim tota substantia est, filius vero derivatio totius et portio.

For Tertullian, the best illustration for how *distinctio/portio* can arise in generation is given by three similar metaphors: "as a root brings forth the ground shoot, and a spring the river, and the sun its beam.'"[40] In these metaphors, we can distinguish the source (the "parent") from the generated (the "son") clearly so that they are not identical: "The root and the shoot are two things, but conjoined; and the spring and the river are two manifestations, but undivided; and the sun and its beam are two aspects, but they cohere.'"[41] The three metaphors, then, capture a mode of generation in which the generated can be a distinct reality beside the generator *without* compromising the unity between the two. In this manner, Tertullian concludes, the Son can be said to be begotten from the Father without being "separated" from him, bringing about divisions to God.

In reaching this conclusion, Tertullian does not refer to God's simplicity (*simplicitas*).[42] Although he forbids any kind of *probolē* that would subject God to divisions—an idea not far from the concept of simplicity developed in the Platonic tradition—Tertullian's reasoning is clearly grounded on the indivisibility of the divine monarchy.[43] But what *APrax.* 8–9 witnesses to is that by the early third century not all Christian writers accepted the Monarchian perspective that an anti-Valentinian rejection of emission is compatible only with the identification of the Father and the Son. Tertullian's awareness of this problem and his attempt to sketch out a solution illustrate that anti-Monarchian writers in this period were acutely aware of the centrality of resolving this issue for the purpose of affirming a theology that makes a clear distinction between Father and Son. This was especially so for those anti-Monarchians who, like Irenaeus, were explicitly committed to divine simplicity (and hence to an anti-Valentinian account of generation). Such anti-Monarchians faced the challenge of upholding their insistence on the distinction between Father and Son without compromising their commitment to divine simplicity and its subsequent implications for the language of generation. As I shall argue in chapters 6 and 7, it is with respect to this problematic that Origen works out the distinctive contours of his thinking on the Father-Son relation.

Historically, the relation between divine simplicity and Monarchianism has been complex. Modern analyses fail to capture the theological issue that arose at the intersection of these two positions in the ante-Nicene period. However, the hunch underlying modern analyses is not entirely irrelevant because during the Monarchian controversy Christians indeed recognized a potential incompatibility—albeit one revealed indirectly through the issue of the language of generation—between divine simplicity and the affirmation of the Father-Son distinction. Monarchians likely raised this issue in defense of their position, although they might not have conceptualized the problem via the Platonic language of simplicity. Anti-Monarchians, in turn, recognized the importance of this issue and had to respond to it. I have argued that in Tertullian's response to the Monarchian criticism, the "proto-Trinitarian" problematic we have seen in Irenaeus is developed into a "fully Trinitarian" problematic. The "ante-Nicene Trinitarian problematic," in short, is the need to maintain an anti-Monarchian distinction between Father and Son while holding onto an anti-Valentinian account of generation that is compatible with divine simplicity. One can look at this problematic from two sides. From one side: is it possible to maintain an anti-Valentinian account of generation that stresses inseparability, consubstantiality, and contemporaneity between generator and generated (and hence is compatible with divine simplicity) without falling into the Monarchian position that the Son and the Father are one and the same? Or, starting from the other side: is it possible to maintain the anti-Monarchian emphasis on the Son's distinction from the Father (such that there are two divine acting subjects in Scripture) without introducing a Valentinian *probolē* that compromises divine simplicity? Or, more succinctly: must we fall into either Valentinian *probolē* or Monarchianism? Hübner's diagnosis, which captures the Monarchian perspective so well, presents this binary as inevitable. But it is precisely the possibility of going beyond this binary that makes the search for a via media between Valentinian *probolē* and Monarchianism an intelligible option in the ante-Nicene period. And given the centrality of divine simplicity in the ante-Nicene Trinitarian problematic and its Platonic pedigree, it is unsurprising that the doctrine has cemented its place in the thought of the greatest theologian and Christian Platonist in this period, Origen of Alexandria.

CHAPTER 5

Divine Simplicity as a Metaphysical-Ethical Synthesis in Origen

The narrative so far has traversed from Plato up to the early third century. This broad coverage set the scene for the remaining three chapters, which have a narrower focus. The aim of these chapters is to examine the role of divine simplicity in the thought of the third-century Alexandrian Christian writer Origen. Adamantius ("the man of steel"), as he is sometimes known, was both a Christian Platonist and a Scriptural exegete. As a Christian Platonist, Origen was committed to divine simplicity, as he drank deeply from the wells of Platonic philosophy. As an exegete of Scripture, Origen developed his commitment to divine simplicity primarily in the context of solving Scriptural problems arising in his daily activity of commentating on and teaching the Christian Scriptures. Furthermore, Origen also saw a commitment to divine simplicity as a result of the imperative of Scripture itself. Both of these aspects of Origen's thought will be stressed in the next three chapters. In this chapter, Origen's Christian Platonism will be emphasized slightly more; in the next two chapters, his identity as an exegete will be highlighted more. But overall, this lack of balance in no way reflects a commitment on my part to interpret Origen as either one or the other; it is simply a limitation due to the lack of space in the present work to provide comprehensive coverage that integrates both aspects. In any case, my decision to stress one or the other is based on the imbalance I have perceived in previous scholarship.

These limitations notwithstanding, the argument I wish to unfold in the remaining three chapters is that in Origen's thought on divine simplicity, various threads narrated in the previous chapters were tied together in a distinctive fashion. In light of my overarching goal, this chapter will first examine Origen's understanding of divine simplicity in both its metaphysical and its ethical connotations in order to paint a picture of the intelligibility of the idea for the Alexandrian. The following two chapters will then show that divine simplicity played a crucial role in shaping Origen's account of the Father-Son relation, acquiring both an anti-Monarchian and an anti-Valentinian function. As we shall see in the final chapter, as an anti-Monarchian committed to divine simplicity, Origen faced the challenge to resolve the ante-Nicene Trinitarian problematic sketched out in the previous two chapters. Consequently, he developed an account of the Son's generation that constitutes a via media between Valentinian *probolē* and Monarchianism.

In this chapter, then, I first offer a nonreductive reading of Origen's doctrine of divine simplicity. My account seeks to attend to the complexity already highlighted in chapters 1 and 2, namely, that divine simplicity exhibits two senses that are closely connected. The first—and, as I have argued, the more original—sense refers to God's perfect constancy, which I denote the *ethical* sense of divine simplicity. This was first set out definitively in *The Republic*. The second refers to the metaphysical sense, which sets out the qualifications required by the identification of God as the supreme first principle of all things. This sense was subsequently developed in the Middle Platonic period. Scholars who have analyzed Origen's doctrine of God tend to focus primarily on the second.[1] This reductive approach does not tell the full story for two reasons. At a basic level, it misses the importance of the ethical meaning of simplicity when it comes to God. But, more crucially, this approach misses the fact that for Origen the metaphysical sense of divine simplicity is *intertwined* with the ethical sense, a link that is crucial in Origen's attempt to identify God as the very nature and ground of spiritual perfection.[2] Thus, not only is Origen's understanding of divine simplicity characterized by the identification of the God of Scripture, whom he conceives, in light of the second rule of theological speech in *The Republic*, as supreme first principle; this identification leads to a synthesis that is indispensable for his theological vision of perfection.[3] It will not be surprising, then, that Origen's philosophical exposition of divine simplicity recapitulates many of the developments traced in chapters 1 and 2.

Given the complexity of my argument, this chapter is structured in a rather schematic manner. I shall take the metaphysical and ethical dimensions of Origen's understanding of divine simplicity in turn in order to highlight the explicit link he draws between the two sets of language. This approach risks overdistinguishing two dimensions of divine simplicity that are in fact integrally linked, but the promise of clarity has been given priority in this instance. In the first part of this chapter, then, I will analyze Origen's account of the metaphysical aspect of divine simplicity, a task most systematically set out in *Peri Archōn* (*On First Principles*) I.1. Along the way I will situate Origen's discussion in light of the polemical and exegetical background for this text, which will add historical nuance to the analysis. In the second part I shall take a closer look at some of Origen's exegetical and homiletical writings in order to reveal that he also possesses a notion of simplicity as self-constancy, one also found in Plato's *Republic* and Philo's *Quod sit deus immutabilis*, upon which he builds a vision of spiritual perfection grounded in God's perfect simplicity. Finally, in the last section I shall turn to a crucial passage in *Peri Euchēs* in which Origen observes an analogy between being metaphysically simple and being ethically simple. According to this analogy, a life of perfect constancy is analogous to an incorporeal existence that is noncomposite and indivisible. Taken together, the three sections offer a nonreductive account of Origen's understanding of divine simplicity that will shed light on the significance of the doctrine for the Alexandrian.

METAPHYSICAL SIMPLICITY

The metaphysical aspect of divine simplicity is most systematically set out in *PArch* I.1, a chapter concerned with the very nature of divinity itself.[4] This chapter, however, first needs to be situated in light of two contexts. The philosophical theology in this chapter bears resemblance to the one found in writers such as Alcinous and Philo. As a Christian "Platonist," Origen most likely inherited a tradition of philosophical thinking about God that was conversant with Middle Platonic theology.[5] Hence Middle Platonism provides the immediate philosophical background for *PArch*

I.1. But Origen's philosophical theology also needs to be read in its exegetical context. This is because Origen's discussions of philosophical theology, including divine simplicity, are frequently situated in the context of interpreting three specific passages in Christian Scripture: Deut. 4:24, John 4:24, and 1 John 1:5. Thus Origen's metaphysical reflections on divine simplicity developed not in a speculative vacuum but rather out of the desire to provide an adequate exegesis of Scripture. It is in light of this twin context that I shall interpret Origen's systematic discussion of divine simplicity in *PArch* I.1.6.

Divine Simplicity in *PArch* I.1: The Immediate Polemical Context

PArch I.1 was written with a polemical agenda in mind. Its purpose was to criticize those who held that God is a body and to provide an alternative theology of divine incorporeality. Origen's anti-corporealist polemic is firmly rooted in the philosophical context of his time. It was common for philosophers in this period to debate about the nature of the first principle.[6] The standard options for interpreting the nature of God in Origen's time are helpfully listed in *ComJn* XIII.123:

> Many have produced lengthy discussions of God and his essence, so that (A) on the one hand some have said that he has a bodily nature which is composed of fine particles and is like ether, but (B) on the other hand (B1) others [have said] that he is incorporeal, (B2) and still others [have said] that he is beyond essence in dignity and power . . .
>
> Πολλῶν πολλὰ περὶ τοῦ θεοῦ ἀποφηναμένων καὶ τῆς οὐσίας αὐτοῦ, ὥστε τινὰς μὲν εἰρηκέναι καὶ αὐτὸν σωματικῆς φύσεως λεπτομεροῦς καὶ αἰθερώδους, τινὰς δὲ ἀσωμάτου καὶ ἄλλους ὑπερέκεινα οὐσίας πρεσβείᾳ καὶ δυνάμει . . .

Three positions are identified: (A) God's essence is like a composite body, (B1) God's essence is incorporeal, and (B2) God is beyond essence. The structure of the passage (μὲν . . . δὲ) makes it clear that Origen conceives a contrast between the first position (A) and the latter two positions (B1 and B2). This is likely because, whereas the first position affirms the corporeality of God, the latter two positions both deny it. As we shall see from *PArch* I.1, there is no doubt that Origen favors the latter two positions over the first.[7] And by affirming divine incorporeality Origen positions himself among the Platonists of his time.[8]

But Origen's interest in engaging with this debate springs from a more specific issue arising in Scriptural exegesis, namely, the applicability of the term ἀσώματον to God. The term ἀσώματον is central in *Peri Archōn*, where Origen explicitly states in the preface (praef. 8–9) that he intends to search for the equivalent of this philosophical term in Scripture.[9] His inquiry, which is initiated in *PArch* I.1, has as its starting point an exegetical problem based on three key passages: Deut. 4:24, John 4:24, and 1 John 1:5. These passages demand philosophical reflection because each may be read as offering an account of the divine essence: Deut. 4:24 says, "God is a consuming fire," John 4:24 says, "God is spirit," and 1 John 1:5 says, "God is light." Given the grammatical structure of these passages ("God is X"), one's interpretation of the key terms ("fire," "spirit," and "light") will inevitably lead one to an account of the divine essence. Now, deciding between the different positions on the nature of God matters hermeneutically with respect to these three passages. If the divine essence is to be understood corporeally, then the terms "fire," "spirit," and "light" must be interpreted literally as referring to corporeal realities. But if the divine essence is incorporeal or God is beyond essence, then the same terms will demand an interpretation beyond their literal sense. In these cases, an alternative reading will be needed to make sense of these passages as descriptions of God. Characteristically, Origen is interested in the debate concerning the nature of the divine essence because this philosophical issue is intertwined with exegesis.

From Origen's point of view, the exegetical issue arising from the three passages is that they are prone to be read as providing evidence of divine *corporeality*, a position he rejects. He is concerned that "fire," "spirit," and "light" are taken by some as referring literally to realities perceptible to the bodily senses. This raises a question, though: who were the opponents of Origen who interpreted the Scripture in this manner? It has been suggested that in *PArch* I.1 Origen probably had in mind "Christian Stoics," not the "unsophisticated anthropomorphites," when he explicitly rebuked his unnamed opponents for their interpretations of Deut. 4:24, John 4:24, and 1 John 1:5.[10] According to Stoic physics, every existent thing is corporeal. This is grounded on the criterion that any existent being must display the power or capacity (δύναμις) of acting or being acted upon. Based on this criterion, the Stoics argue that all existent things must be corporeal because only bodies can act or be acted upon. This does not mean that bodies are the only items in Stoic ontology. But it does mean that for the Stoics, principles (*archai*) that account for the cosmos are corporeal: God is the active principle, whereas unqualified matter is the passive principle.[11] Hence, in the Stoic scheme, God is a co-principle with matter, acting together with it to generate all existent things. It is difficult to say whether it is fair to accuse the Stoics of making God a material principle, possessing a body.[12] Nevertheless, this accusation was common among Platonists in Origen's time.[13] This polemical interpretation of Stoic theology appears frequently in Origen's corpus and is summarized well in *Contra Celsum*:

> The Stoics who maintain that God is a body . . . introduce a corruptible first principle which is corporeal [ἀρχὴν φθαρτὴν εἰσάγοντος τὴν σωματικὴν]. According to this last view, of the Stoics, even God is a body [ὁ θεὸς . . . ἐστι σῶμα], and they are not ashamed to say that He is capable of change [τρεπτὸν] and complete alteration [δι' ὅλων ἀλλοιωτὸν] and transformation [μεταβλητὸν], and in general liable to corruption [ἁπαξαπλῶς δυνάμενον φθαρῆναι] if there is anyone to corrupt Him; as there is nothing which can do so He is fortunate enough not to be corrupted.[14]

Although a late work, *Contra Celsum* testifies that Origen has been concerned with Stoic theology explicitly. This lends some initial plausibility to the suggestion that he was earlier concerned with those who read Deut. 4:24, John 4:24, and 1 John 1:5 through the lens of Stoic physics in *PArch* I.1. This conclusion is strengthened if we turn to examine another section from this same work, *CCels.* VI.69–71. The context of this passage is Celsus's accusation that the Christian teaching of the incarnation, making God known to creatures through a kind of corporeal process, is unworthy of the divine.[15] In response, Origen accuses Celsus of failing to understand the Christian position correctly. What is striking is that Origen's response in *CCels.* VI.69–70 contains a number of points that are also found in the earlier work, *PArch* I.1:

1. God is incorporeal and thus invisible. The Son of God made God known by being the image of the invisible God (*CCels.* VI.69; *PArch* I.1.8).
2. The invisible God may be perceived by the "heart," that is, the "mind" (*CCels.* VI.69; *PArch* I.1.9).
3. God shares his Spirit with those who can participate in him (the saints). But God's Spirit is not to be conceived of as being cut into parts, divided up, and distributed to the saints (*CCels.* VI.70; *PArch* I.1.2).
4. Deut 4:24 is not to be interpreted literally. God is not a corporeal fire, and he does not consume corporeal things. Rather, the "wood or hay or stubble" (1 Cor. 3:12) consumed by God refers to sins (*CCels.* VI.70; *PArch* I.1.2).
5. Based on 2 Cor 3:6, we are to read certain passages (John 4:24 and Deut. 4:24) according to the spirit, not according to the letter (*CCels.* VI.70; *PArch* I.1.2).
6. Speaking to the Samaritan woman, Jesus taught that God is not to be worshiped in flesh and in material places. Rather, God is to be worshiped in spirit (understood in an incorporeal sense) (*CCels.* VI.70; *PArch* I.1.4).

These parallels suggest that Origen's response to Celsus here simply rehearses anti-corporealist arguments developed earlier in *PArch* I.1. Origen's response also touches on the key term in John 4:24—"spirit" (πνεῦμα)—which is central in the Stoic account of conflagration.[16] In *CCels.* VI.71, at the summit of his response, Origen argues that Celsus's chief error is lumping Christians and Stoics together when it comes to the term "spirit."[17] Because, like the Stoics, Christians have made πνεῦμα a key term in their theology, Celsus infers that the Christians must have understood the term corporeally as did the Stoics.[18] Origen recognizes the problem created by the shared centrality of the term "spirit" in Christian and Stoic theology. His response is to summarize Stoic teaching in order to differentiate it from Christian teaching:

> According to the opinion of the Stoics, who maintain that the first principles are corporeal, and who on this account hold that everything is destructible and venture even to make the supreme God Himself

> destructible (unless this seemed to them to be utterly outrageous), even the Logos of God that comes down to men and to the most insignificant things is nothing other than a material spirit. But in the view of us Christians, the divine Logos is not material. The Stoics may destroy everything in a conflagration if they like. But we do not recognize that an incorporeal being is subject to a conflagration, or that the soul of man is dissolved into fire, or that this happens to the being of angels, or thrones, or dominions, or principalities, or powers.[19]

This passage shows Origen's familiarity with the Stoic doctrine of cosmic conflagration. His criticism of the Stoics in the passage I quoted earlier (*CCels.* I.21) is likely derived from the thought that if God is involved in the process of cosmic conflagration, then God is inevitably subjected to "change, complete alteration, transformation and corruption."[20] Origen's well-developed response to Celsus further illustrates that Stoic physics was the central background to the Alexandrian's exegesis of πνεῦμα in John 4:24.

Summing up the foregoing evidence, we are led to the following view of the polemical context of *PArch* I.1. As an exegete and philosopher, Origen was sensitive to the problem of divine corporeality caused by Deut. 4:24, John 4:24, and 1 John 1:5. He was deeply aware of the philosophical debates of the time concerning the nature of the first principle(s) and how it was relevant to the exegesis of these passages. In particular, as the response to Celsus has shown, Origen was aware that Stoic physics might lead some to interpret key terms in Scripture (in Deut. 4:24, "fire," in John 4:24, "spirit") as grounds for affirming divine corporeality. This constellation of issues in Origen's mind formed the likely context for *PArch* I.1, an attempt to develop an alternative that counters the possibility of a "Christian Stoic" theology based on the three key passages. As we shall see, this is the task Origen set for himself in *PArch* I.1.

Origen's Commitment to the Second Rule of *The Republic* in His Polemics

It is unlikely that we can reach any greater certainty regarding the identity of the opponents in *PArch* I.1. Origen's critique of divine corporeality is not directed exclusively at the Stoics but also at the Epicureans, for instance.[21] But what is clear is that Origen's greatest concern is affirming a robust doctrine of divine incorporeality against the claim that God is a body. Origen's own philosophical theology, including his exposition of divine simplicity, must be read as an attempt to set out an alternative. But before we analyze *PArch* I.1.6, it is helpful to see that Origen's polemical insistence on divine incorporeality springs from his commitment to the second rule of the pattern of theological speech in *The Republic*. Underlying his critique of the Stoics is his conviction that it is not possible to believe in God's perfect incorruptibility while holding that God has a body. As we have seen, Origen insists that everything that is corporeal is subjected to change, complete alteration, transformation, and corruption.[22] This quartet of terms is repeated in *CCels.* III.75.[23] The Stoics might not have endorsed the logic that the corruptibility of God follows as a consequence of holding to divine corporeality. But in Origen's reading, divine corporeality necessarily leads to a God who is mutable and subject to variation. Origen's critique of the Stoics reveals that he is ultimately committed to the second rule in *The Republic*: theological speech that is worthy of God must not postulate that change and a multiplicity of forms are part of the divine nature.[24]

In *CCels.* IV.14, we find testimony to Origen's enduring commitment to this rule. In this passage Origen is responding to Celsus's criticism of the Christian account of God's descent into the world through the incarnation as inappropriate to the nature of divinity. The starting point of Celsus's theology is precisely the Platonic rule in question: God "exists in the most beautiful state," and hence he is unchangeable. For Celsus, if God is to descend into the world, then surely this subjects God to change. The kind of change Celsus has in mind is very precise: it is a change "from good to bad, from beautiful to shameful, from happiness to misfortune, and from what is best to what is most wicked." In other words, Celsus is arguing that the incarnation will bring the most undesirable kind of change to God: change from one state to its contrary. But why, according to Celeus, should God be exempted from such changes? Mortal and immortal beings differ, he contends, in that it is only the former that are subjected to "change and remoulding," whereas an immortal being's nature is "to remain the same without alteration." So if God is immortal—which Celsus takes for granted—then God is not be able to undergo change. So Celsus's theology can be summed up thus: (1) God exists in the most perfect state, (2) the realm of corporeal reality demands everything to be subjected to change and remolding, and (3) the divine nature is immortal and remains always the same without change. On this basis, Celsus concludes that it would be inappropriate for God to be associated with the realm of corporeal reality, as in the Christian doctrine of the incarnation, because God's perfect incorruptibility would be compromised.

Celsus's theology is clearly grounded in Plato's second rule in *The Republic*.[25] He was simply drawing out the implication of the rule for God's relations to the world. Origen's response to Celsus's reasoning, however, is illuminating. Origen affirms Celsus's methodological principle that an immortal, self-same God cannot suffer any change from the perfect state to its contrary. Origen is thus equally committed to the second rule of theological speech in *The Republic*. But from Origen's perspective, Celsus's main error lies in his hermeneutics. Like the Christian Stoics and simple anthropomorphites, Celsus has failed to pass beyond the "letter" of Scripture. The Scriptural account of the incarnation does not imply that God was subjected to change when he "descended." Rather, God descends in terms of his care for human affairs: "While remaining unchanged in essence, He comes down in his providence and care."[26] According to Origen, God's descent into human affairs is to be interpreted *symbolically*.[27] The sense in which God has "descended" is analogical to the way we commonly say that teachers come down to the level of children for the sake of their education or wise men come down to those who are beginners in philosophy. These examples provide a sense of descent without necessarily conveying a physical descent. For Origen, this is how one should understand the language of divine descent in Scripture—for it would make no sense for the God who fills heaven and earth to be limited in his presence to a localized place.[28] So if Celsus had gone beyond the "letter," he would have reached the conclusion that the incarnation in no way implies the idea that in "descending" God's immortal and self-same nature was changed to its contrary state.

Origen then repeats the same argument at the level of the doctrine of God. He argues that Celsus has failed to distinguish the Christian doctrine of God from various corporeal notions of the divine. Epicurean doctrines, for instance, hold that the divine is compounded of atoms and is liable to dissolution. Epicurean theology thus presents the gods as concerned with throwing off the atoms that may cause their destruction. The idea is that only certain specific atoms remain stable in composition, whereas others do not, and so it is necessary for the gods to throw off the ones that do not. In virtue of this process, the Epicurean gods are subjected to the kind of change Celsus had in mind. Similarly, the Stoic notion of divinity takes on different states during different stages of the dynamics of world history: at the conflagration stage, the divine substance is entirely composed of the ἡγεμονικόν (guiding principle), whereas at the stage of new world order, it becomes a part of the cosmos—a divine organism that is immanent in the cosmos. In Origen's reading, the Stoic divinity is also subjected to the kind of change Celsus had in mind. But unlike Epicureans and Stoics, Origen argues, Christians likewise affirm the Platonic pattern for theological speech, albeit on the basis of the divine Scriptures.[29] On the basis of Mal. 3:6 and Ps. 101:28 (LXX), Christians teach "the true conception of God's nature, as being entirely incorruptible, simple, uncompounded, and indivisible" (τὴν φυσικὴν τοῦ θεοῦ ἔννοιαν ὡς πάντη ἀφθάρτου καὶ ἁπλοῦ καὶ ἀσυνθέτου καὶ ἀδιαιρέτου).[30] Here divine simplicity is posited as a characteristic of divine incorporeality. If the gods of the Epicureans and Stoics are liable to dissolution and division, the God of the Christians is simple and free from the possibility of corruption. Furthermore, unlike the Epicureans and Stoics, Christians distinguish simple and intelligible reality from composite and sense-perceptible reality. For Christians, the "God of the universe is mind. . . . He transcends mind and being, and is simple and invisible and incorporeal."[31] Once again, Celsus's overly simplistic approach has led to his failure to distinguish Christian theology from theologies that clearly affirm divine corporeality.

The foregoing analysis of *CCels* IV.14 thus confirms that Origen clearly shares with Celsus the demand for theological language to be shaped by the second rule of *The Republic*. This commitment, in turn, forms the backdrop of Origen's polemic against attributing corporeality to God. Origen ultimately rejects divine corporeality because it is incompatible with God's perfect constancy. It is not surprising, then, that simplicity, the notion at the heart of the second rule in *The Republic*, features prominently in Origen's polemic in *PArch* I.1. In what follows, I shall read Origen's exposition of divine simplicity in *PArch* I.1.6 as an attempt to counter a theology of divine corporeality and its associated hermeneutics with a robust doctrine of divine incorporeality that is fully compatible with the second rule of *The Republic*.

The Philosophical Case for Divine Simplicity in *PArch* I.1

Origen's central focus in *PArch* I.1.6 is to clarify the distinction between God and corporeal beings. His central strategy is to follow what we have seen in the Middle Platonist Alcinous, namely, to identify God as the supreme first principle, source of all composite and sense-perceptible (hence corporeal) realities, a simple intellectual (hence incorporeal) existence. This identification suffices to differentiate God from corporeal realities. Like many of his Middle Platonic and Christian predecessors we have encountered in the previous chapters, Origen maintains this distinction by comparing the operations of the divine mind with the operations of human minds. Thus the central question posed in *PArch* I.1.6 is this: if God is simple, what is the necessary consequence in terms of the nature of his operations?

According to Origen, a simple God is distinguished from ordinary corporeal beings in that his actions can suffer no delay or hesitation due to factors associated with corporeality. In *PArch* I.1.6 Origen unfolds this claim through two basic premises about the divine nature. First, God does not require physical space for his acts because he is not conditioned by the limitations imposed by corporeality. Second, God does not need physical magnitudes in order to act.[32] These premises are likely rooted in Middle Platonic negative theology.[33] As we have seen, Alcinous's theology was strongly shaped by a theological reading of the first hypothesis of Plato's *Parmenides*, according to which what is truly one is that which is not many and is without parts (*Parm.* 137c–d). This claim has a series of implications, of which four are particularly relevant to Origen's argument in *PArch* I.1.6. Noncomposition (1) is without limits (*Parm.* 137d), (2) has no extension or shape (*Parm.* 137d–138a), (3) is nowhere, that is, not contained in space (*Parm.* 138a–b), and (4) is not in time, that is, cannot be or become older or younger (*Parm.* 140e–141d). Hence, if something is truly one, then one must abstract these restrictions from it.[34] As in Alcinous, the negative theology formulated through this method of abstraction is often combined with the (Aristotelianizing) identification of God as the supreme mind. Taken together, these implications help set out an account of God as a simple mind (i.e., the most supreme of all intellects) who is without limits, extension, and shape, not restricted in physical space or time. While Origen does not pursue the method of abstraction rigorously as Philo or Clement of Alexandria does, nevertheless *PArch* I.1.6 reflects his clear reliance on Middle Platonic theology to provide a concrete notion of divine incorporeality.

In light of this background, let us turn to examine Origen's argument on the nature of divine operations. The bulk of *PArch* I.1.6 is spent establishing the plausibility of the two premises mentioned above. First, the mind does not require physical space to move because, by its very nature, intellectual operations are not affected by physical space. Consequently, a purely simple mind possesses its own sphere of operations unaffected by physical restrictions. For Origen, this is evident even from the nature of human minds:

> It is certain, even from the observation of our own mind, that mind does not need space to move according to its own nature. For if it abides within its own sphere, and nothing from any cause occurs to obstruct it, it will never be slowed down at all, by reason of difference in place, from performing its own movements; nor, on the other hand, does it gain any addition or increase of mobility from the quality of [particular] places.[35]

Origen gives an example to illustrate his point. He asks his reader to consider a man traveling by sea in a boat tossed by the waters. In this specific location, our mind would seem to be less effectual in its operations compared to when we are on land. In this instance, does it mean that the difference of physical place has affected the way our mind functions? For Origen, the answer is no. The difference in this case is caused not by the nature of the particular physical locations but by the movement and disturbance of the *body*. The man traveling by sea suffers diminishing mental capacities because it is against the nature of the human body to live at sea. Consequently, while at sea, the man is not able to sustain his intellectual operations as on land because his *body*, to which his mind is conjoined, suffers diminishing ability to enable the mind to function freely. Therefore, the following two accounts must be distinguished:

1. The human mind functions less well at sea than on land because intellectual operations are prone to be affected by physical locations
2. The human mind functions less well at sea than on land because it is conjoined with the body, and the body's capacity to facilitate intellectual operations *is* prone to being affected by physical locations.

In other words, the cause of the discrepancy between our mental activities on land and at sea is found not in the mind, but in the body being affected by physical locations. Hence, in the case of the human mind, it appears that intellectual operations are affected by physical locations, but the discrepancy is due to the fact that humans are mind-body composites. Origen thus draws from this illustration the conclusion that even in the case of human minds, intellectual operations are not by nature affected by physical locations.

God's mind, however, differs from human minds: "God, who is the beginning of all things, is not be regarded as a composite being, lest perchance there be found, prior to the first principle itself, elements, out of which whatever is called composite has been composed."[36] Here Origen explicitly identifies God, the purely simple mind, as the first principle of all things. This identification implies that God must be *prior* to all things—the origin and source of everything that has come after him. Hence God is most appropriately called μονάς (unity) or ἑνάς (oneness) because he is the first being, who alone is truly one. Anything other than the first is merely one among many. Given that God is the first, there can be absolutely nothing prior to God. In the above passage, God's priority is closely linked to simplicity in a way similar to what we have seen in Alcinous: if God is composed of parts, then each of the elements would have had to be prior to God. Origen thus also supposes the kind of reasoning we saw previously in the *Phaedo*. If something is a composite, then its existence as a whole is posterior to the individual parts because the whole is dependent on the putting together of all the parts. This implies that the individual parts need to exist prior to the composite whole not merely temporally, but causally. In a composite, then, the parts have a causal priority over the composite whole. It follows that the claim that God is the *first* principle cannot be made compatible with the claim that God is composite. Consequently, if God is the first principle of all things, then God cannot be a composite of mind and body. Now, as Origen has argued, the only restriction on human mental operations that is imposed by physical locations results from the fact that humans are mind-body composites. But since this restriction does not apply to God due to divine simplicity, God's operations must be purely effectual and suffer no delay due to restrictions imposed by physical locations. This concludes the argument for the first premise, that God does not require physical space to act.

Now let us turn to Origen's argument for the second premise, that God does not need physical magnitudes to act. Mind, by its very nature, is free from any corporeal attributes whatsoever: physical magnitudes, bodily shapes, colors, or anything of this kind. Just as mental operations act in a sphere distinct from physical space, so mental magnitudes that measure the strengths of mental operations are also distinct from physical magnitudes. All magnitudes that measure and circumscribe bodies are therefore not applicable to an existence that is purely intellectual. Unlike the eye, which grows in physical magnitudes—it expands and contracts—the mind does not grow in physical magnitudes when it operates. Instead, the mind grows with respect to *intellectual* magnitudes as opposed to physical magnitudes and a sense of growth (e.g., aging). Origen gives the following example: mind grows not as one ages physically but rather through education. The first point to note, then, is that the growth of mental magnitudes is not necessarily concomitant to the growth of physical magnitudes (e.g., age in this example).

As in the argument for the first premise, Origen proceeds to discuss the case of human minds in which the independence of mental magnitudes from physical magnitudes is somewhat impeded. He similarly accounts for this impediment by the fact that humans are mind-body composites. While in principle a mind could grow in intellectual magnitudes entirely free from physical magnitudes, humans are not able to carry out from birth the exercises necessary to sharpen the power of the mind. This is because human bodily parts are weak, in the first instance, with respect to their ability to enable the mind to grow effectively in intellectual magnitudes. No concrete example is supplied by Origen, but one could easily imagine what he might have had in mind. Consider a child who gets physically tired after long hours of mathematical exercises. The intellectual exercises tire her body, making her not "able to endure the force of the mind's working." Or consider a baby who is not yet able to receive verbal instructions. In this case, its physical immaturity prevents it from receiving instructions necessary for growth in intellectual magnitudes. Origen's point is that in the case of humans, our physical conditions do indeed affect our capacity to grow intellectually because we are mind-body composites. But the human case notwithstanding, the distinction between intellectual and physical attributes implies that it is in principle possible to envisage a mind that is entirely without restrictions imposed by physical magnitudes. God is precisely such a mind due to his simplicity. Hence, divine simplicity implies that God is able to operate entirely independently from physical magnitudes.[37] This concludes the argument for the second premise, that God does not require physical magnitudes to act. This conclusion, in turn, further affirms that divine operations are totally unimpeded by corporeal conditions given divine simplicity.

The Exegetical Case for Divine Simplicity in *PArch* I.1

Origen's philosophical case for divine simplicity is further accompanied by an exegetical case. As I stressed earlier, his concern for divine incorporeality in *PArch* I.1 is occasioned by an exegetical concern with interpreting Deut. 4:24, John 4:24, and 1 John 1:5. For Origen, the philosophical doctrine of divine simplicity finds its basis in the teachings of the Scriptures. In *PArch* I.1.4 Origen sets out his exegetical case: there is no doubt that Jesus's response to the Samaritan woman in John 4:24 indicates that God is incorporeal. He writes:

> To this belief, then, of the Samaritan woman, who thought that because of the privileges of material places, God was less rightly or rightly worshipped either by the Jews in Jerusalem or by the Samaritans on Mount Gerizim, the Saviour answered that one who would follow God must refrain from all preference for material places, and spoke thus: "The hour is coming when neither in Jerusalem nor on this mountain shall true worshippers worship the Father. God is spirit, and those who worship him must worship him in spirit and in truth." See also how appropriately he has associated truth with spirit: he called [God] spirit to distinguish him from bodies, and truth to distinguish him from a shadow or an image.

In this passage Origen is offering a reading of John 4:24 in the context of the whole conversation between Jesus and the Samaritan woman. The woman believes that right worship is attached to a material place. But Jesus's response to her goes beyond simply pointing out her faulty understanding of worship. Rather, Origen interprets Jesus's response as offering a diagnosis of the Samaritan woman's faulty theology: she has a materialistic understanding of God, from which her faulty belief about worship is derived. God, however, is "spirit." This phrase, then, captures Jesus's insistence, contrary to the Samaritan woman's materialistic theology, that the divine nature must be distinguished from corporeal natures. This exegesis suggests that this passage teaches that God must be incorporeal. In Origen's mind, then, John 4:24 offers a clear exegetical foundation for the metaphysical doctrine of divine simplicity set out in *PArch* I.1.6.

The use of John 4:24 showcases the exegetical case for divine simplicity only partially. Origen further argues that the Greek philosophical term ἀσώματον can be found in Scripture under the name ἀόρατον (invisible). While the two terms obviously differ in name, Origen argues that they are identical in sense: both ἀσώματον and ἀόρατον signify the reality of "any substance in which neither colour nor form nor touch nor magnitude is to be understood, to be visible to the mind alone."[38] For Origen, there is ample Scriptural evidence that there is indeed such a correspondence:

> Perhaps these assertions [viz., regarding divine incorporeality] may seem to have less authority with those who wish to be instructed in divine things from the holy Scriptures, and who seek to have it proved to them from that source how the nature of God surpasses the nature of bodies. See, then, if the Apostle also does not say the same thing when, speaking of Christ, he says, "who is the image of the invisible God, the firstborn of every creature" (Col. 1:15). Not, as some suppose, that the nature of God is visible to some and invisible to others; for the Apostle does not say, "the image of God who is invisible to men" or "invisible to sinners," but pronounces, with absolute constancy, on the very nature of God, saying, "the image of the invisible God." And John, also, saying in the Gospel, "No one has seen God at any time" (John 1:18), clearly declares to all who are able

> to understand that there is no being to which God is visible; not as if he were a being visible by nature and yet eludes and escapes the gaze of the frailer creatures, but because by nature it is impossible for him to be seen.[39]

The argument here rests on the exegesis of Col. 1:15 and John 1:18. According to Origen, here Scripture does not apply the term ἀόρατον to God in a relative sense. In other words, God is not merely visible to one and invisible to another. Rather, ἀόρατον is applied to God in an absolute sense, meaning that by his very nature he is invisible—he does not possess a nature that admits of being seen. That which is visible can be seen in no other way than "by its shape and size and colour, which are properties of bodies."[40] Thus, whenever Scripture declares that the divine nature is invisible, then it amounts to implying that God is incorporeal. In this manner, the doctrine of divine simplicity may be grounded exegetically given that, as we have seen in *PArch* I.1.6, divine simplicity is just a way to unpack divine incorporeality. Origen's philosophical case for divine simplicity is therefore accompanied by an exegetical foundation that, in his mind, can be found if one attends to Scripture carefully.[41]

ETHICAL SIMPLICITY

Origen develops metaphysical qualifications of divine simplicity along the lines we have seen in chapter 2. But the simplicity of God is not simply a metaphysical aside for Origen; it lies at the heart of his vision of spiritual perfection. Like Philo, Origen speaks of spiritual perfection as most appropriately reflected by the sense of absolute oneness, that is, in the sense of perfect constancy—a quality at the heart of the meaning of divine simplicity in *The Republic*. The second part of this chapter will be devoted to illustrating how Origen develops this sense of ethical simplicity, which serves as the basis of a vision of spiritual perfection. In this vision, the perfection of words and humanity itself is ultimately measured by the standard of God's perfect simplicity. Hence Origen's vision of spiritual life is inseparable from his doctrine of God. This examination thus unveils the centrality of ethical simplicity in Origen's theology, located at the heart of his vision of spirituality.

The Basic Idea

Origen's vision of perfection draws on the contrast between one and many. He takes this contrast as containing a deeper meaning beyond what we might call its literal sense. This claim arises out of his close attention to the grammatical structure of Scripture, especially to the use of the singular and the plural.[42] In many places Origen observes that Scripture's use of the singular and the plural points toward a deeper theological meaning in a given passage. In these instances, the contrast between one and many denotes a deeper theological contrast between perfection (goodness) and imperfection (lack of goodness). Origen thinks such passages call for a hermeneutic that unveils this deeper layer of meaning. It is in this context that Origen develops an ethical interpretation of one and many. Origen's framework can be illustrated by the following fragment from *Selecta in Genesim* on Genesis 11:

> "Come, let us go down and confound their language, that they may not understand one language of his neighbor" (Gen. 11:7). The confusion of tongues is a sign of evil, whereas this is truly a sign of virtue, when "there was one heart and one soul of all believers" (Acts 4:32). Thus you will find, observing the Scriptures, that wherever there is a multitude of number [πλῆθος ἀριθμοῦ], that wherever there is schism [σχίσμα], that wherever there is division [διαίρεσις] and internal discord [διαφωνία], and the like, it is a sign of evil [κακία]. But where there is unity [ἑνότης], and harmony [ὁμόνοια], and many miracles in the Word, there virtue [ἀρετῆς] is made known.[43]

In this fragment Origen picks up on the numerical plurality of languages (tongues) found in Genesis 11. God's decision to confuse the tongues of men indicates the presence of evil on earth. This is because this act results in a multitude of number (πλῆθος ἀριθμοῦ)—a reality that is referred to in the plural. According to Origen, numerical plurality is always presented as a sign of evil in Scripture, which associates multiplicity with a group of terms that connote a lack of unity among many beings or things. "Schism," "division," and "internal discord" all refer to cases in which many beings or things are not held together by a more fundamental unity. In this sense, then, the multitude of tongues in Genesis 11 is a sign of evil among those confused by God. In contrast, the description of the disciples in Acts 4:32 reflects paradigmatically how Scripture uses oneness as a sign of virtue. Acts 4:32 refers to the believers as having "one heart and one soul" in order to indicate the profound virtuous quality, unity, and harmony, of the early Christian community. Since the contrast between multitude (Gen. 11) and oneness (Acts 4:32) is interpreted ethically, in this fragment Origen is not really focusing on numerical plurality as is seemingly indicated by the presence of the plural in Genesis 11. Rather, he is attending to how Scripture is using the plural as a sign that points toward the evil character among those confused by God. Similarly, while Acts 4:32 certainly refers to many disciples numerically, Origen is not primarily interested in the literal sense of numerical oneness indicated by the description "one heart and one soul." Rather, his interpretation attends to how this use of the singular in Scripture serves as a sign that points to the virtuous quality of the community in Acts 4. What this illustrates, then, is Origen's insistence on attending to an ethical sense of the singular and plural in Scripture beyond their respective literal senses.

This fragment on Genesis 11 sketches the basic contours of Origen's ethical interpretation of one and many. On the one hand, perfect reality, characterized by virtue, possesses unity and harmony. Unity in this ethical sense is used by Scripture as a sign of those who are virtuous. On the other hand, imperfect reality is many, characterized by schism, division, and internal conflicts. Multiplicity in this ethical sense is used by Scripture as a sign of those who are imperfect (evil, sinful, etc.). One important implication that follows from this hermeneutical approach is that both one and many in their ethical senses must be distinguished from their literal counterparts. The use of the ethical sense of oneness will not be restricted to single subjects—those who are numerically one. Similarly, the application of multiplicity in its ethical sense also will not be restricted to multiple subjects (many in the numerical sense). In this way, as we shall see, Origen utilizes the ethical interpretation of one and many to unveil deeper theological meanings in many passages of Scripture. To see this in action, I shall now turn to examining how he applies this framework to three themes: word, man, and God.

εἷς λόγος: The One Word and Many Words

In a fragment of the *Commentary on John* preserved in the *Philocalia*, Origen wrestles with the spiritual appropriateness of his endeavor to compose many books of his commentary. It seems that certain passages in Scripture do not recommend the making of many books. Ecclesiastes 12:12 reads: "My Son, beware of making many books." Further, Proverbs 10:19 states that "in the multitude of words you shall not escape sin, but he who restrains his lips is prudent." In light of these passages, which potentially call into question Origen's book-making endeavors, he poses this question: what is the "multitude of words" that Scripture condemns? The meaning of this phrase needs to be inquired into carefully, Origen argues, because one cannot take it literally to mean numerically more than one word. This interpretation is absurd because, if it were true, then even men such as Solomon and Paul, who were speaking "holy and saving words," would not escape the condemnation issued by Scripture. They would be considered guilty of sin since both spoke many words in their profitable teaching.[44]

How, then, can this conundrum be resolved? Origen turns to considering the "multitude of words" beyond its literal sense. According to Origen, there are two kind of words. On the one hand, there is the perfect Word of God, which is not multiple. This is because Scripture has deliberately referred to this Word in the singular and not in the plural. In John 1:1 we read, "In the beginning was *the Word*," not "words" or "a multitude of words." However, the fact that the Word is singular does not mean that it is free from all kinds of multiplicity: "There is one Word consisting of many aspects" (λόγος γὰρ εἷς συνεστὼς ἐκ πλειόνων θεωρημάτων).[45] Origen is well aware that multiple aspects can be attributed to "the Word." But this multiplicity does not compromise its oneness, because "each of these aspects is a part of the whole Word" (ἕκαστον θεώρημα μέρος ἐστὶ τοῦ ὅλου λόγου). So the Word of God is one in a sense that does not exclude multiplicity absolutely. On the other hand, besides the Word of God there are words (λόγοι) that are to be referred to in the plural. The multiplicity associated with the λόγοι is contrasted with the oneness of the divine Word. For λόγοι possess a multiplicity that lacks the final unity possessed by the Word of God in spite of its multiple aspects:

> [For they, i.e., λόγοι, are] in no way a unit, and in no way are they harmonious and one, but because of disagreement and conflict, they have lost their unity and have become numbers, perhaps even endless numbers.
>
> Οὐδαμοῦ γὰρ ἡ μονάς, καὶ οὐδαμοῦ τὸ σύμφωνον καὶ ἕν, ἀλλὰ παρὰ τὸ διεσπᾶσθαι καὶ μάχεσθαι τὸ ἕν ἀπ' ἐκείνων ἀπώλετο, καὶ γεγόνασιν ἀριθμοί, καὶ τάχα ἀριθμοὶ ἄπειροι.[46]

The kind of unity and multiplicity involved in the contrast between the one Word and multiple words must be treated carefully. The Word of God is one, even though it consists of numerically multiple aspects. It is even described as having these multiple meanings as parts (μέρη). The Word, which possesses multiple aspects numerically, is one since its aspects are unified into a single Word. The problem with the λόγοι does not concern their numerical multiplicity. Rather, Origen understands λόγοι as containing a plurality in which conflict and division are found. Thus, for Origen, the difference between the Word of God and the λόγοι comes down to the fact that while the former possesses a final unity amid numerical multiplicity, the latter do not. On this basis, the "multitude of words" in the warnings found in Ecclesiastes 12:12 and Proverbs 10:19 therefore cannot be understood literally.

Instead, Origen suggests that the multiplicity in the "multitude of words" is to be interpreted according to its ethical sense. Many saints spoke many words, but that is not a sign of their sinfulness. This is because what differentiates the singular word and the multitude of words resides in the *nature* of the words uttered. So in the case when many words are spoken, whether these words are to be described in the singular or the plural depends on whether there is a final unity and harmony within the nature of these words. If many words are spoken in accordance with godliness and truth, then even though there is a multitude of words, they can be called *one word* (εἷς λόγος) collectively: "According to this we may say that he who utters anything whatsoever contrary to godliness speaks much, while he who speaks the things of the truth, even though he speak so exhaustively as to omit nothing, even speaks one word, and the saints, making the one Word their constant aim, do not fall into the vice of much speaking."[47] Hence, the problem Scripture raises regarding the making of many books and the speaking of many words is not tied up with the speech of numerically multiple words. Rather, the problematic multiplicity pertains to the nature of the words in question. If the words in question reflect the truth and godliness, as in the case of words uttered by the saints, then even though there are many words, they are appropriately described as being one Word. It is the making of imperfect words that Scripture forbids.

In support of this reading, Origen highlights that Scripture is full of examples in which one and many are not used in their literal sense but rather their ethical sense. For instance, what does Christ mean when he asks his disciples to "search the Scripture" (in the singular) in order to find his presence?[48] Does he mean that they should find him in one specific book of Scripture? This does not make sense, Origen argues, because Christ asks his disciples to find him in all the books of Scripture and not only in a particular portion.[49] According to Origen, the many books of Scripture are described in the singular here because the nature of the words contained therein reflects the perfect reality—a reality ultimately characterized by unity in truth and goodness. So while there are many books of Scripture—the Pentateuch, Prophets, Psalms, and so on—we are to find Christ in one book. Further, Scripture also describes the opposition between the one word and the multitude of words: The holy words are contained in one book, whereas many books are brought to those judged by God.[50] Thus Scripture in many places teaches that the singular Word and the multitude of words contain a deeper ethical sense: perfect words that are godly and virtuous are described by Scripture in the singular, whereas imperfect words that are ungodly and evil are described in the plural, denoting their multiplicity, which characterizes the division and internal conflict inherent in their nature.

Vir Unus: Singular and Plural Pronouns in Scripture

Origen also develops an ethical interpretation of the contrast between one and many in the context of anthropology. According to Origen, Scripture provides numerous examples in which the perfect and imperfect natures of man are contrasted by the deliberate use of singular and plural pronouns. In a number of passages he observes that there is a shift in pronouns from the singular to the plural *for the same subject* in question. Instead of interpreting these changes as textual inconsistencies, he argues that they should be interpreted in light of the ethical sense of one and many. The contrast between singular and plural pronouns is not a mistake but a deliberate device. When a plural pronoun is used, Scripture is pointing to the imperfect nature of those who are addressed. But when a singular pronoun is used, Scripture is stressing the perfect nature of those who are addressed. So the shift of pronouns in Scripture for Origen signposts a theological lesson about the distinct natures of perfect and imperfect man.

A number of examples illustrate how Origen carries this exegesis out. In the ninth homily on Ezekiel he observes that Ezekiel 16 seems to be rebuking the same addressee (Jerusalem), and so it seems that Scripture is repeating the same message for no good reasons. However, he observes that in the same chapter the pronoun shifts from the singular (*Pater tuus Amorrhaeus, Mater tua Chettaea*, Ezek. 16:3) to the plural (*Mater vestra Chettaea, Pater vester Amorrhaeus*, Ezek. 16:45) in God's naming of Jerusalem's ancestry. According to Origen, this shift of pronouns is not accidental:

> There the words are, as it were, addressed to one person; here as if to many. . . . When sin is diffused and evil goes forth more widely and sinners share their sins among themselves, then there is not a single sinner, but in one there are many, just as in the beginning when there was a commencement of transgressing, there were not yet so many as the multitudes that now exist.[51]

So even though Ezekiel 16 is addressing one person (Jerusalem interpreted figuratively), the plural pronoun is used to indicate the multiplicity contained in her sinful nature. In the one sinner there are paradoxically many sinners because of the contagiousness of sin. The nature of sin is that it multiplies and spreads. Here, clearly, the multitude in question goes beyond the literal sense. The one sinner can be called many because of the multitude that is characteristic of sin itself. Here we have a reversal of what we have seen previously when Origen points out that even though numerical multiplicity of aspects is present in the Word of God, there is an ultimate unity that warrants calling the Word one according to its perfection. In the passage on Ezekiel, even though there is numerical singularity, the one sinner contains, potentially, many sinners in herself. Hence Jerusalem is addressed by the plural pronoun according to her sinfulness. Just as the ethical sense of oneness can accommodate numerical multiplicity, so the ethical sense of multiplicity can accommodate numerical singularity. In this passage, then, Origen clearly takes the multiplicity in question in its ethical sense, denoting the nature of sin.

In *Homily on Ezekiel* 9.2, Origen further elaborates the respective natures of sin and virtue on the basis of an ethical interpretation of one and many. The language here is very close to that of the Genesis fragment we have seen previously: imperfection is associated with multiplicity, schisms, heresies, and dissensions, whereas perfection is associated with solitariness and unity. Origen's language here, though, is even more striking: "The beginning of all evils is multiplicity," he writes. Acts 4:32 is once again invoked as the paradigmatic Scripture account of perfection. What is new in this passage is that Origen elaborates the dynamic process of salvation in relation to the ethical sense of one and many:

> If we are to be saved, we must in unity "become perfect in the same mind and in the same thought" (1 Cor. 1:10). We must be "one body and one spirit" (Eph. 4:4). But if we are such that unity does not circumscribe us . . . and we are still being torn apart and divided by evil, we are not going to be where those are who are drawn back into union. For as the Father and the Son are one (John 10:30), so those who have one Spirit are confined into a union. For the Saviour says: "I and the Father, we are one" (John 10:30), and "Holy Father, just as I and you are one, . . . they may be one in us' (John 17:11–12). And one reads in the Apostle: "Until we all attain to the perfect man and to the measure of the age of fulness in the unity of Christ"; and again: "Until we all attain to the unity of the body and spirit of Christ" (Eph. 4:13). From this it is signified that virtue makes one from many, and that we need to become one through it and to flee from the multitude.[52]

According to this passage, perfect unity characterizes the soteriological *telos* for the believer, as indicated by Scripture. So even though sinners possess multiplicity characterized by division, through virtue they may flee multiplicity and *become one*. This is possible because "virtue makes one from many." This passage thus sets out a soteriological vision in terms of the ethical sense of one and many: it is possible to overcome one's multitude (denoting imperfection) toward unity (denoting perfection). While sin is indicated by multitude, it is possible to be transformed from multiplicity toward unity through virtue.

The same soteriological vision is even more clearly set out in a passage from the lost *Commentary on Hosea*, which is preserved in *Philocalia* VIII. Commenting on Hosea 12:4, Origen notes a similar example of shifting pronouns, this time proceeding from the plural to the singular. Characteristically, he contends that this is not to be interpreted as an error in the copy of the text but rather to be understood as signposting a theological lesson. He turns to Genesis 2:16–17 to note that a similar pattern of shifting pronouns is observed.[53] In that passage God is giving commands to Adam. God begins by addressing Adam in the singular when he is giving positive commands: "Of every tree in the garden you may freely eat [βρώσει φαγῇ]" (Gen. 2:16). However, when God turns to the negative commands—regarding what Adam is forbidden to eat—he addresses Adam in the plural: "Of the tree of the knowledge of good and evil, ye shall not eat of it [οὐ φάγεσθε]: for in the day that ye eat [φάγητε] thereof, ye shall surely die [ἀποθανεῖσθε]" (Gen. 2:17). The reason for the shift from the singular to the plural, Origen explains, is that in the case of the positive commands, God is speaking of the way that would preserve the lives of those who would obey them. As a result, those who would keep the positive commands are one in virtue of their single-minded obedience to God's command, though they might be many in the literal sense (as seen in the example of Acts 4:32). However, in the case of the negative commands, God is speaking of laws regarding sin and transgression. The nature of such things is, as we have seen, associated with multiplicity. And so God refers to those who would sin and transgress his laws in the plural. In light of this observation, Origen suggests that the Genesis text reveals the principle that when Scripture is speaking of realities related to goodness and virtue, the singular is used and when it is speaking of realities related to sin and transgression, the plural is used. He then returns to the Hosea passage and attaches a soteriological thrust to this principle:

> And so it is with the present passage. When they still weep and make supplication to God, the plural is used—"They wept and made supplication to me" [Ἔκλαυσαν καὶ ἐδεήθησάν μου]; but when they find God, He no longer uses the plural—"There He spake, not with them [πρὸς αὐτούς]," but "with him" [πρὸς αὐτόν]. For by finding God and by

> hearing His Word, they have already become one [ἕν γεγόνασιν]. For the individual when he sins is one of many, severed from God and divided, his unity gone [Ὁ γὰρ εἷς ὅτε ἁμαρτάνει πολλοστός ἐστιν, ἀποσχιζόμενος ἀπὸ θεοῦ καὶ μεριζόμενος καὶ τῆς ἑνότητος ἐκπεσών]; but the many [οἱ . . . πολλοὶ] who follow the commandments of God are one [εἷς].[54]

According to this remarkable passage, those who are separated from God—who have fallen into sin and transgression—are addressed in the plural because this indicates their true nature. Before receiving salvation, a sinner was addressed in the plural because he was severed from God, the source of unity and oneness. Hence the unity of the person was gone. Nevertheless, the situation changes when he finds God and hears the Word of God. This encounter with God effects a transformation from many to one such that now the man is called *one man*, since those who have found God have become one (ἕν γεγόνασιν). Thus, while Origen sharply distinguishes perfect and imperfect men through the language of one and many, the man who is many can overcome his imperfect multiplicity through a proper encounter with God, the perfect source of unity.

One and many, then, are core terms Origen uses to speak of spiritual transformation. But a critical issue remains: why is it intelligible to associate the righteous man with oneness and the imperfect man with multiplicity? A passage from the *First Homily on 1 Samuel* will shed light on the issue. In *Hom1S* I.4, occasioned by 1 Sam. 1:1, Origen is concerned by a variant among various copies of the text. It seems that while some copies have "there was a certain man" (*erat vir quidam*), other copies have "there was one man" (*erat vir unus*). Origen argues in favor of the latter by offering an ethical interpretation of one and many. It is more correct to adhere to *erat vir unus* because Scripture is using *unus* to teach a theological lesson about the nature of the righteous man since rendering the verse *erat vir quidam* will remove the "title of praise," *vir unus*, attributed to the righteous man. Here, then, Origen clarifies why this title cannot be attributed to the sinful man, who is said to be many and not one:

> We, who are sinners until now, are not able to acquire the title of praise, because each one of us is not one, but many. For consider with me the face of someone who is angry at one moment, sad the next.

> Shortly afterwards, he is joyful, then troubled again, and then again calm. At one time, he enquires about divine things and the acts pertaining to eternal life, while shortly after, he strives towards things pertaining to greed or worldly glory. Behold, how that man whom we believe to be one person is not one at all. Instead, there seem to be many persons in him, as many as there are behaviors, since even according to the Scriptures, "the fool changes like the moon" (Sir. 27:11 LXX).[55]

The sinner is many because he is subjected to changes that turn him from one state to another. But Origen's stress here is not on the possibility of any change but on changes from one state to its contrary. The sinner is many because he is subjected to many mutually conflicting states. At one time he could be happy and yet sad soon after. At one time he could be striving for divine things and yet soon after moved toward worldly glory. Due to such changes, the sinner can never remain one. Internal division, then, is the ruling characteristic that qualifies a person to be described as many. Paradoxically, internal division turns the numerically one into what is truly many. In contrast, the *vir unus* is not subjected to changes that bring about in him one state at one time and its contrary at another time. Perfect constancy, then, is what qualifies a person to be described as one. Once again, paradoxically, this oneness has the effect of transforming the numerically many into one, as in Acts 4:32, where the multitude of believers are described as having "one heart and one soul." For although the Church is composed of many in the numerical sense, there is a perfect constancy of character among them. This is why the Church is described as one man, *vir unus*, the perfect one who shall receive the prize from God.

The *Homily on 1 Samuel* I.4 clarifies the intelligibility of Origen's application of one and many in his anthropology. Further, this passage crucially connects Origen's ethical sense of oneness with the notion of simplicity in *The Republic*. Origen's distinction between the perfect and the imperfect man in this passage resembles the distinction between the forms and particulars in *The Republic*. The form of beauty captures perfect beauty because its contrary, ugliness, can never be attributed to it. Similarly, the perfect man for Origen is one who is perfectly consistent with his own nature such that contraries cannot be found in him. Origen's *vir unus*, then, is simple in the sense attributed to the divine in *The Republic*. Conversely, the imperfect sinner is many because he lacks this simplicity. It is therefore the ethical sense of simplicity that ultimately grounds the intelligibility of Origen's use of one and many in his anthropology. From this observation it is no surprise that at the summit of Origen's vision of spiritual perfection is the perfectly simple God, through whom all sinful humans, characterized by multiplicity, are to become one.

One God: The Self-Same Unchanging Reality

In the same discussion on the *vir unus* in *Hom1S* I.4, Origen identifies the ethical sense of oneness (and its contrary) as most perfectly found in God. But what does divine oneness entail? So far I have indicated that Origen's understanding of the ethical sense of oneness is not an absolute rejection of multiplicity. Rather, multitude in the ethical sense refers to subjection to diverse conflicting states—thoughts, feelings, behaviors, and so on. Verbal multiplicity is imperfect because it lacks internal unity; hence, one word could stand in opposition to another. The sinner is many because he is internally divided, acting in contrary ways. So a reality described as many in the ethical sense is imperfect because it does not possess an ultimate unity that holds the multiplicity together and prevents the possibility of internal conflict caused by diverse contrary states. This state of affairs, according to Origen, is what stands in contrast with God, who is described in Deut. 6:4 as one: "Hear O Israel! The Lord your God; God is one [*Deus unus est*]." In Origen's reading, here the oneness spoken of by Scripture goes beyond its literal sense. God is called one not simply according to number: "God is to be believed to be above all number." Rather, "one" refers to God's immutability, as indicated by Ps. 101:28 (LXX), where God is said to be "the same" (*idem ipse*), and in Mal. 3:6, God says of himself: "I do not change" (*non immutor*). It is in light of these verses that the "one" in Deut. 6:4 should be understood. God stands in contrast to the "many" because he is never subjected to the possibility of acting in contrary ways. Rather, God is truly one because he is ever self-same without being other than who he is. As a result, "That which does not change is said to be one." This constellation of ideas points to what I have already hinted at earlier in Origen's response to Celsus, namely, that the Alexandrian identifies the simple God of *The Republic* as the God of the Scriptures (Mal. 3:6).

Perfection, therefore, is appropriately described as one because God is one. God's perfect oneness, or ethical simplicity, constitutes the basis for Origen's ethical interpretation of one and many. *Vir unus* is an appropriate phrase to use to praise the perfect righteous man because he is the true imitator of God.[56] In other words, since the righteous man does not act in contrary ways and is not subjected to internal division, he truly reflects the simplicity of God. Likewise, the Word of God is one in that its diverse aspects display unity and harmony among them, lacking mutual conflicts. On the contrary, evil and imperfect realities are called "many" in order to reflect how their natures are contrary to the divine simplicity. Due to the presence of internal divisions, everything described by Origen as "many"—a single sinner, many words, and so on—lack the simplicity most perfectly reflected by God. Origen's ethical interpretation of one and many thus ultimately springs from treating God's perfect simplicity as the measure of perfection in all things. The nature of things can be one or many in the literal sense, but their ultimate natures are signified by one and many in the ethical sense, measured by the perfect simplicity of God. In the *Homilies on Leviticus* Origen remarks that "he who is holy is of God alone . . . but he who is a sinner and unclean is of the many."[57] This statement sums up Origen's ethical understanding of one and many: whatever is holy is of God alone, thus one, but whatever is imperfect is contrary to God, hence many.

THE METAPHYSICAL-ETHICAL SYNTHESIS

The foregoing analysis reveals two aspects of Origen's understanding of divine simplicity. On the one hand, as the supreme first principle of all things, God is a simple intellectual existence. On the other hand, as the measure of perfection, God displays perfect constancy, never acting in contradictory ways. These two aspects are nonetheless not disconnected parts of Origen's thinking. In this final section I shall turn to showing that Origen indeed explicitly connects the two aspects of this thinking in a crucial passage in his treatise *Peri Euchēs* (*On Prayer*).

In *PEuch* XXI.2 Origen considers the purpose of Jesus's preface to the disciples in Matt. 6:7 before he teaches them how to pray. The disciples, Jesus exhorts them, are not to be like the gentile, who "uses vain repetitions." What does Jesus mean by "vain repetitions," Origen asks? His explanation is illuminating:

> It seems indeed that he who speaks much "uses vain repetitions," and he who "uses vain repetitions" speaks much. *For no material or bodily thing is single: but every one of them, though reckoned single, is split up and cut in pieces and divided into several parts, having lost its unity.* Virtue is one, vice is many; truth is one, falsehood is many; the true righteousness is one, ways to counterfeiting it are many; the wisdom of God is one, the wisdoms "of this world" and "of the rulers of this world, which are coming to nought," are many; the word of God is one, those who are estranged from God are many.
>
> καὶ ἔοικέ γε ὁ πολυλογῶν βαττολογεῖν, καὶ ὁ βαττολογῶν πολυλογεῖν. οὐδὲν γὰρ ἓν τῆς ὕλης καὶ τῶν σωμάτων, ἀλλ' ἕκαστον τῶν νομιζομένων ἕν ἔσχισται καὶ διακέκοπται καὶ διῄρηται εἰς πλείονα τὴν ἕνωσιν ἀπολωλεκός· ἓν γὰρ τὸ ἀγαθὸν πολλὰ δὲ τὰ αἰσχρὰ, και ἓν ἡ ἀλήθεια πολλὰ δὲ τὰ ψευδῆ, καὶ ἓν ἡ ἀληθὴς δικαιοσύνη, πολλαὶ δὲ ἕξεις ταύτην ὑποκρίνονται, καὶ ἓν ἡ τοῦ θεοῦ σοφία, πολλαὶ δὲ αἱ καταργούμεναι τοῦ αἰῶνος τούτου καὶ τῶν ἀρχόντων τοῦ αἰῶνος τούτου, καὶ εἷς μὲν ὁ τοῦ θεοῦ λόγος, πολλοὶ δὲ οἱ ἀλλότριοι τοῦ θεοῦ.[58]

Origen's interpretation of "vain repetitions" here resembles how he interprets the sense of "multitude of words" in Proverbs 10:19, as we have seen previously. The multitude in the one who "speaks much" is clearly understood in the ethical sense, referring to the imperfect and fallen nature of *logoi* characterized by mutual conflicts. But in the second sentence Origen develops a fresh point. He draws an analogy between the sense of multitude contained in "vain repetitions" and the nature of what is material and corporeal, since nothing of this sort is one. This analogy is valid due to the inherent instability in material and corporeal things. While Origen does not elaborate this in detail, it is not difficult to fill in what he had in mind. We have seen that for something to be many in the ethical sense means that it is subject to internal division. The man who is joyful at one time and sad at another time is aptly considered "many" because his nature is divided, open to being in contrary states. This state of affairs clearly resembles the nature of bodies, which are always subjected to being "split up," "cut in pieces," and "divided into parts."[59] Hence, the sense in which the multitude lacks self-constancy finds a natural counterpart in bodies, which lack permanent immutability. Conflicts and schisms, which are characteristic of the multitude in the ethical sense, thus mirror corporeal divisions and dissolutions. It is this resemblance that enables Origen to draw an analogy between those who are ethically many and corporeal realities. In light of this, the purpose of the second sentence in this passage is to clarify the nature of the "multitude" in question, akin to the numerous passages we examined in the second part of this chapter, but this time through an analogy with corporeality: Corporeality highlights the crucial feature of imperfection signified by the "multitude of words," namely, the lack of simplicity due to conflicts and divisions.

But we may go further. *PEuch* XXI.2 also suggests conversely that one who is perfectly one must be associated with incorporeality. Hence, this passage can be read as evidence that Origen holds the metaphysical and ethical senses of simplicity together in a *synthesis*. While he does not explicitly make this point in the passage, two observations drawing from what we have seen in this chapter will further support this claim. First, if such a synthesis exists, then a defense of divine incorporeality (*metaphysical* simplicity) will inevitably be a central feature of any theology that seeks to implement the second rule in *The Republic*, which is concerned with God's constancy (*ethical* simplicity). This is indeed the case in Origen, as we have seen, in his reply to Celsus in *CCels.* IV.14. Second, the close connection between divine self-constancy and divine incorporeality is further reflected by Origen's use of Ps. 101:28 (LXX) and Mal. 3:6 as the Scriptural basis for both divine self-constancy (*Hom1S* I.4) and divine incorporeality (*CCels.* IV.14). Mal. 3:6, in fact, fully captures Origen's understanding of divine simplicity as a metaphysical-ethical synthesis: the simple God is one, remaining ever the same. To say that God is simple is to affirm the self-same reality of divinity, perfectly constant in goodness and free from division resulting from corporeal composition. The appropriateness of Mal. 3:6 in both contexts further signals the inseparability of divine self-constancy and incorporeality in Origen's thinking. In light of this, I suggest that *PEuch* XXI.2 calls for a nonreductive reading of Origen's doctrine of divine simplicity as a metaphysical-ethical synthesis. God's metaphysical simplicity and ethical simplicity cannot be analyzed as two separate, disconnected aspects of Origen's theology. Rather, for

Origen, the God of Scripture is simple (perfectly constant) in the sense of *The Republic*, a sense that is reflected precisely by the simplicity (incorporeality) that follows from being the supreme first principle of all things.

Origen's account of divine simplicity ties together various philosophical threads. First and foremost, he is committed to a Christian doctrine of God fully compatible with the second rule of *The Republic*, which requires the divine to be portrayed as simple in the sense of perfect constancy. This commitment needs not be exclusively attributed to Origen's Platonism since it has obvious Christian Scriptural sources in Mal. 3:6 and Ps. 101:28 (LXX). But this commitment also leads Origen to develop a set of metaphysical qualifications of divine simplicity already seen in Alcinous and Philo: God is a simple intellectual reality, incorporeal, primordial, and noncomposite. Corporeal qualities are absent from God; in no way are God's acts restricted by these qualities. Consequently, Origen also stresses a point highlighted earlier in Alcinous and Philo: God's purely intellectual operations can in no way be conceived in anthropomorphic terms. Origen's theology has thus absorbed the crucial developments I have identified in the Middle Platonic period regarding the philosophical meaning of divine simplicity: Origen identifies the simple God of *The Republic* as the supreme first principle of all things. However, once again, these commitments need not be attributed exclusively to Origen's Platonism since they also have obvious Christian Scriptural sources such as John 4:24 and Col. 1:15. In this chapter, therefore, I have demonstrated that Origen's commitment to divine simplicity flows equally from Platonism and Scriptural exegesis. The metaphysical-ethical synthesis I have described is not the result of one or the other exclusively; rather, it flows from the integrity that Origen has created between the two.

Further resonances with Philo abound in almost every part of Origen's attempt to build a vision of spiritual perfection upon God's simplicity. A few points are worth highlighting. Origen's analysis of the multitude in the imperfect man and God's immutability in *Hom1S* 1.4 corresponds closely to Philo's analysis in *Deus* 20–32. Moreover, like Philo, Origen attempts to transpose the second rule of theological speech in *The Republic* to the context of biblical interpretation. His ethical interpretation of one and many examined in the second part of this chapter is the result of this undertaking. Finally, Origen's account of one and many offers a soteriological vision of spiritual transformation that is bound up with his doctrine of God's simplicity, a point already hinted at by Philo. These similarities are by no means exhaustive. But this list indicates how Origen's approach to divine simplicity amounts to a further transposition of ideas from Philo's Jewish context into the ante-Nicene Christian context.

This chapter advances my overall narrative by painting a nonreductive account of Origen's commitment to divine simplicity, in order to shed light on the intelligibility of his attempt to regulate the language of the Father-Son relation by the doctrine. If my analysis in this chapter is correct, then nothing short of a metaphysical-ethical synthesis suffices to make sense of Origen's understanding of divine simplicity. His commitment to divine simplicity is not merely a commitment to divine incorporeality, safeguarding God's metaphysical supremacy over creatures. This is because this insistence, in turn, is inseparably connected to an affirmation of God's self-constancy, safeguarding his supremacy in goodness over creatures. Thus, when we turn to Origen's use of divine simplicity to regulate the language of the Father-Son relation, what is at stake is whether Christianity can offer a coherent theology according to which God is perfect goodness, supreme creator, *and Triune*.

CHAPTER 6

Divine Simplicity as an Anti-Monarchian Principle of Differentiation between the Father and the Son

In this chapter I examine the first significant way Origen's commitment to divine simplicity shapes his thinking on the Father-Son relation. Origen draws on divine simplicity to differentiate the Father from the Son. It is the Father alone who is simple; the Son, as Christ and Savior, admits multiplicity in a sense that the Father does not. This scheme is set out in a crucial passage in Origen's *Commentary on John*:

> God, therefore, is altogether one and simple. Our Saviour, however, because of the many things, since God set him forth as a propitiation and firstfruits of all creation, becomes many things, or perhaps even all these things, as the whole creation which can be made free needs him.
>
> ὁ θεὸς μὲν πάντῃ ἕν ἐστι καὶ ἁπλοῦν. ὁ δὲ σωτὴρ ἡμῶν διὰ τὰ πολλά, ἐπεὶ προέθετο αὐτὸν ὁ θεὸς ἱλαστήριον καὶ ἀπαρχὴν πάσης τῆς κτίσεως, πολλὰ γίνεται ἢ καὶ τάχα πάντα ταῦτα, καθὰ χρῄζει αὐτοῦ ἡ ἐλευθεροῦσθαι δυναμένη πᾶσα κτίσις.[1]

The idea of ordering two divine principles based on the simplicity/multiplicity contrast is commonplace in Origen's period among philosophers.[2]

Numenius, for instance, taught that "the first god . . . is simple, and being together with himself throughout can never be divided. The second . . . god, however, is one. He comes into contact with matter, but it is dyadic and, although he unifies it, he is divided by it."[3] Inspired probably by a reading of the first and second hypotheses in Plato's *Parmenides*, Numenius differentiates between the first principle (a simple unity) and the second principle (a complex unity that is not purely simple). Similarly, Clement of Alexandria thought that "God is the One (*Str.* 5.12.81 et passim) and . . . beyond the world of ideas (*Str.* 5.6.38). The Logos is also one, a complex unity into which the believer is united (*Str.* 4.25.156f). The Father is simple, and purely single reality; and the Son is complex, a single reality in multiplicity."[4] In a similar way, Origen in the above passage uses simplicity to articulate a "fairly pronounced difference in status" between the Father and the Son.[5] Divine simplicity, then, leads Origen to what might be termed a *hierarchical* account of the Father-Son distinction.

It is tempting to approach Origen's hierarchical understanding retrospectively in light of later controversies in the fourth century. Ever since Epiphanius of Salamis, questions have been raised regarding the orthodoxy of Origen's Trinitarian theology in a retrospective vein: was Origen a "proto-Arian" or "subordinationist"?[6] This possible reading of Origen, in turn, triggers reactions from scholars who, wishing to defend Origen, undertake the opposite yet equally retrospective approach to portray the Alexandrian as a precursor of Nicene Trinitarian theology.[7] But Origen's hierarchical account of the Father and the Son may also be read primarily in light of his own third-century polemical context.[8] This context is made clear by Origen's heresiological reports:

> Many people who wish to be pious are troubled because they are afraid that they may proclaim two Gods and, for this reason, they fall into false and impious beliefs. They either (1) deny that the individual property [ἰδότητα] of the Son is other than [ἑτέραν] that of the Father by confessing him to be God whom they refer to as "Son" [υἱὸν] in name at least [μέχρι ὀνόματος], or (2) they deny the divinity of the Son and make his individual property [τὴν ἰδιότητα] and determinate essence to be different from the Father [τὴν οὐσίαν κατὰ περιγραφὴν . . . ἑτέραν τοῦ πατρός].[9]

> Moreover, not without danger may those be associated with the Church's membership who say that (2) the Lord Jesus was a man, foreknown and predestined, who before his coming in the flesh had no substantial and proper existence [*qui ante aduentum carnalem substantialiter et proprie non extiterit*], but that, because he was born human, he possessed only the deity of the Father within him [*Patris solam in se habuerit deitatem*]. The same applies to those . . . (1) wishing to avoid the appearance of saying that there are two Gods, and yet having no intention of denying the deity of the Saviour, [who] claim that the Father and the Son have one and the same substance [*unam eandemque subsistentiam Patris et Filii adseuerant*]. That is to say, they indeed say that the deity receives two names according to the diversity of causes [*duo quidem nomina secundum diuersitatem causarum recipientem*], yet there exists a single ὑπόστασις [hypostasis], that is, one underlying person with two names [*unam personam duobus nominibus subiacentem*].[10]

> There are, for example, all the heretics who certainly announce the Father and the Son and the Holy Spirit; but they do not announce well or faithfully. For either (2) they wrongly separate the Son from the Father, when they say that the Father is of one nature and the Son is of another nature, or (1) they wrongly confuse them, when they imagine . . . that he [God] is merely referred to by three names.[11]

Taken together, these reports outline the primary errors regarding the Father-Son relation available in Origen's time.[12] On the one side, labeled (1) above, some have overstressed the unity between the Father and the Son so as to dissolve the proper distinction between them. This group, likely to be Monarchians, have sacrificed the individual personality of the Son for the sake of monotheism. On the other side, labeled (2) above, others have instead overemphasized the distinction between the Father and the Son. This group, likely to be psilanthropists, have postulated that the Son is a mere man, thus different in essence (or nature) from the Father.[13] While the two groups have emphasized opposite tendencies, Origen puts them together because he recognizes that both deny the pre-existence of the divine Son of God.[14] Origen's own heresiological catalogue, then, reveals Monarchianism to be one of the major theological currents in his third-century context that preoccupied his Trinitarian thinking.

In this chapter I suggest that what has frequently been called Origen's "subordinationism," namely, his hierarchical understanding of the Father-Son distinction, is better understood as his anti-Monarchianism.[15] Origen's tendency to stress the transcendence of the Father over the Son is more aptly seen, in his third-century context, as an attempt to counter the Monarchian identification of Father and Son. In light of the wider context, my central thesis is that Origen's use of divine simplicity as a principle of differentiation between Father and Son constitutes an anti-Monarchian theme. Hence, my primary goal in this chapter is to set out a case for situating Origen's hierarchical account of the Father-Son relation in his own third-century theological context in order to better highlight the intelligibility of his use of simplicity to distinguish the Father from the Son as an anti-Monarchian emphasis.[16]

ORIGEN'S CRITIQUE OF MONARCHIANISM

Determining the precise nature of Origen's anti-Monarchianism is not straightforward. This is because, as an exegete, he criticizes the Monarchians only in passing, that is, as part of the task of Scriptural interpretation. Origen therefore does not set out a systematic case against Monarchianism as such. As a result, he rarely elaborates on the terms of his critique. But Origen's critical remarks on Monarchianism scattered across his corpus possess one striking feature. In his description of Monarchian theology he utilizes several technical terms related to Trinitarian theology. He claims that the Monarchians reject the following kinds of distinctions between the Father and the Son:

a. Distinction with respect to hypostasis (καθ' ὑπόστασιν)
b. Distinction with respect to personal property (κατ' ἰδιότητα)
c. Distinction with respect to substrate (καθ' ὑποκείμενον)
d. Distinction with respect to essence (κατ' οὐσίαν)

In this first section I shall set out Origen's anti-Monarchianism by analyzing the content of his critique of Monarchianism in terms of these four types of distinctions.[17]

The clearest aspect of Origen's anti-Monarchianism is found at the level of ὑπόστασις. In *CCels.* VIII.12 Celsus objects to the Christian practice of worshiping Jesus as another alongside the one supreme God. In reply, Origen cites John 14:11 and 10:30 to show that Christians do not worship two gods because the Father and the Son are one God. But immediately Origen feels the need to clarify himself with respect to the Monarchian undertones in his response. He turns to reject the Monarchian interpretations of John 14:11 and 10:30 to safeguard his reply to Celsus from being misinterpreted in a Monarchian fashion:

> "For the Father," he [Jesus] says, "is in me and I in the Father" (John 14:11; 17:21). If, however, anyone is perturbed by these words lest we should be going over to the view of those who deny that there are two *hypostases*, Father and Son, let him pay attention to the text "And all those who believed were of one heart and soul" (Acts 4:32), that he may see the meaning of "I and my Father are one" (John 10:30). Accordingly we worship but one God, the Father and the Son, and we still have a valid argument against the others. . . . Therefore we worship the Father of the truth and the Son who is the truth; they are two distinct hypostatic realities [δύο τῇ ὑποστάσει πράγματα], but one in mental unity, in agreement, and in identity of will [ἓν δὲ τῇ ὁμονοίᾳ καὶ τῇ συμφωνίᾳ καὶ τῇ ταὐτότητι τοῦ βουλήματος].

"Those who deny that there are two hypostases," no doubt, refers to Monarchians, who affirmed a single divine ὑπόστασις due to their commitment to monotheism. Hence they refused distinct individual existence to divine persons, thereby denying the distinction between the Father and the Son καθ' ὑπόστασιν. Here, at the level of hypostasis, we know exactly what alternative Origen had in mind, namely, that the Father, Son, and Holy Spirit are three distinct divine ὑποστάσεις.[18] Thus, at the level of ὑπόστασις, the content of Origen's critique of Monarchianism can be determined with precision.

Next, we turn to ἰδιότης. According to the first of the heresiological reports quoted at the beginning of this chapter (*ComJn* II.16), Monarchians also denied that the Son possesses an individual property (ἰδιότης) that distinguishes him from the Father. Monarchians likely argued that if (a) the Father and the Son are both divine and (b) each possesses individual property, then we will end up with two beings, each of whom personally possesses *divine* properties. Hence, the attribution of distinctive ἰδίοτης to the Son leads to ditheism. Against this view, Origen criticizes the Monarchians for maintaining a merely nominal distinction between the Father and the Son: If the Son does not possess his own individual property, then he could be differentiated from the Father only as one divine name is distinguished from another name.[19] But why is it problematic to deny the Son's possession of individual properties that distinguish him from the Father?

We gain further precision as to Origen's critique from his comments on the opposite error in this passage. As we have seen, Origen frequently pits the Monarchian position against an opposite, equally problematic, psilanthropist position that overemphasizes the distinction between the Father and the Son. Origen's description of this second position in *ComJn* II.16 *prima facie* raises an interpretative issue.[20] On the one hand, he accuses the Monarchians of rejecting the Son's possession of ἰδίοτης. But on the other hand, he accuses the psilanthropists of affirming the Son's possession of individual property. On first reading, Origen seems to end up with a contradiction here: how could both the rejection and the acceptance of the Son's possession of individual property be wrong? This issue can be resolved only if we read the passage more carefully. It seems that in his critique of the second position, Origen is rejecting the combination of two conditions that make this position an overemphasis of the Father-Son distinction. Not only does the second position hold that the Father and the Son are distinct κατ' ἰδιότητα. The problematic claim is that the Son's distinct property and individual essence are radically *other* than those of the Father. For psilanthropists, the Son, possessing distinct human existence (including human properties), has no share of divine property in himself (hence *psilanthropos*, that is, merely human). Origen's critique of the psilanthropists does not contradict his critique of Monarchianism but rather further clarifies it. The psilanthropists' error is that while they affirm the Son's possession of his distinctive individual properties, they refuse to recognize that he possesses any *divine* properties. This clarifies that when Origen frames the Monarchian error as a denial of the Father-Son distinction κατ' ἰδιότητα, he is simply referring to the Monarchian refusal to affirm that the Son possesses *divine* properties in a substantive rather than nominal manner. At the level of ἰδίοτης, we can infer that Origen is willing to affirm that the Father and the Son each possesses divine properties individually.

Next we turn to οὐσία. It seems that Monarchians argued for their position based on the observation that both Father and Son are called "light" in Scripture. If Scripture calls both by the same term, then do the Father and the Son share the same essence? If two horses are both "horses" because they share one common essence (οὐσία), then did Scripture teach by the same logic that there is no distinction between the Father and the Son with respect to essence (κατ' οὐσίαν)? In response, Origen writes:

> Now since the Savior here is "light" in general, and in the catholic epistle of the same John, God is said to be light, one thinks it is confirmed from that source too that the Father is not distinct from the son in essence [τῇ οὐσίᾳ μὴ διεστηκέναι]. But another who has observed more accurately and speaks more soundly will say that the light which shines in the darkness and is not overcome by it, and the light in which there is no darkness at all are not the same [οὐ ταὐτὸν εἶναι].[21]

As is clear from this passage, Origen even accuses Monarchians of rejecting the Father-Son distinction in essence (τῇ οὐσίᾳ). Origen does not explain the significance of his use of οὐσία language here, nor does he clarify what alternative he had in mind. Orbe suggests that here Origen is affirming the opposite thesis, namely, that the Father is distinct from the Son in essence (τῇ οὐσίᾳ).[22] Does Origen's anti-Monarchianism here imply that the Father and the Son are two οὐσίαι? On the basis of this passage alone, it is unclear whether Origen affirms the opposite. What is clear is that for Monarchians, the fact that the same Scriptural term, "light," is applied to both the Father and the Son implies that they are one in οὐσία. If this is indeed an accurate representation of Monarchianism, then Origen's anti-Monarchianism amounts to his rejection of this move. For Origen, the fact that both the Father and the Son are called "light" in Scripture need not imply that there is only *one* light. If we observe the use of "light" in Scripture carefully, we must indeed distinguish two lights.[23]

In making this move, Origen is simply repeating the strategy commonly found among anti-Monarchians, namely, to show that on the basis of close grammatical reading, the wider narrative of Scripture could make sense only if we postulate two divine subjects. But from this passage it is difficult to gain further precision as to whether Origen uses the term οὐσία in the same way as the Monarchians, if indeed the latter used οὐσία as a technical term in formulating their position.

Further clarity on the implication of Origen's anti-Monarchianism on Trinitarian terminologies, however, is found in a passage that largely recapitulates what we have seen so far. Moreover, this passage also introduces the last technical term, ὑποκείμενον. In *ComJn* X.246 Origen provides testimony that Monarchians draw on John 2:19 in combination with other New Testament passages to argue that their position can be deduced from reading Scriptural data about Jesus's resurrection as a coherent whole:

> Those, however, who are confused on the subject of the Father and the Son bring together the statement, "And we are also found false witnesses of God, because we have testified against God that he raised up Christ, whom he did not raise" (1 Cor. 15:15) and words like these which show him who raises to be different [ἕτερον] from him who has been raised, and the statement, "Destroy this temple, and in three days I will raise it up" (John 2:19). They think that these statements prove that the Son does not differ from the Father in number [μὴ διαφέρειν τῷ ἀριθμῷ], but that both being one, not only in essence, but also in the underlying substance [ἓν οὐ μόνον οὐσίᾳ ἀλλὰ καὶ ὑποκειμένῳ], they are said to be Father and Son in relation to certain differing aspects [κατά τινας ἐπινοίας], not in relation to their reality [οὐ κατὰ ὑπόστασιν λέγεσθαι].[24]

In John 2:19 the Son teaches that he will raise himself up, whereas in 1 Cor. 15:15 Paul teaches that it is God—the Father—who raised Christ up after his crucifixion. For Monarchians, the only coherent reading of these two passages is to say that the one who has raised himself up in the Son is indeed the Father himself. Orbe has taken this passage as revealing something about Origen's global account of how various Trinitarian terms relate to each other.[25] This seems plausible, since in the above passage Origen's critique of the Monarchians is precise: the Monarchians fall into error by affirming that the Father and the Son are one in οὐσία and ὑποκείμενον and that "Father" and "Son" signify simply two ἐπίνοιαι and not ὑπόστασεις.[26] It is possible, then, to infer from this that Origen wishes to signal his preference for an anti-Monarchian alternative based on these terms: the Father and the Son are two οὐσίαι, ὑποκείμενα and ὑπόστασεις. Our textual evidence, however, clearly supports only the conclusion in relation to ὑπόστασις, where an alternative is explicitly developed by Origen in a Trinitarian context. A less speculative interpretation, however, is that the use of multiple terms in this passage arises as the result of Origen's desire to accentuate the severity of the potential threats contained in Monarchianism. This passage nonetheless cements the centrality of Monarchianism in Origen's understanding of key Trinitarian terms in relation to the distinction between Father and Son. In Origen's mind, the Monarchian position may be described with reference to the denial of the distinction between Father and Son with respect to all four key terms relevant to Trinitarian theology: ὑπόστασις, ἰδίοτης, οὐσία, and ὑποκείμενον.[27] Furthermore, Origen clearly formulates the alternative, anti-Monarchian, position in terms of the language of the Father and the Son as two ὑποστάσεις.

This brief survey confirms Origen's anti-Monarchian credentials. Monarchianism is rejected due to its affirmation of monotheism at the expanse of the distinction between Father and Son. Apart from ὑπόστασις, I have suggested that the precise content of Origen's anti-Monarchian alternative is far from clear. What remains to be clarified, then, is the kind of Father-Son distinction Origen proposes to counter Monarchianism. One approach is to attempt a reconstruction of Origen's philosophical understanding of Trinitarian terminologies.[28] The result of such investigations is illuminating but inevitably speculative. In what follows I shall offer a slightly less speculative approach. Without postulating the philosophical meaning attributed by Origen to ὑπόστασις, ἰδίοτης, οὐσία, and ὑποκείμενον, another promising approach is to reconstruct Origen's account of the Father-Son distinction by reading his theory of Scriptural titles in its anti-Monarchian context. As I shall argue, given that Origen's theory emerges from an anti-Monarchian context, it is possible to infer from this theory the desirable sense in which the Son should be distinguished from the Father in an anti-Monarchian manner.

ORIGEN'S HIERARCHICAL FATHER-SON DISTINCTION AS AN ANTI-MONARCHIAN EMPHASIS

In his *Commentary on John* Origen sets out a detailed analysis of Scriptural titles. Three types of Scriptural titles can be found in this discussion: (1) titles the Father possesses absolutely and the Son derivatively, (2) titles the Father possesses in the Son and the Son possesses absolutely, and (3) titles the Father does not possess and the Son possesses contingently. This scheme enables Origen to differentiate the Father from the Son in a hierarchical manner in various ways. The aim of this section is to show how Origen's use of divine simplicity to differentiate between the Father and the Son is intelligible only in light of his account of patrological and Christological titles.

Absolute Patrological Titles

In the first group we have titles for which the Father is the sole source and form. The classical examples frequently discussed by Origen are goodness, divinity, and immortality. With respect to these terms, the Father's essence (οὐσία) is essentially identical to them. This is usually expressed linguistically in Greek by the presence of the prefix αὐτο- or the definite article. The implication of this first group of titles is not restricted to the Father but extends to the Son as well. According to Origen, the Son possesses this group of titles only derivatively. In other words, the Son participates in the Father in order to acquire these titles. The first group of titles thus fills out in a crucial manner how the Father-Son distinction is a *hierarchical* one for Origen: with respect to this group, the Father is essentially what the Son is only by participation. This is why I call these titles absolute patrological titles.

In Origen's mind, the hierarchical nature of the Father-Son relation with respect to this group is grounded on a tightly connected Scriptural logic, drawing particularly on the following passages: (a) John 1:1–2, (b) John 14:28, (c) John 17:3, (d) Mark 10:18, (e) 1 Tim. 6:16, and (f) 1 John 1:5. This Scriptural logic lies at the heart of what is unique to Origen's scheme in comparison with other Middle Platonic or Neo-Platonic differentiations between the "first" and the "second" god. Thus, if we want to fully grasp Origen's scheme, we need to pay close attention to how he treats this tightly connected network of passages.

The Basic Intuition: John 14:28 and Mark 10:18

We begin by establishing the core intuition: the Father is *greater* than the Son. For Origen, the radical transcendence of the Father is grounded in two key passages: John 14:28 and Mark 10:18. From these, taken together, Origen infers that there must be a radical contrast between the Father and the Son in order to make sense of these words issued by the Savior. In *ComJn* XIII.151, we have the clearest articulation of this inference made by Origen from these two verses:

> We are obedient to the Saviour who says, "The Father who sent me is greater than I" (John 14:28) and who, for this reason, did not permit himself to accept the title "good" (Mark 10:18) when it was offered to him, although it was perfectly legitimate and true. Instead, he graciously offered it up to the Father, and rebuked the one who wished to praise the Son excessively. This is why we say the Saviour and the Holy Spirit transcend all created beings, not by comparison, but by their exceeding pre-eminence. The Father exceeds the Saviour as much as (or even more than) the Saviour himself and the Holy Spirit exceed the rest (πάντων μὲν τῶν γενητῶν ὑπερέχειν οὐ συγκρίσει ἀλλ' ὑπερβαλλούσῃ ὑπεροχῇ φαμὲν τὸν σωτῆρα καὶ τὸ πνεῦμα τὸ ἅγιον, ὑπερεχόμενον τοσοῦτον ἢ καὶ πλέον ἀπὸ τοῦ πατρός, ὅσῳ ὑπερέχει αὐτὸς καὶ τὸ ἅγιον πνεῦμα τῶν λοιπῶν).[29]

For Origen, John 14:28 and Mark 10:18 clearly indicate that it is possible to praise the Son "excessively" so that one regards him as greater than the Father in an inappropriate manner. These two passages suggest that the Son did not want anyone to mistakenly elevate him to the level comparable with that of the Father. To do so would violate monotheism. This point is explicitly developed further, in relation to John 14:28, in *CCels.* VIII.14. According to Celsus, Christians are merely paying lip service when they say that they worship God alone. Celsus thinks Christians endorse Jesus as the Son of God, implying that they exalt Jesus to the same level as that of God the Father. In response, Origen directly rebukes some Christian believers for the view they might have deviated to, namely, that "the Saviour is the greatest and supreme God."[30] This view is incorrect, however, because it contradicts Jesus's teaching in John 14:28. This verse is read by Origen as clearly ruling out the possibility of treating the Son of God as greater—that is, more worthy of worship—than the Father. Here Origen is not entirely clear about whether, based on John 14:28, he would also rule out the possibility of treating the Son as co-equal with the Father, as the greatest and supreme God. But from the context it is safe to assume that he interprets John 14:28 as meaning nothing less than that the Father alone is the greatest and supreme God. As a result, against Celsus, Origen argues that Christians do in fact "pay great reverence" to the Father and worship him alone.

There seems to be a slight hesitation on Origen's part regarding whether the transcendence of the Father over the Son is either similar to, or even greater than, the Son's transcendence over creation. On this point, for instance in *ComJn* XIII.151-53, he does not specify which view he thinks is more correct. Elsewhere Origen seems to assert the opposite view, namely, that with respect to goodness the Son exceeds the rest of creation more than the Father exceeds the Son.[31] This ambiguity notwithstanding, what is clear is that Origen thinks that John 14:28 and Mark 10:18 teach that the Father's greatness over the Son must be preserved: "He [the Son] is not to be comparable with the Father in any way (οὐ συγκρίνεται κατ' οὐδὲν τῷ πατρί)."[32]

Developing the Intuition: 1 Timothy 6:16, 1 John 1:5, and John 1:3

John 14:28 and Mark 10:18 set the exegetical foundation for the basic intuition that there must be a sense in which the Father is greater than the Son. This intuition is then supported by a few verses that, while not as explicit as John 14:28 and Mark 10:18, nonetheless give further evidence of the Father's radical transcendence over the Son. Moreover, this group of verses further clarify the sense in which the Father is greater than the Son: the Father possesses a specific group of Scriptural titles that are absent in references to the Son.

First, in *ComJn* II.123–25 Origen combines Num. 14:28 and 1 Tim. 6:16 to argue that it is the Father who alone possesses life as *absolute immortality*. The Son, in contrast, does not possess life in this manner. According to Origen, Num. 14:28 ("As I live, says the Lord") teaches that "living in the proper sense . . . occurs with God alone."[33] This "living in the proper sense" is what 1 Tim. 6:16 is teaching about God, "who alone has immortality." Origen argues that the sole privilege of possessing immortality in this verse must be attributed to the Father alone. This is because even the Son does not possess such immortality since he died for the sake of all who need salvation.[34] If the Son has immortality that is "absolutely unchangeable and immutable," how can he be said to have "tasted death for all"? Origen concludes from 1 Tim. 6:16 that it is the Father who possesses life absolutely because immortality in the absolute sense is absent from the Son. Consequently, Origen differentiates the Father's absolute immortality from the sense in which the Son is said to be "life."[35]

Further Scriptural support for the transcendence of the Father over the Son is also found in 1 John 1:5, which states that "God is light; in him there is no darkness at all." Once again, Origen asks: to whom should we attribute this statement? He argues that it is not possible to say that there is no darkness in the Son because of his involvement in the salvific economy:

> We shall now more daringly add further to those words that if "him who knew no sin he made sin on behalf of us" (2 Cor. 5:21), that is the Christ, it could not be said of him, "There is no darkness in him." For if Jesus condemned sin "in the likeness of sinful flesh" (Rom. 8:3) by taking up the likeness of sinful flesh, it will no longer be completely accurate to say of him, "There is no darkness in him."[36]

This daring interpretation of 1 John 1:5 reflects that Origen finds it not possible to present a clear-cut division between the Son apart from the salvific economy and the Son who is involved in the salvific economy. Since the Son is involved in taking on our sins, infirmities, and even death for our benefit, he cannot be said to be "without darkness." Hence, only the Father could be the subject of the statement "There is no darkness in him." The Father, then, is pure light, in contradistinction with the Son, who is the "light of men" (John 1:4), "true light" (John 1:9), and the "light of the world" (John 8:12)—a light pursued by darkness.[37] So 1 John 1:5, when read in conjunction with John 1:3, supplies the Scriptural evidence that the Father is light in an absolute sense that is absent from the Son. This amounts to yet another way Origen draws on Scripture to defend the transcendence of the Father over the Son.

Origen's interpretation of 1 Tim. 6:16 and 1 John 1:5 as evidence of the Father's transcendence over the Son depends on an account of the Son in relation to his involvement in the salvific economy. Inevitably, the divine titles contained in these verses can be most appropriately applied to the Father alone. Origen is clearly aware of the potential objection to this procedure: is it not problematic to say that the Son does not possess, as the Father does, absolute immortality and freedom from darkness? In response, Origen writes:

> In the sense that the Father "alone has immortality," because our Lord, on account of his love for man, took up death on behalf of us, in the same sense the Father alone has the quality expressed in the statement, "There is no darkness in him," since the Christ, because of the benefit which follows for men, took our darkness upon himself that by his power he might destroy our death, and completely destroy the darkness in our soul.[38]

This passage illustrates why Origen has no problem with interpreting 1 Tim. 6:16 and 1 John 1:5 as suggesting that the Father is in some way greater than the Son. According to Origen, the Son's worthiness for human worship rests primarily on his willingness to take on sin and death for mankind—not, therefore, on the basis of equality with the Father by nature. In fact, as we shall see, Origen sees the Son as teaching exactly the opposite—that he should not be treated as equal with the Father. It is then solely the Father whose worthiness of worship is grounded in his absolute immortality and purity as light. Consequently, Origen interprets 1 Tim. 6:16 and 1 John 1:5 as unequivocally lending further weight to his hierarchical understanding of the Father-Son relation, in which qualities such as "life" and "light" are possessed absolutely by the Father alone.

The Formalized Scheme: John 1:1–2 and John 17:3

We can now sketch out Origen's formalized scheme that captures what we have seen so far. In *ComJn* II.12–18 the basic intuition that the Father is greater than the Son in divinity finds a more definitive statement on the basis of John 1:1–2 and John 17:3. According to Origen, the triad of propositions in John 1:1–2 contains a unique ordering that indicates something profound about the nature of the Son's divinity.[39] Since we find the proposition "and the Word was with God" in the second place before the proposition "and the Word was God," Origen postulates that "the ordering of the propositions could be so for the purpose that we might understand that the Word has become God because he is "with God" (ἵνα δυνηθῇ ἀπὸ τοῦ πρὸς τὸν θεὸν εἶναι ὁ λόγος νοηθῆναι γινόμενος θεός).[40] In other words, the content of the second proposition (that the Word was "with God") provides the basis for the validity of the third proposition (that the Word was God). It is in clarifying this logic that Origen elaborates a formalized statement of his hierarchical understanding of the Father-Son relation. He observes that in John 1:1–2 John used the Greek article in one place but not in another. We have "the Word" but only "God," without the article.[41] John is not ambivalent about the rules of the Greek article; rather, he is making a substantial theological point: "For he [John] adds the article when the noun 'God' stands for the uncreated cause of the universe, but he omits it when the Word is referred to as 'God.' And as 'The God' and 'God' differ in these places, so, perhaps, 'the Word' and 'Word' differ."[42] In this reading, the difference between "The God" and "God" is that with the article, one names the source (ἡ πηγὴ) for something.[43] "The God" who is "over all" (ὁ ἐπὶ πᾶσι θεὸς) is the source of divinity. He is ὁ θεός, because the article is used for the "first" (τῷ πρώτῳ) that serves as the source of that thing of which it is the first. But the Word should not be called "The God" because he is God in virtue of being "with God," as the ordering of the second and third propositions in John 1:1–2 indicates.[44] Rather, the Word has "drawn divinity into himself" through participation in the Father's divinity.[45] The implication, then, is that the Word could not be regarded as the source of divinity himself. The structure of John 1:1–2, as well as the absence of the article attributed to the Son in these verses, thus indicates for Origen that John is teaching a differentiation between "The God," in whom divinity is grounded on himself and thus greater, and "God" (the Son) in whom divinity is grounded on participating in "The God" and thus lesser. Here, then, we have a more formalized account of the transcendence of the Father over the Son in Johannine terms.[46]

Origen draws on further Johannine inspiration to explain this formalized statement of the intuition already found in John 14:28. According to Origen, the Son's prayer to the Father in John 17:3 clearly indicates the language that "The God" is also called the "true God" or "very God." In *ComJn* II.17 he writes:

> We must say to them that at one time God, with the article, is very God (αὐτόθεος), wherefore also the Savior says in his prayer

> to the Father, "That they may know you the only true God" [μόνον ἀληθινὸν θεόν] (John 17:3). On the other hand, everything besides the very God, which is made God by participation in his divinity, would more properly not be said to be "The God," but "God" [πᾶν δὲ τὸ παρὰ τὸ αὐτόθεος μετοχῇ τῆς ἐκείνου θεότητος θεοποιούμενον οὐχ ὁ θεὸς ἀλλὰ θεὸς κυριώτερον ἂν λέγοιτο].

This passage further clarifies how the Origenian scheme works. On the one hand, in John 17:3 "The God" refers to the "true God" to whom the Savior prayed. A simple inference implies that "The God" is the Father of the Son. This God is "very God" (αὐτόθεος) in the sense that his divinity serves as the source of divinity for himself as well as for any other who is called "god." On the other hand, the "many gods" mentioned by Scripture are made God by participation in the divinity of "The God."[47] These gods who obtained their divinity in such a manner are said to be "besides the very God" (παρὰ τὸ αὐτόθεος). By combining John 1:1–2 and John 17:3, Origen concludes that the Word is God in the latter sense: since the Son participates in the Father ("The God" and "true God"), he is said to be divine. The language of "The God," "true God," and "very God" therefore offers a way to formalize the basic intuition found in John 14:28 and Mark 10:18, namely, that the divinity of the Father must be greater than, and differentiated from, the divinity of the Son.

The formalized scheme serves as the framework for the whole group of Scriptural titles that indicate a hierarchical understanding of the Father-Son relation. So the Father is the *source* and *form* with respect to goodness (Mark 10:18), divinity (John 1:1–2, 17:3), immortality (1 Tim. 6:16), and light (1 John 1:5).[48] These titles are attributed to the Father absolutely. The Son possesses these titles only derivatively, in virtue of his participation in (being "with") the Father. As a result, this group of titles indicates a precise sense of how the Father is greater than the Son (John 14:28), as I shall turn to elaborating in a moment.

Christological Titles

In the second place, we have a group of titles that occupies probably the most complex place in Origen's thought. Classic examples in this group are σοφία, λόγος, and ἀλήθεια. The Father's relation with this group is complex and somewhat undeveloped by Origen. As Orbe has speculated, Origen might have understood this group of titles as attributed to the Father only *potentially* and to the Son *actually*.[49] The Father, then, possesses this group of titles *in the Son*. That is to say, with respect to this group, the Son is the Father's perfections subsisting in actuality. The Son, in turn, is the one who possesses these titles absolutely. This is why I refer to this group as absolute sonship titles. With respect to these titles, the Son takes on the role of source and form. This is analogous to the role assumed by the Father with respect to the absolute patrological titles.[50] This point is usually expressed by Origen linguistically by the use of the Greek definite article for these titles whenever they are applied to the Son. The absolute sonship titles further clarify the sense in which the Father and the Son are distinct: whereas the Father does not possess this group of perfections save in the Son, the Son is the source and form of these titles.

But there is another reason why this group is called absolute sonship titles. This is in relation to the fact that the status of Christological titles in Origen cannot be understood with reference to the Father-Son relation alone apart from the Son-creation relation. According to Origen, Scripture attributes many titles to Jesus Christ, but they do not all possess the same significance. It is necessary to distinguish between two kinds of attributions.[51] Titles that indicate an essential aspect of Christ are attributed to him in an unqualified manner (ἁπλῶς). Titles that belong to Christ only with respect to his role in the salvation of fallen souls are attributed to him "for us" (ἡμῖν), in a qualified manner. Methodologically, Origen does not provide any straightforward ways to determine the exact nature of each Christological title. Typically, he investigates all the Scriptural data in order to draw his own conclusion for each title. His investigations reveal many possibilities. Some titles are attributed to Christ both absolutely and "for us"; others are attributed to Christ only "for us."[52] This complexity notwithstanding, in the *Commentary on John* two distinct groupings of Christological titles emerge. Origen identifies one group of titles attributed to Christ both absolutely and economically. It is in this group that we find the absolute sonship titles—wisdom, Logos, power, justice, and truth. This group of titles is attributed to Christ *absolutely* in that they reveal something about Christ apart from his role in the salvific economy. This, then, is a second sense in which titles such as wisdom, Word, and truth are referred to as absolute sonship titles. Since Christ is the source and form of these attributes, he also holds these titles "for us" whenever these attributes are sometimes also said to be found in other created beings in Scripture. The absolute sonship titles, then, are attributed to Christ both absolutely and economically.

Origen identifies another group of titles attributed to Christ *only* economically, and as such they are said to "come to be" in Christ only for the purpose of the salvific economy. This second group includes titles such as "firstborn of the dead," "shepherd," "door," "way," "life," "light of men," and many others.[53] The important point about this second group is that each title denotes a particular economic role Christ plays in relation to us. Consequently, they communicate to us who Christ is only with reference to the benefits he bestowed upon creatures in the economy. Hence I call these titles relative soteriological titles. I shall now turn to examining the absolute Sonship titles first, then the relative soteriological titles.

Absolute Sonship Titles: The Divine Aspects of Christ

In *ComJn* XXXII.387 Origen summarizes the primary absolute sonship titles: "To seek Jesus is to seek the Word, and wisdom, and justice, and truth, and the power of God, all of which Christ is." These five titles are attributed absolutely to Christ throughout the *Commentary on John*. Origen describes them as belonging to "the divine aspects in Jesus."[54] It is with respect to Word, wisdom, justice, truth, and power that Christ is most appropriately regarded as divine. This point is most clearly expressed in Origen's discussion of the death of Jesus Christ. According to him, the possibility of being killed and dying cannot be ascribed to Christ according to his absolute titles. Only with respect to his humanity can Christ admit the possibility of death.[55] This illustrates the point that for Origen the absolute sonship titles signify the divinity of Christ.

These titles, however, are attributed not only to Christ but also to other created beings. The five titles mentioned in *ComJn* XXXII.387 are also attributed to Christ "for us." Christ serves as the source and form of these attributes, whereas creatures obtain them only through participating in Christ. With respect to the five absolute sonship titles, we find a hierarchical participatory structure also present in the absolute patrological titles. Instead of the Father, the Son is truly the single source and absolute standard vis-à-vis the absolute sonship titles. Consequently, these titles can be attributed to all created things only if they truly participate in Christ. From this participatory structure there is a sense that, with respect to his absolute titles, Christ relates to the rest of creation in a manner analogous to how the Father relates to him.[56] Just as the Father is the source of Christ's divinity, so is Christ the source of wisdom, reason, power, justice, and truth for the rest of creation. We shall now turn to specific examples to illustrate this point.

We begin with wisdom, for which Christ serves as source in two senses.[57] First, it is as wisdom that Christ is said to be the source of all creaturely existence—in other words, as creator. According to Origen, all things were created because of the "creation" of wisdom in Prov. 8:22. Further, in Ps. 103:24 (LXX) we read that "God created all things in wisdom." Joining Prov. 8:22 with Ps. 103:24 (LXX), Origen concludes that it is because of the creation of wisdom that all created things could exist, "since it has a share in the divine wisdom according to which it has been created."[58] So creatures exist because they participate in wisdom, and wisdom serves as the source of their existence. There is a further sense in which wisdom serves as a source. Creatures are said to be "wise" because they participate in Christ, the fullness of wisdom. While each wise person receives wisdom from Christ according to their capacity for wisdom, all receive wisdom through participation in Christ.[59] Thus for Origen, the absolute sonship title "wisdom" grounds the double fact that (1) all things exist by participating in Christ as wisdom and (2) all wise beings are said to be wise only by participating in Christ.

Origen's discussion of wisdom invokes the participatory structure familiar to his discussion of divinity, but he does not refer explicitly to the language of source and archetype, which is found in his discussion of Christ's second absolute title, "Word."[60] For Origen, just as "The God" (or the true God) relates to every other "god" as the archetype, so does the Word of God relate to the reason in every other rational being as the archetype. He writes: "As the Father is very God and true God in relation to the image and images of the image (wherefore also men are said to be 'according to the image,' not 'images'), so is the very Word in relation to the reason in each one. For both hold the place of a source (Ἀμφότερα γὰρ πηγῆς ἔχει χώραν); the Father, that of divinity, the Son, that of reason."[61] As Word, Christ "holds the place of a source." This language automatically invokes the participatory structure we have seen in Origen's discussion of wisdom. Every rational creature possesses reason only insofar as they participate in the source of reason, Christ as Word. Once again, each receives reason from Christ according to their capacity. In the first place are the prophets, to whom the Word has "come to be," who participate in the "Word in the beginning—the Word "with God" and "God the Word."[62] The prophets truly possess reason since they have truly grasped the Word in himself. In the second place are believers who participate in the "Word made flesh," those who know nothing "except Jesus Christ and him crucified." In Origen's reading, believers have mistakenly presupposed that "the Word which became flesh was the totality of the Word, who know Christ only according to the flesh." Presumably, these are those who knew only the "letter" and not the "spirit" of Scripture. In the third place are those who follow the schools of Greek philosophy, who devote themselves to "words" (λόγοι) and participate in some way in "the Word," supposing that these "words" transcend every word. Finally, there are those who believe in words (λόγοι) that do not participate in "the Word" in any way at all but are altogether corrupt and godless. Origen describes them as those who "do away with providence which is self-evident and more or less perceptible to the senses, and which approve some other goal than the good."[63] Origen thinks this scheme reveals how Christ is "the Word" in a manner analogous to how the Father is "The God": just as the Father is the single source of divinity from which all other gods receive their divinity, so Christ does as the Word serve as the single source of reason from which all reason in rational creatures is derived.[64]

The participatory structure we have seen with respect to wisdom and Word is also found in Origen's discussion of Christ as "truth."[65] The *aporia* that forms the context of his discussion concerns the consistency between John 1:17 and John 14:6: is it contradictory to say that Jesus Christ is the truth himself and that truth "came through Jesus Christ"? Origen's solution turns to the same participatory structure we have seen in the case of "Word":

> For one does not himself come into existence through himself. We must understand, however, that the ultimate truth itself [ἡ αὐτοαλήθεια ἡ οὐσιώδης] and, if I may put it this way, the archetype of the truth

> in rational souls [πρωτότυπος τῆς ἐν ταῖς λογικαῖς ψυχαῖς ἀληθείας], from which images of that truth, as it were, have been impressed on those who understand the truth, did not come through Jesus Christ nor through anyone at all, but came through God. Just as the Word which was in the beginning with God did not come through someone, and wisdom, which "God created as the beginning of his ways" (Prov. 8:22), did not come through someone, so neither did the truth come through someone.[66]

Here Origen differentiates between the archetype of the truth—Christ himself in John 14:6—and truths based on the archetype (as its images). The former did not come through Christ since "one does not himself come into existence through himself." Rather, it came through God, i.e., the Father. In much the same way that we should consider Word and wisdom, truth came from God and not from someone else. Truths based on the archetype, however, came through Christ because it was on the basis of Christ, the archetypal truth, that many truths—the truths of men—came forth. Further, to be "in the truth" means to participate in Christ. Scripture states that the truth is not in the devil not because he does not hold any true opinion at all but because he does not participate in *the* truth, namely, Christ. To participate in the truth, then, is to participate in Christ, who said, "I am the truth" (John 14:6).

This participatory structure extends to the other two absolute titles of Christ, namely, justice and power. First, 1 Cor. 1:30 and Ps. 10:7 (LXX) for Origen indicate that the archetypal justice is Christ. The justice of each person is "formed from that justice, so that many justices come into existence in those who are saved" (ἀπ' ἐκείνης δὲ τῆς δικαιοσύνης ἡ ἐν ἑκάστῳ δικαιοσύνη τυποῦται, ὡς γίνεσθαι ἐν τοῖς σῳζομένοις πολλὰς δικαιοσύνας).[67] Second, Phil. 4:13 suggests that Paul derives his power from Christ Jesus, who is the power of God (1 Cor. 1:24).[68] It follows that all those who are said to possess power derive their power from participating in the archetype and source of power, Christ himself.

As we have seen, with respect to absolute sonship titles, Christ stands as the archetype and source. This implies that there is a sense in which Christ is analogous to the Father as *purely one*. The Father is one and simple because he is the source and archetype of everything that he is (e.g., goodness, divinity, etc.). Similarly, the Son is one with respect to all that he is absolutely (wisdom, word, justice, etc.). In other words, the move Origen makes between the one true Word and many false words (*logoi*) that we saw in chapter 5 is also applicable to the relation between the one truth and many truths, one wisdom and many wisdoms, and so on. Origen does not explicitly articulate the oneness of the Son with respect to all five of his absolute titles. But, from what he does say about some of the absolute titles as well as his constant grouping of these titles, it is not unreasonable to infer that Christ's oneness as source and archetype extends to all five of his absolute titles.

In *ComJn* II.37–41 Origen attempts to explain why the prologue of John's Gospel speaks of "the Word" and not "the Word *of God*." Origen thinks this is not trivial but indicates the fact that there is only one Word—the Son, the single source and archetype of reason. According to Origen, if it were written in John 1:1 that "in the beginning was the Word *of God*," it would indicate that there are many words: the Word of God, word of men, word of angels, etc. In other words, specifying the Word as the Word of God would have proposed that Jesus Christ is one word among many other words. However, this is absurd because it would lead to the postulate that there are several things that properly possess the title "Word," that is, as the source and archetype of reason. Origen thinks that consideration of the nature of truth will help establish the absurdity of this: there is only one proper standard of reason because the truth is one. No one would dare to argue, for instance, that the truth of God is one thing and the truth of angels another. Hence, the truth of God, as archetype and source of truths, is one and not many. Elsewhere, in language reminiscent of the ethical sense of one and many discussed in chapter 5, Origen suggests that whoever stands "in the truth" (i.e., in the archetype of truth) is "single and simple," whereas whoever stands outside the truth is "complex and manifold."[69] Now, given that the truth is one, he argues that it is absurd to think that there can be many words that can be identified as *the* Word or indeed many wisdoms or justices that are identified as *the* Wisdom and *the* Justice:

> Now if truth is one, it is clear that its elaboration and demonstration, which is wisdom, would reasonably be thought of as one, since everything considered wisdom would not properly be called wisdom if it

> did not possess the truth [οὐ κρατούσης τῆς ἀληθείας]. And if truth is one and wisdom is one, the Word also, who announces the truth and wisdom simply and openly to those capable of apprehending it, would be one.[70]

The essence of this argument is that if the truth is one, then the wisdom with which we elaborate and demonstrate the truth must also be one if what wisdom demonstrates is indeed truth itself. This is because whatever is in possession of truth is properly so called only if it possesses the same oneness as the truth. Likewise, the Word with which we announce the truth and wisdom must also take hold of this same oneness. Thus, the standard for truth, wisdom, and word (their archetype and source) is one. Put differently, that to which the Greek article can be given must be one and not many. This last point reinforces what we have seen in this section: the Son's relation to his absolute sonship titles mirrors exactly the Father's relation to his absolute patrological titles.

Relative Soteriological Titles

The third group of titles are best termed relative soteriological titles since these are titles the Son possesses purely "for us." According to Origen, this group belongs exclusively to the Son in his role as Savior. Origen contemplates whether this group will remain applicable to the Son if the soteriological purpose of the titles is made redundant in the eschatological age.[71] This is because soteriological titles are understood by Origen as attributed to the Son purely "for us"—in other words, in a purely *relative* manner. Hence, the soteriological titles do not belong to the Son's essence; they are perhaps best conceived of as the Son's contingent properties. It is clear that the Father does not possess any of the titles in this group at all. The soteriological titles, then, will be crucial for further differentiating between the Father and the Son.

According to Origen, Christ acquired many titles that are purely relative to his soteriological role because creatures needed him to have them for their salvation.[72] Christ became the "light of men" because those who were darkened by evil needed to be illuminated by him in order to return to God. He became "the firstborn from the dead" because of men's sin and their fall into corruption. Christ became a shepherd because men became like "senseless beasts" who needed someone to lead them back to God. For Origen thinks that each title must be investigated thoroughly because it is possible to come to a false or incomplete picture of the economy if a thorough investigation of the differences between the titles is not carried out. Methodologically, the multiplicity of soteriological titles is crucial for Origen's approach to understanding the salvific economy revealed in Scripture. The multiple relative titles is attributed to Christ only "for us"—economically—because these titles indicate a unique aspect of Christ in which he is needed in the salvific economy. Origen expresses this point in a bold and striking manner. If men had not fallen into darkness, Christ would not have become the "light of men" since there would be no need for Christ to be a light for them.[73] If Adam and Eve had not sinned, and consequently led humanity into corruption and death, there would be no need for Christ to die and to descend into Hades. As a result, he would not be properly given the title "firstborn of the dead."[74] Christ would not be a shepherd if men had not become comparable to "senseless beasts."[75] Origen thus clearly considers the multitude of titles attributed to Christ as purely due to the need to save the fallen creatures. Consequently, the soteriological titles differ from the absolute titles in that the latter are attributed to Christ's very nature himself apart from his role in the salvific economy.

A further aspect of this difference between the relative soteriological and the absolute sonship titles is that while the latter belong to Christ absolutely—there is no sense in which they "came to be" in him—this is not true of the former.[76] As Origen notes, an ordering of Christological titles must be put in place to grasp the theological significance of these titles:

> Once we have collected the titles of the Son, therefore, we must test which of them came into existence later, and whether they would have become so numerous if the saints had begun and continued in blessedness. For perhaps wisdom alone would remain, or word, or life, and by all means truth, but surely not also the other titles which he took in addition because of us.[77]

With respect to Christological titles, then, it is crucial not only to investigate whence a particular title came into existence in Christ but also to ask the general question regarding which titles are absolute and which are soteriological so that we can discern which would remain if men had not sinned.[78] A good example of how Origen carries out his investigation is found in his discussion of the title "life."[79] According to Origen, it is clear from John 1:4 that "life" came into existence in Christ. What this means is that there must be an ordering between the title "Word"—which appears in John 1:1–3—and "life," which appears only in John 1:4. Observing carefully the logic of the Johannine prologue, Origen argues that if "life" was equated with the "light of men," then it must be the case that the "life that was made" in Christ belongs to him not absolutely but only for us.[80] Insofar as "life" is concerned as a title, it is a purely soteriological title. As such, "life" "comes into existence after the Word, being inseparable from him after it has come into existence" (τῷ λόγῳ ἐπιγίνεται, ἀχώριστος αὐτοῦ μετὰ τὸ ἐπιγενέσθαι τυγχάνουσα).[81] This example indicates that Origen thinks that in general Christ took on soteriological titles "in addition" to his absolute titles for the purpose of fulfilling his role in the salvific economy. These titles are *contingent* upon the salvific need of men and should be differentiated from the absolute titles that indicate, as we have seen, the "divine aspects" of the Son. The relative titles thus are best conceived as titles that do not belong to the Son's essence (οὐσία) but are merely his contingent individual properties (ἰδίοτητες).

The multiplicity that Christ took on—the titles that are purely "for us"—clearly differentiates the Son from the Father in a significant way. For Origen, the multiplicity of soteriological titles captures the fact that Christ has a unique role in the economy, acting as *the* way that lead the lost back to God.[82] This role is uniquely played by Christ and not by the Father. Thus the Son's relative title contains within it a crucial anti-Monarchian emphasis, namely, that the Son is to be distinguished from the Father with respect to his role in the salvific economy, not merely with respect to the fact that the he is lesser than the Father in terms of the absolute patrological titles (goodness, divinity, immortality, etc.). I shall expand on these two aspects of Origen's account of the Father-Son distinction in the following section.

Origen's overall account of patrological and Christological titles can now be summarized schematically as in figure 6.1.

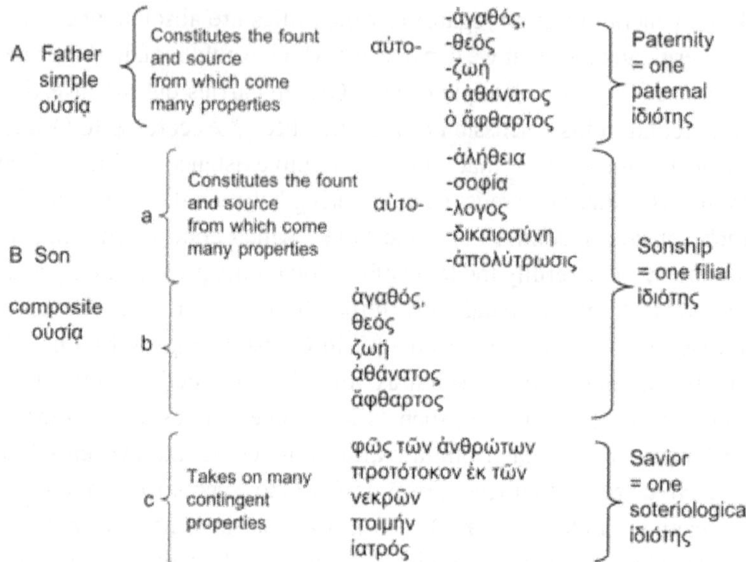

Figure 6.1. A Schematic Presentation of Origen's Account of Patrological and Christological Titles

Source: Expansion of a diagram found in Orbe, *Hacia*, 1:443.

Note: A = absolute patrological titles; Ba = titles the Son receives from the Father; Bb absolute sonship titles; Bc = relative soteriological titles

Origen's Anti-Monarchianism

Building on the work of Orbe, figure 6.1 indicates a number of ways Origen's theory of Scriptural titles fills out the content of the Father-Son distinction.[83] By unfolding these possibilities captured in the above diagram, it will be possible to arrive at a more precise determination of the content of Origen's anti-Monarchianism, his insistence on the distinction between the Father and the Son. It is in the context of Origen's anti-Monarchianism where one can pinpoint more precisely how divine simplicity differentiates the Father from the Son.

The Transcendence of the Father over the Son as an anti-Monarchian Emphasis: Patrological Titles

The patrological titles reveal the first sense in which Origen distinguishes the Father and the Son in a hierarchical manner. The Father is the single fount and source of goodness, divinity, immortality (A in figure 6.1). In this role he is simple in the sense of *The Republic*: perfect goodness itself, self-constant, and immutable.[84] The Son receives these qualities (Bb) derivatively, that is, through participation in the Father. Since the Son is not fount and source—the form—of the absolute patrological titles, he is not simple. This does not imply that the Son is not good and immutable. But it is as the image of the Father that he acquires these qualities.[85] Origen's account of the absolute patrological titles thus reveals that it is the Father who is most truly simple in the sense of *The Republic*.

It is possible to show explicitly that Origen developed this emphasis on the Father's transcendence over the Son as an anti-Monarchian emphasis. For *ComJn* II.12–20, where he develops the formalized account of the Father's transcendence, clearly possesses an anti-Monarchian context. In this section Origen explicitly addresses the Monarchians twice. First, as we have seen in *ComJn* II.16, he criticizes the Monarchians explicitly. It is in the next paragraph, beginning with the words Λεκτέον γὰρ αὐτοῖς, that he immediately turns to developing the formalized scheme for distinguishing between "The God" (= the Father) and "God" (= the Son) on the basis of John 17:3. This suggests that he set out the hierarchical scheme directly in response to Monarchian theology. Second, having set out the scheme, in *ComJn* II.19 Origen explicitly anticipates what resembles an objection from the Monarchians: does the differentiation between "true God" and "God" compromise monotheism? This point arises because Origen's scheme not only differentiates between the Father and the Son; it actually envisages a more general differentiation between "The God" and everything else that Scripture calls "gods," including the Son.[86] This opens up Origen's scheme to the objection of polytheism. Does the differentiation between "The God" and "God"—thus implicitly affirming the appropriateness of applying the title to more than one being—lead to the degradation of the term "God"? It is worth briefly examining Origen's response here since it further highlights how Origen's stress on the Father's transcendence over the Son emerges as part of his attempt to defend a hierarchical account of the Father-Son relation against Monarchian criticisms.

Origen's response is to postulate an exegetical case for the existence of a hierarchy of divinity in general. According to Origen, the exegetical starting points for a hierarchy of divinity are Ps. 49:1 (LXX) and Ps. 135:2

(LXX), in which we find the phrase "The God of gods." For Origen this phrase implies that Scripture teaches the existence of other gods besides "The God" and the Son of God. Other gods must exist in order for "The God" to be God of something existent. Further, we learn in Matt. 22:32 that "he is not God of the dead, but of the living." Origen reads this verse as indicating that "the gods," of whom "The God" is God (as described by the Psalmist), are *living* beings. Last, but not least, the Apostle Paul seems to acknowledge the existent of these "gods" in 1 Cor. 8:5 by saying, "just as there are many gods." This network of passages led Origen to postulate the existence of "the gods" as a third order (below "The God" and the Son) in the hierarchy of divinity.[87]

So, according to Origen, apart from God the Father, all that are called "god" in Scripture draw their divinity from the Father as their source. The Son, who is God in virtue of being "with The God" in John 1:2, is the first who "has drawn divinity into himself" by receiving the divinity of the Father. In a similar manner, "the gods" obtain their divinity through participating in the divinity of the Father. It is in the mode of reception of divinity that we find the main difference between the Son and "the gods." The Son, on the one hand, receives his divinity by being "with The God," whereas "the gods" are deified through the "ministry" of the Son.[88] Moreover, in Origen's scheme, "the gods" are further divided into two orders: first, those who are gods by participating in "The God" (through the ministry of the Word), and second, those who are "said to be gods, but are not gods at all."[89] The last category refers to those are simply idols and the term "god" is falsely applied to them. We can then summarize Origen's hierarchy of divinity in table 6.1.

The line in table 6.1 represents the break between "The God" and "God." Everything that is called "God" in Scripture obtains divinity by participating in the Father. It is important to remember that the four orders

Table 6.1. Origen's Hierarchy of Divinity

1. God the Father = "The God," "true God," "very God" (source of divinity)

---

2. God the Son: "God" in virtue of being "with The God" in the beginning.
3. Those who are god by participating in "The God" through the ministry of the Son of God (e.g., the heavenly bodies, created human beings)
4. Those who are said to be god but are not gods at all (e.g., idols)

listed here for Origen refer to four senses of how the noun "God" is applied, not four distinct groups of subjects that are properly called divine since, in actual fact, only the first three groups are correctly named "God." Mindful of the Monarchian critique, Origen argues that this hierarchy of divinity by no means implies polytheism. Scripture indeed testifies to the many gods. But this affirmation by no means compromises monotheism because, in Origen's understanding, even though there are many gods, there is only a single source of divinity, namely, the Father.[90] As a result, even though many are called "God" in Scripture, there is only one "true God."[91] Monotheism, on this account, is entailed by the claim that there is only *one true source of divinity.* Origen favors this understanding of monotheism as more exegetically accurate, drawing upon 1 Cor. 8:5–6, where Paul affirms that "indeed there are many 'gods' . . . yet for us there is one God, the Father." If this passage is read literally—which Origen did—then it implies that a proper affirmation of Scriptural monotheism may hold the existence of many gods together with the affirmation of one God. It follows, then, that the hierarchy of divinity does not contradict the Scriptural testimony of monotheism; consequently, the Monarchian objection is not fatal to a hierarchical understanding of divinity.[92]

Origen's formalized account of the Father's transcendence over the Son in *ComJn* II, then, is sandwiched by Monarchian concerns. It is the Monarchian danger that introduces the theme in this section of the *Commentary.* And it is the Monarchian objection to the theme that gives rise to the response from Origen that follows. At the level of patrological titles, Origen's "subordinationism" is therefore most appropriately understood as an anti-Monarchian motif.

The Transcendence of the Father over the Son as an Anti-Monarchian Emphasis: Christological Titles

The Father and the Son are further distinguished with respect to the Christological titles. Returning to *ComJn* I.119 we find that the Father is "one and simple," whereas the Son "because of the many things . . . becomes many things." The key issue here, then, is to determine the "many things" that are uniquely attributed to the Son but not to the Father. There are several possibilities to account for how simplicity differentiates the Father from the Son. First, it could be that the Father is simple in the sense that he possesses only one *type* of property, whereas the Son possesses multiple types of properties. The "many things" in this case would refer to distinct types of properties (Ba + Bb in figure 6.1) in the Son. So the Son would be composite in that this multiplicity is present in his essence (οὐσία).

Second, it could be that the Father is simple in the sense that the only relation he possesses to his properties is as their source and form. In this manner, the Father possesses absolutely the self-sameness required by simplicity. This is due to the familiar logic we have seen previously: if something is a form of "X," it always remains the same with respect to "X" and there is no possibility for the contrary of "X" to be present in it. Under this construal of simplicity, the Son would be both simple and complex. On the one hand, he possesses simplicity with respect to absolute Sonship titles (Bb). However, on the other hand, with respect to the titles he receives from the Father (Ba) and his relative soteriological titles (Bc), the Son is not their source and form. Rather, the Son stands in a different kind of relation to these properties. The Son, then, would not be *purely* simple because he would not be a simple source vis-à-vis *all* his properties. In this case, the "many things" that render the Son multiple would refer to the properties to which he does not stand as source and form, namely, the attributes he receives from the Father (Bb) and his relative soteriological titles (Bc).

Third, it could be that the Father is simple in the sense that he does not possess any attributes that are purely relative to the salvific economy. Relative soteriological titles violate immutability, which is essential for simplicity, because they are *contingent* on the existence of creation. As we have seen, Origen regards these titles as "coming to be" in Christ. In this third sense, then, the Son is not simple since he acquires many soteriological titles that subject him to such contingency. In this case, the "many things" that render the Son multiple would be specifically his relative soteriological titles (Bc).

Which is the most likely explanation of *ComJn* I.119? Orbe argues for the first option in his attempt to reconstruct Origen's anti-Monarchian claim that the Father and the Son are distinct with respect to personal property (κατ' ἰδιότητα) and to essence (κατ' οὐσίαν). According to Orbe, whereas in the Father there is only one "simple and polyvalent property," in the Son we have a composite of several substantial properties (i.e., Ba + Bb).[93] In this interpretation, the diagram above outlines speculatively the precise content of Origen's anti-Monarchian distinctions. Orbe's interpretation is not implausible but faces an exegetical problem. In this passage the Son's lack of simplicity is due to the many things (τὰ πολλά) that *he becomes for the sake of creatures* since he takes on these things "as the whole creation which can be made free needs him" (καθὰ χρῄζει αὐτοῦ ἡ ἐλευθερούσθαι δυναμένη πᾶσα κτίσις).[94] It seems odd, then, that the soteriological titles (Bc) are left out, as this passage suggests that they must be a crucial part of the "many things" that render the Son non-simple. Orbe's failure to account for these titles is understandable since he was preoccupied strictly with determining the content of Origen's insistence that the Father and the Son are distinct κατ' οὐσίαν. The soteriological titles are certainly contingent to the Son's οὐσία, and this explains why Orbe leaves these out in his interpretation of *ComJn* I.119 as a strict comparison between the Father and the Son at the level of οὐσία. Orbe's concern with arriving at a strictly *ontological* characterization of the Father-Son distinction thus unwittingly prevents his interpretation from accounting for the full complexity of *ComJn* I.119.[95]

It is equally tempting, however, from the soteriological significance of the "many things" in *ComJn* I.119, to opt for the third option outlined above and conclude that Origen considers the Son to be multiple on the basis of his relative soteriological titles (Bc) alone—in other words, on the basis of his contingent ἰδίοτητες. Prima facie, this makes sense because, as we have seen, the relative titles subject the Son to contingency and thus are said to "come to be" in the Son. Being subjected to such "becoming" would certainly violate immutability and hence account for the Son's lack of simplicity. But this interpretation is also overly simplistic because what Origen had in mind, as I shall show now, is something like a combination of the second and third options above. This is because the "many things" in *ComJn* I.119 must include Christ's absolute sonship titles (Ba), a point clearly indicated by Origen's interpretation of this phrase in *ComJn* I.51–62.

In this section Origen discusses the meaning of the phrase "good things," triggered by the verse "how beautiful are the feet of those who announce good things" (Isa. 52:7 *apud* Rom. 10:15). Origen defends the claim that the plural phrase "many good things" actually refers to the singular person Jesus Christ himself: "Let no one be surprised if we have understood Jesus to be announced by the plural 'good things.' For when we have understood the things of which the names which the Son of God is called are predicated, we will understand how Jesus, whom these whose feet are beautiful preach, is many good things."[96] To illustrate this point, Origen lists Scriptural titles according to which one can conceive Jesus as a good thing: life, light, truth, way, resurrection, door, wisdom, power, Word, crucified, righteousness. On this list we find both absolute sonship titles (life, truth, wisdom, power, Word) and relative soteriological titles (light, way, resurrection, door, crucified). Since each of these titles represents one aspect of how Christ brings a particular benefit to us, if they are taken together, the list shows that Jesus Christ is apt to be called "many good things." This discussion is crucial for understanding *ComJn* I.119 because in the paragraphs leading up to this passage (*ComJn* I.112–118) Origen seems to indicate that he is developing his previous comments on Isa. 52:7 earlier in the book.[97] Hence, the "many things" in *ComJn* I.119 should be interpreted in light of Origen's comments on "many good things" in *ComJn* I.51–62. The absolute sonship titles, therefore, should be included in the "many things" that render the Son multiple and not simple.

How, then, should we understand the Son's distinction from the Father through the "many things"? A hint is given by *ComJn* I.62: "It is the same thing, therefore, to say that the apostles preach the Saviour and that they preach good things. For he is the one who received from the good Father that he be good things, in order that each one who received through Jesus the thing or things he is capable of, might engage in good things." According to this passage, the identification of Christ as "many good things" highlights his unique role assigned by the Father in the economy of salvation. The Father intends the Son to be many good things so that, through the Son, creatures may acquire these qualities. This suggests that the "many things" that render the Son multiple, and hence distinct from the Father's simplicity, are due to his distinctive role as the mediator between God the Father and creation. This point is further developed in a crucial passage in *ComJn* VI.107 that is situated as part of a discussion on the phrase "make straight the way of the Lord (John 1:23)." Here Origen is interested in clarifying the meaning of the title "way" attributed to Christ. This "way" leads to "life," but not for everyone. The majority, who are "carnal," instead constrict the way, according to Scripture (Matt. 7:13–14). There is a reason that Scripture gives multiple titles to the Son, Origen explains: "The Saviour, who contains all virtue, is multiple in his aspects. For this reason he is the way for the one who has not yet arrived at the goal but is still advancing, but for him who has already put off all that is dead, he is life." Scripture assigns many things to Christ because not all who need him have the same needs. Christ is both "way" and "life": for those who are still searching for salvation, Christ is the "way" since they need to be led toward the good Father, but for those who are advancing in the search, Christ is their "life." Hence, it is due to the distinctive needs of creatures for Christ that he "becomes many things."[98]

It is safe to conclude, then, that the "many things" refer to titles that the Son possesses "for us." This interpretation implies that relative soteriological titles are obviously included in the "many things" since they are attributed to the Son purely "for us," that is, for the purpose of the salvation of creatures. But this interpretation also explains why Origen includes absolute sonship titles such as wisdom, Word, and truth in the "many things" since the Son possesses these titles both absolutely *and* "for us."[99] Thus, this set of titles brings about a true multiplicity in the Son, as is required by the distinctive needs presented by creatures at different stages of spiritual progress. Consequently, it is Christological titles attributed to the Son "for us" that distinguish him from the simplicity of the Father.

We can elaborate this point with greater precision still. Returning to figure 6.1, it is (Ba) and (Bc) that constitute the "many things" that render the Son distinct from the Father in *ComJn* I.119. While many terms, such as goodness, divinity, and immortality, are attributed to the Father, Origen, like Alcinous conceives the Father as the source and form of all his attributes. The absolute patrological titles, then, are not to be conceived as realities that possess existence independent from the Father. In this sense, the Father is purely one and simple. The Son, in a limited sense, is also one. As we have seen, the Son's multiple aspects are to be conceived as one.[100] Christological titles are not many in the ethical sense as we saw in the previous chapter since no divisions or conflicts exist between them. But the Son, in Origen's thought, assumes a unique mediatory role in the economy, assigned by the Father, to distribute the multiple good things that serve the needs of creatures at different stages of spiritual maturity. This role accounts for the need for multiple titles attributed to the Son "for us," some only in this manner (Bc) and others only partially (Ba). These titles, therefore, are the "many things" that give the Son a multiplicity absent in the simple Father.

At the level of Christological titles, I suggest that Origen's hierarchical distinction between the Father and the Son also possesses an anti-Monarchian shape. In chapter 4 I highlighted the fact that the Monarchians tend to collapse the salvific economy from a partnership between two acting subjects to an act by a single actor.[101] Origen's account of Christological titles hence accomplishes something that Monarchians have failed to do so, namely, to explain how the Son is to be distinguished from the Father κατ' οἰκονομίαν. The Father's role in the economy is not one that would introduce multiplicity in him. Rather, it is the Son's role to become many for the sake of creatures. Inasmuch as the originator of salvation must be differentiated from the mediator and savior, so must the Son be distinguished from the Father κατ' οἰκονομίαν.[102] Divine simplicity thus gives content to Origen's anti-Monarchianism by offering a way to capture the distinctive economic roles assigned to the Father and the Son respectively.

Origen, as we have seen, is a committed anti-Monarchian. His anti-Monarchianism is difficult to pin down. While it is clear that Origen regards it heretical to deny the Father-Son distinction at the level of ὑπόστασις, ἰδίοτης, οὐσία, and ὑποκείμενον, it is difficult to obtain certainty about his own understanding of the distinction between the Father and the Son in these terms (except for ὑπόστασις). In this chapter I have argued that Origen's anti-Monarchianism can be *indirectly* understood through his account of Scriptural titles. The result is that Origen's "subordinationist" motifs, his hierarchical understanding of the Father-Son distinction, reveal themselves as integral parts of his anti-Monarchianism. It is in this context that divine simplicity has acquired a central role in shaping Origen's hierarchical-anti-Monarchian understanding of the Father-Son distinction. I have offered a plausible reading of the relevant sources that grant a degree of precision regarding how divine simplicity serves as a principle of differentiation between the Father and the Son in *ComJn* I.119.[103] Origen's commitment to divine simplicity, then, has a distinctively anti-Monarchian function. This constitutes the first significant way divine simplicity has given shape to Origen's thinking about the Father-Son relation.

What is remarkable in Origen's scheme is the possibility of a positive theological account of multiplicity. As we saw in chapter 5, in line with the Platonic tradition, the simplicity-multiplicity distinction is often used by Origen to signify a contrast between perfect and imperfect reality. But in Origen's Trinitarian thought, the Son's lack of simplicity is not due to imperfections in him. Rather, the Son's multiplicity is grounded on the genuine multiple needs of creatures who are situated at different stages of spiritual progress. The Son's multiplicity, then, arises from his unique role as a mediator between the Father and the rest of creation—in other words, it is the result of Origen's anti-Monarchianism. But it ultimately springs from the Son's concern with leading creatures back to the Father. This insight, it seems to me, captures the originality of Origen's scheme.

CHAPTER 7

Divine Simplicity as an Anti-Valentinian Principle of Unity between the Father and the Son

My aim in this final chapter is to identify a second way divine simplicity has formed Origen's account of the Father-Son relation. The previous two chapters charted Origen's commitment to divine simplicity and his use of this doctrine to inform his anti-Monarchianism, respectively. Origen's commitment to divine simplicity, like that of Irenaeus, also shapes his language of the Son's generation. To be precise, divine simplicity equally leads Origen to place an emphasis on safeguarding the unity between the Father and the Son in his account of the Son's generation. But, as I argued in chapter 4, an anti-Monarchian committed to the doctrine of divine simplicity faces the "ante-Nicene Trinitarian problematic," that is, the challenge of maintaining an anti-Monarchian affirmation of the Father-Son distinction while upholding an anti-Valentinian account of the Son's generation from the Father that follows from divine simplicity. In this final chapter I shall turn to showing how Origen's account of the Son's generation can be read as an attempt to resolve this problematic by steering a via media between Monarchianism and Valentinian *probolē*. To do so I will detail how Origen's account of the Son's generation satisfies the anti-Valentinian conditions required by simplicity set out in chapter 3 while maintaining the anti-Monarchian concern for the Son's distinct individual existence.

Origen's account of the Son's generation has been thoroughly examined by scholars. Some analyze it systematically around important themes.[1]

Others tend to focus on drawing out the significance of Origen's teaching on this theme for fourth-century theology.[2] Less often explored, though, is the role played by the third-century polemical landscape in shaping Origen's account.[3] In this chapter I do not seek to present a comprehensive analysis of Origen's account of the Son's generation as a whole. Instead I offer a focused reading of *PArch* I.2 in light of its anti-Valentinian and anti-Monarchian contexts. Situating *PArch* I.2 in these contexts will bring a fresh perspective on how certain features of Origen's understanding of the Son's generation have been developed shaped by polemical concerns. Consequently, a contextualized understanding of Origen's account within its third-century milieu will emerge.

Divine simplicity's role as an *anti-Valentinian* emphasis is much less obvious in Origen than in Irenaeus. Two passages that resemble Irenaeus's anti-Valentinian polemic can be found in the *Peri Archōn*.[4] But the reliability of our texts of these passages is questionable because it is well known that Rufinus's Latin rendering of the work is especially problematic when it comes to the Son's relation to the Father.[5] Given this thorny issue, some brief remarks are in order to detail how I aim to establish my thesis in this chapter. In the first part I shall draw on internal and external evidence to establish Valentinian *probolē* and Monarchianism as relevant polemical concerns in *PArch* I.2. On the one hand, I highlight that Origen explicitly rejects Valentinian *probolē* based on simplicity in the *Peri Archōn*. While Rufinus is not always reliable on the Son's generation, there is no reason to doubt the explicit anti-Valentinian polemic in the translation as authentic. This, then, justifies my anticipation of anti-Valentinian considerations, similar to the ones in Irenaeus, in Origen's account of the Son's generation in *PArch* I.2. On the other hand, I highlight key evidence that lends plausibility to my anticipation of anti-Monarchian concerns in the background of that text. We know Origen was concerned with the Monarchian account of the procession of the Word in his Alexandrian period.[6] Further, explicit anti-Monarchian polemic can be found in *PArch* I.2.2. Once again, while Rufinus might be unreliable on other details in this chapter, I see no reason to doubt the authenticity of the explicit anti-Monarchian polemic presented therein. Having secured my identification of Origen's polemical concerns, in the second part of the chapter I will show that Origen's account of the Son's generation in *PArch* I.2 satisfies the three key conditions that follow from divine simplicity, as highlighted in chapter 3. But Origen's implementation of these conditions is considerably more complex than in Irenaeus. I argue that if we attend closely to how Origen formulates his concerns (*PArch* I.2.4), it reveals that his account of the Son's generation (*PArch* I.2.5–13) can be read as an attempt to resolve the "ante-Nicene Trinitarian problematic." Consequently, Origen's use of divine simplicity as a principle of unity between Father and Son must be situated within his attempt to maintain a via media between Valentinian *probolē* and Monarchianism.

THE POLEMICAL CONTEXT SURROUNDING ORIGEN'S ACCOUNT OF THE SON'S GENERATION IN *PERI ARCHŌN*

It is difficult to assess the value of the text of *PArch* I.2 as an account of Origen's thinking on the Father-Son relation. The text promises a unique vantage point from which to look into Origen's thinking on this theme as it contains his most systematic discussion on Col. 1:15, Heb. 1:3, and Wis. 7:25–26—the three central passages in his understanding of the Son. *PArch* I.2 is especially valuable for grasping Origen's exegesis of Wis. 7.25–26 since little systematic analysis of this passage exists elsewhere in the Origenian corpus. Though *ComJn* offers a more systematic account of Origen's theory of *epinoiai*, *PArch* I.2.5–13 remains a unique source of his account of the Father-Son relation, especially with respect to the Son's generation. Yet, Rufinus's Latin translation of *PArch* I.2 is generally considered unreliable on Origen's Trinitarian thought.[7] For example, Tzamalikos has highlighted that Origen's precise conception of time and its implication regarding the God-Logos-Creation relation are simply lost in Rufinus's Latin. Rufinus simply did not grasp the significance of Origen's language, in which the tenses of verbs as well as temporal qualifiers like "before," "after," "eternal," and so on, must be used carefully in order to specify the God-Logos-Creation relation.[8] *PArch* I.2, then, is one of the chapters that suffer most from Rufinus's lack of comprehension of Origen's theory of time. As a result, the value of Rufinus's text of this chapter for comprehending Origen's Trinitarian thought needs to be treated with caution because what we have likely contains a muddled rendering of Origen's account of the Father-Son relation.

Is it possible, then, to make use of *PArch* I.2 as a source of Origen's account of the Son's generation? In my view, this chapter is not useless as a source of Origen's Trinitarian thought. Tzamalikos harshly concludes that *PArch* can be drawn upon only when an extant Greek text has witnessed to the same ideas found in Rufinus's Latin text.[9] The merit of this approach lies in its attention to the most reliable testimonies of Origen's teaching, but it also leaves out valuable insights that could be gained only from *PArch*. For instance, it is in this chapter that clearly Origen's develops his account of the Son's generation as a via media between Monarchianism and Valentinian *probolē*. In what follows, I suggest that there is no reason to doubt that the anti-Monarchian and anti-Valentinian polemic in *PArch* I.2 are genuine. I shall argue that on these themes Rufinus's text is a reliable witness given that what we have in it agrees with is known about Origen's engagement with these polemical contexts. I shall now turn to substantiating this claim.

Anti-Valentinian Polemic in *Peri Archōn*

Origen is committed to the simplicity of God the Father. It is therefore not surprising that he is concerned with purging every materialistic connotation associated with the Son's begetting. While he consistently rejects the materialistic notion of generation, he never explicitly identifies his opponents who hold this view. Sometimes he refers to them as heretics (*haeretici*).[10] Other times he simply refers to them by the generic plural "some" or "those."[11] Several attempts at more precise identification, however, have been made by scholars. Orbe argues that Origen had the Valentinian notion of *prolatio*/*probolē* in mind.[12] Samuel Fernández, along with Cécile Blanc, simply identifies Origen's target as "Gnostics."[13] I think further precision on this might be possible. According to Jerome, Origen debated a Valentinian named Candidus. Jerome provides us with a brief summary of the content of this debate:

> There exists in Greek a dialogue between Origen and Candidus the defender of the heresy of Valentinians. . . . Candidus maintains that the Son is of the substance of the Father, falling into the error of asserting a *Probolē or Prolatio*. On the other side, Origen, like Arius and Eunomius, refuses to admit that He is produced or born, *lest God*

> *the Father should thus be divided into parts*; but he says that He was a sublime and most excellent creation who came into being by the will of the Father like other creatures.

> Habetur dialogus apud Graecos Origenis et Candidi, ualentinianae haereseos defensoris. . . . Dicit Candidus Filium de Patris esse substantia, errans in eo quod προβολήν, *id est prolationem*, adserit. E regione Origenes, iuxta Arium et Eunomium, repugnat eum uel prolatum esse uel natum, *ne Deus Pater diuidatur in partes*, sed dicit sublimem et excellentissimam creaturam uoluntate extitisse Patris, sicut et ceteras creaturas.[14]

Jerome's report is undoubtedly polemical, as he attempts to align Origen with "Arianism."[15] However, there is no reason to doubt the authenticity of his report because its content corresponds closely to the language found in *PArch* on the materialistic notion of begetting:

> God the Father, since he is both *indivisible and inseparable* from the Son, generated the Son *not, as some suppose, by an act of separation from himself.* For if the Son is something emitted from the Father, and if this expression signifies something resembling the offspring of animals and human beings, then both he who separated and he who is separated are of necessity bodies. For we do not say, as the heretics suppose, that a part of God's substance was changed into the Son.

> Deus pater cum et *indivisibilis sit et inseparabilis* a filio, *non per prolationem ab eo*, ut quidam putant, generatus est filius. Si enim prolatio est filius patris, prolatio vero dicitur quae talem significat generationem, qualis animalium vel hominum solet esse progenies, necessario corpus est et is, qui protulit, et is, qui prolatus est. Non enim dicimus, sicut haeretici putant, partem aliquam substantiae dei in filium versam.

> Περὶ πατρός, ὡς ἀδιαίρετος ὢν καὶ ἀμέριστος υἱοῦ γίνεται πατήρ, οὐ προβαλὼν αὐτόν, ὡς οἴονταί τινες. εἰ γὰρ πρόβλημά ἐστιν ὁ υἱὸς τοῦ πατρὸς καὶ γέννημα ἐξ αὐτοῦ, ὁποῖα τὰ τῶν ζῴων γεννήματα, ἀνάγκη σῶμα εἶναι τὸν προβαλόντα καὶ τὸν προβεβλημένον.[16]

There are two noteworthy similarities between Jerome's report of Origen's dialogue with Candidus and the discussion of the Son's generation in *PArch* IV.4.1. First, Jerome reports that Origen rejects Valentinian *probolē* since it violates simplicity—lest God be divided into parts. This is identical to Origen's critique in *PArch* IV.4.1 of those who supposed that the generation of the Son was by an act of emission from the Father (*per prolationem ab eo*). This passage seems to recapitulate the point made earlier in the work where Origen attacks those who "depict for themselves certain emanations, so as to name the divine nature in parts and divide the God and Father as far as they can" (*qui prolationes quasdam sibi ipsi depingunt, ut divinam naturam in partes vocent et deum patrem quantum in se est dividant*).[17] This comparison suggests that Candidus's Valentinian notion of *probolē* could be the view Origen criticizes in *PArch* I.2.6 and IV.4.1.[18] Second, Jerome reports that Origen's response to Candidus is found in his teaching that the Son was a "sublime and most excellent creation [*creaturam*]" who "came into being by the will of the Father like other creatures" [*sicut et ceteras creaturas*]." We need not trust Jerome's polemical portrayal of Origen's doctrine here. As we saw in the previous chapter, Origen's conception of the Son is a great deal more sophisticated than the "Arian" doctrine Jerome tries to portray. But one detail from Jerome's report is illuminating: in response, Origen seems to have stressed the nature of the Son's generation as "by the will of the Father (*uolutate . . . patris*)." This expression matches exactly with what we find in the two places in *PArch* where we find Origen criticizing the materialistic notion of the Son's generation. In both passages we find Origen teaching that the Son's generation is "like an act of will proceeding from the mind."[19] These two observations suggest that the view of Candidus was a likely background to Origen's discussion of the Son's generation in *PArch*.

Chronologically, this identification is plausible since the *Dialogue with Candidus*, the hypothetical Origenian work that recorded this debate, is dated to before Origen's departure from Alexandria (~231/32) if we identify it, as Pierre Nautin did, with the first dialogue mentioned by Origen in his letter to his friend Alexander.[20] If *Dialogue with Candidus* was indeed the first work mentioned by Origen in his letter to his friend Alexander, then, given that the *PArch* is usually dated during the 220s (i.e., before the end of the Alexandrian period),[21] Candidus certainly qualifies as a plausible candidate for the anti-Valentinian context underlying Origen's account of the Son's generation in *PArch.* I am inclined to think that Origen probably did have Candidus in mind given the similarity of language between Jerome's report and *PArch* I.2.6 and IV.4.1. But given our scanty information on Candidus, this remains plausible but not certain. What we can safely conclude, though, from the comparison between Jerome's report and *PArch,* is that it is highly likely that Valentinian *probolē* constitutes a key polemical context surrounding Origen's reflection on the Son's generation in the *PArch.*[22]

A final observation will strengthen my case that Origen was explicitly concerned with Valentinian *probolē* in his reflection on the Son's generation in *PArch.* According to Jerome, Candidus holds that the "Son is of the substance of the Father" (*Filium de Patris esse substantia*). In the *Commentary on John,* Origen criticizes a similar view when he turns to John 8:42b: "I have proceeded and come from God" (Ἐγὼ ἐκ τοῦ θεοῦ ἐξῆλθον καὶ ἥκω).[23] Commenting on this verse, Origen discusses two different interpretations of what it might mean for the Son to say that he has "proceeded" from God in this verse. Origen's preferred interpretation is that this phrase refers to the Son's incarnation, taking on the "form of a servant" (Phil. 2:7). Origen points out that the verb ἐξ-έρχομαι has the connotation of a "quasi-local" departure and separation.[24] Such a connotation can be appropriately applied only to describing the Son's incarnation, where there is a sense in which he has "proceeded from God" by coming to us. However, Origen mentions a different interpretation that was available in his time:

> Others, however, interpret the statement, "I proceeded from God," to mean, "I have been begotten by God." These must say consequently that the Son has been begotten of the Father's essence [ἐκ τῆς οὐσίας . . . τοῦ πατρὸς γεγεννῆσθαι τὸν υἱόν], as one might understand this also in the case of those who are pregnant, and that God is diminished and lacking, as it were, in the essence that he formerly had, when he has begotten the Son.[25]

According to Origen, some have interpreted ἐξῆλθον in John 8:42b as referring to the Son's literally proceeding out of the Father's essence. Given the "quasi-local" connotation of the verb, Origen argues that this interpretation cannot avoid the inevitable materialistic connotation of the language. This interpretation, then, inappropriately conceives of the Son's generation in a manner analogous to that of a human offspring generated out of one who is pregnant. In the case of human generation, indeed the offspring proceeds out of the pregnant woman such that the latter is diminished due to the removal of the offspring that she formerly possessed. For Origen, the language of ἐκ τῆς οὐσίας necessarily points to a materialistic understanding of begetting.[26] Both the process of begetting and the begotten in this case must be corporeal and composite. Thus, when applied to the generation of the Son of God, the language of ἐκ τῆς οὐσίας subjects the Father to division and violates his simplicity. As expected, Origen rejects the interpretation immediately. Now those who held this interpretation of John 8.42b are not identified by Origen, but the view he criticizes is similar to the one reported by Jerome: the Son is "of the substance of the Father" (*Filium de Patris esse substantia*).[27] While *ComJn* XX is less likely than *PArch* to be concerned with Candidus directly given that it was written in Origen's Caesarean period,[28] nonetheless it seems to target the Valentinian position that the Son was generated out of the Father's substance.[29] It seems that Origen's anti-Valentinian concern about the Son's generation likely remained beyond his Alexandrian period. The direct relevance of this concern in Origen's thinking about the Son's generation in *ComJn* XX lends further weight to my claim that Valentinian *probolē* forms a key polemical context for his account on the same theme in his earlier work, *PArch* I.2.

Therefore, I suggest that Valentinian emission likely constitutes the target of Origen's polemics in *PArch* against the materialistic notion of generation. As a result, anti-Valentinian polemic also likely underlies Origen's account of the Son's generation in *PArch* I.2. It would be appropriate, then, to read this chapter as sharing with Irenaeus a similar concern against Valentinian *prolatio*/*probolē*, namely, that it would violate the divine simplicity.[30] It follows that one should expect *PArch* I.2 to set out an alternative account of the Son's generation that is compatible with divine simplicity.

Anti-Monarchian Polemic in *PArch*

As an anti-Monarchian, it is not surprising that Origen is also concerned with Monarchianism in his reflection on the generation of the Son. The Monarchian account of the procession of the word forms the second polemical background underlying *PArch* I.2. I shall be brief here because the case has been expertly set out previously by Ronald Heine.[31] As we have seen, Monarchians reject various distinctions between the Father and the Son. This view seems to be accompanied by an account of the Son's generation based on an exegetical tradition with respect to Ps. 44:2 (LXX).[32] In this account, the Son's generation is framed by an analogy with the human uttered word. Origen reports this account in *ComJn*:

> It is worthwhile to consider those who disregard so many names and treat this one [Logos] as special. And again, they look for an explanation in the case of the other names, if someone brings them to their attention, but in the case of this one they believe they have a clear answer to what the Son of God is, when he is named Word. This is especially obvious since they continually use the verse, "My heart uttered a good word," as though they think the Son of God is an expression of the Father occurring in syllables [οἰόμενοι προφορὰν πατρικὴν οἱονεὶ ἐν συλλαβαῖς κειμένην εἶναι τὸν υἱὸν τοῦ θεοῦ]. And in accordance with this view, if we inquire of them carefully, they do not give him a hypostasis [ὑπόστασιν αὐτῷ . . . οὐ διδόασιν] nor do they elucidate his essence [οὐδὲ οὐσίαν αὐτοῦ σαφηνίζουσιν]. I do not yet mean that his essence is this or that, but in what manner he has essence [οὐδέπω φαμὲν τοιάνδε ἢ τοιάνδε, ἀλλ'ὅπως ποτὲ οὐσίαν].[33]

As Heine has pointed out, the disagreement on whether the Logos is substantial or insubstantial constitutes the crucial difference between anti-Monarchians and Monarchians.[34] According to the account in the above passage, the Son's generation is akin to the utterance of a human word as sound. If this model is preferred, then it secures the Monarchian position that the Son does not possess individual subsistence on his own. This connection between Monarchianism and the Son as an "uttered word" was already noted by Tertullian:

> For you refuse to consider him substantive in objectivity, as being a substance which is himself [*non vis enim eum substantivum habere in re per substantiae proprietatem*], that he may be seen to be an object [*res*] and a person [*persona*], and so may be capable, inasmuch as he is another beside God, of causing there to be two, the Father and the

> Son, God and the Word: for what, you will say, is a word except voice [*vox*] and oral sound [*sonus oris*] and . . . smitten air intelligible in the hearing, for the rest an empty something, void and incorporeal?[35]

The Monarchian model of the Son's generation, then, takes Ps. 44:2 (LXX) as offering an account of the generative relation between Father and Son that justifies the refusal to attribute distinct individual existence to the Son.

It is noteworthy, then, that the Monarchian account of the Son's generation forms one of the key contexts for the first two books of the *Commentary on John*. This is significant since it is in these two books that Origen develops his systematic consideration of Christological titles, on the basis of which he builds his discussion of Christology in *PArch* I.2. In particular, in *ComJn* I.280–88, Origen offers an explicit critique of the use of Ps. 44:2 (LXX) in support of the use of "uttered word" as a model for the Son's generation.[36] Though we do not find such an argument in *PArch* I.2, two observations highlight that the anti-Monarchian polemic in Book I of *ComJn* likely also underlies the consideration of the Son's generation in *PArch* I.2.[37] First, Origen's approach to Christological titles in Book I of *ComJn* is animated by his concern with "de-centering" Logos as a special title.[38] This is because, according to Origen, those who propose that the Son was an "uttered word" were led to this problematic account of generation because they were unduly focused on Logos as a special title. In response to this, Origen replaces Word with wisdom as the supreme title of the Son. Word as a title, he contends, must be understood in relation to wisdom. Further, he argues that Word is only one among many Christological titles. It follows, from this "de-centering" of Logos, the Monarchians were insufficiently attentive to the multiplicity of Christological titles in Scripture, leading them to become fixated with Word as a special title for understanding the Son's generation. This explains why in *ComJn* I Origen stresses the nature of Christ as "many things," as we saw in the previous chapter, as an anti-Monarchian emphasis. Now in *PArch* I.2, a reproduction of this anti-Monarchian "de-centering" of the Word is present, albeit in a simplified form. Origen's Christological discussion in *PArch* I.2.1–3 proceeds in a manner that parallels the one found in *ComJn* I.90–124: he begins with wisdom. Then, parallel to what he does in *ComJn* I.111–15, in *PArch* I.2.2–3 he elaborates how the Word should be understood as a title in relation to wisdom. Finally, in *PArch* I.2.3–4 he proceeds to several key titles that come after wisdom and Word in the order of Christological titles: life, truth, resurrection, and finally, way. The structural parallels between *ComJn* I and *PArch* I.2 point to the more systematic discussion of the former as a foundation for the more concise discussion of the latter. This, in turn, suggests that the polemical context of the former likely carries over to the latter. More definitive is my second observation, that in *PArch* I.2 Origen expresses his anti-Monarchian concern explicitly: "Let no one, however, suppose that when we call him the wisdom of God, we mean something unsubstantial."[39] This indicates that, as in *ComJn* I.151, cited above, the Monarchian account of the Son as a word uttered by the Father is at the back of Origen's mind when he composes his account on the Son's generation in *PArch* I.2. These two observations, then, suffice to secure the centrality of anti-Monarchian concerns as the second key polemical background to *PArch* I.2.

ORIGEN'S VIA MEDIA BETWEEN VALENTINIAN *PROBOLĒ* AND MONARCHIANISM IN *PERI ARCHŌN* I.2

With Irenaeus, Origen insists that divine simplicity rules out Valentinian *probolē*. If God is simple, then he cannot suffer the kind of divisions implied by Valentinian *probolē*. But, with Tertullian, he also rejects the Monarchian account of the Son's generation as an uttered word. The Son is a distinct hypostasis. So one would also expect that in developing an anti-Valentinian account of the Son's generation, Origen would be concerned with safeguarding the Son's distinct individual existence. In *PArch* I.2.4 he frames his account of the Son's generation precisely around what I have called the "ante-Nicene Trinitarian problematic":

> But whereas the offspring of humans or of other animals, whom we see around us, correspond to the seed of those of whose seed they are or of those in whose wombs they are formed and nourished, having from these whatever it is that they have taken and bring into the light of day when they are born, *it is abominable and unlawful to equate the God and Father, (A) in the begetting of his only-begotten Son and*

> *(B) in his giving [him] subsistence, with any generation of humans or other animals*; but it must be something exceptional and worthy of God, for which can be found no comparison at all, not merely in things, but even in thought or imagination, such that a human mind could apprehend how the unbegotten God becomes Father of the only-begotten Son.

> Verum quoniam hi, qui apud nos videntur hominum filii vel ceterorum animalium, semini eorum a quibus seminati sunt respondent vel earum in quarum utero formantur ac nutriuntur, habentes ex his quicquid illud est, quod in lucem hanc assumunt ac deferent processuri: *infandum autem est et inlicitum deum patrem (A) in generatione unigeniti filii sui atque (B) in subsistentia eius exaequare alicui vel hominum vel aliorum animantium generanti*; sed necesse est exceptum aliquid esse et deo dignum, cuius nulla prorsus comparatio non in rebus solum sed ne in cognitatione quidem vel sensu inveniri potest, ut humana cogitatio possit adpraehendere quomodo ingenitus deus pater efficitur unigeniti filii.[40]

In a key sentence, which I have italicized above, Origen announces programmatically the problem he is attempting to resolve in *PArch* I.2.5–13. The main problem is caused by what he perceives to be two ways to impiously attribute anthropomorphic connotations to the Father. First, it is inappropriate to regard the Father, in the generation of his Only-Begotten son, as akin to a human generator. Origen likely has in mind the standard polemical account of Valentinian *probolē* here. The first impious way, then, is to think of God the Father as generating in an animal-like manner such as in Valentinian emissions. Second, it is inappropriate to regard the Father, in granting his Only-Begotten Son subsistence, as akin to a human generator. The phrase *in subsistentia eius*, I suggest, indicates that Origen likely had in mind here the same issue we have seen previously in Tertullian's *APrax*. 8. As seen in chapter 4, Tertullian observes a potential Monarchian critique against the anti-Monarchians' position: if the Son possesses his own distinct individual existence, does this position mean that the Father is divided? The problem, then, is that the anti-Monarchian affirmation of the Son's distinct individual existence potentially entails an animal-like account of generation. In the above passage Origen seems to be rejecting the possibility of drawing this conclusion. The presence of the phrase *in subsistentia eius* shows that Origen is clearly aware of this potential problem as he sets out his own account of the Son's generation. The final part of this passage suggests that Origen intends to resolve this problem in an anti-Monarchian manner. In the face of this problem, instead of concluding with the Monarchians that a distinct hypostasis should not be attributed to the Son, what is required is an "exceptional" process that accounts for the generation of the Son *while maintaining* the Son as a distinct individual existence, begotten from the Father in a manner that is compatible with the Father's simplicity. If this reading is correct, then Origen's problematic in *PArch* I.2.5–13, programmatically set out in the above passage, is similar to the "ante-Nicene Trinitarian problematic": how is it possible to construct an account of the Son's generation that (1) preserves the simplicity of the Father, and (2) maintains the Son's individual existence as a result? In other words, how does one find a via media between Valentinian *probolē* and Monarchianism? If this is right, then the dual concern of maintaining an account of the Son's generation that is compatible with divine simplicity (anti-Valentinian emphasis) without compromising the Son's distinct hypostasis (anti-Monarchian emphasis) should be at the forefront of Origen's thinking throughout *PArch* I.2.

In what follows I shall argue that this dual concern indeed frames Origen's distinctive account of the Son's generation in *PArch* I.2.5–13. To be precise, I shall turn to examining the basic structures of Origen's thinking on this theme in order to highlight that he is committed to maintaining the same conditions (inseparability, consubstantiality,[41] contemporaneity) we have seen in Irenaeus. But I shall frequently stress that Origen's implementation of these conditions goes beyond that of Irenaeus, as might be expected from his additional concern with maintaining the anti-Monarchian affirmation of the Son's distinct hypostasis.

Implementing Inseparability: *Tanquam a Mente Voluntas*

If God is simple, then he cannot generate that which is separate from him. Inseparability, as we have seen in the work of Irenaeus, implies that God cannot generate in the manner of human begetting or mental activities.

These two examples highlight what is required for a process of generation to preserve the simplicity of the generator: the generated must in some sense be identical with the generator.[42] But Irenaeus's "identity thesis" language was not adequate for Origen. If the simple could generate only that which was identical to itself, this would lead directly to Monarchianism. This is because Irenaeus's language does not differentiate the sense in which something that possesses a *distinct* individual existence from the sense in which something possesses a *separate* individual existence. Or, putting it in Tertullian's terms, Irenaeus's analysis lacks differentiation between *divisio*/*distinctio* and *pars*/*portio*. Origen's approach is to outline an "exceptional" process in which God could generate his Only-Begotten Son so that the Son would not have a separate existence while ensuring that the Son acquired a distinct hypostasis. This approach can be read as an attempt to safeguard the following two theses:

> Anti-Valentinian thesis: The Son must be identical to the Father *in some sense* in order to preserve the simplicity of the Father.
>
> Anti-Monarchian thesis: The Son must possess a distinct individual existence (= hypostasis) and as such must not be *totally* identical to the Father himself.

Origen's task, then, is to maintain the two theses in a coherent manner without contradictions. The solution, the "exceptional process" Origen had in mind in *PArch* I.2.4, is aptly summed up by the phrase *tanquam a mente voluntas*: the generation of the Word is "like the act of will from the mind."[43]

In *PArch* I.2.6 Origen introduces the language of the will proceeding from the mind:

> If "all that the Father does, the Son also does likewise" (John 5:19), then by the fact that the Son does all things like the Father, the image of the Father is formed in the Son, who is assuredly born of him, as an act of his will proceeding from the intellect. And therefore I consider that the will of the Father ought to be sufficient for the subsistence of what he wills; for in willing he uses no other means than that which is produced by the counsel of his will. In this way, then, the subsistence of the Son is also begotten by him.

> Si enim *Omnia quae facit pater, haec et filius facit similiter*, in eo quod omnia ita facit filius sicut pater, imago patris defomatur in filio, qui utique natus ex eo est velut quaedam voluntas eius ex mente procedens. Et ideo ego arbitror quod sufficere debeat voluntas patris ad subsistendum hoc, quod vult pater. Volens enim non alia via utitur, nisi quae consilio voluntas profertur. Ita ergo et filii ab eo subsistentia generatur.

To probe the details of Origen's account more precisely, the meaning of the term *voluntas* needs to be determined since this term contains a significant ambiguity. Does it refer to (1) the Father's very act of willing (i.e., his faculty of will), (2) the object of the Father's act of willing (i.e., that which is willed by him), or (3) the result of the Father's act of willing?[44] Since the notion of the Son as begotten from the will of God became tainted after the fourth-century controversies surrounding Arius and "Arianism," this is a point at which one would expect to see Rufinus's editorial hand. Hence, Rufinus's Latin translation of *PArch* cannot be entirely trusted here.[45] In light of this, I shall turn to a set of extant Greek passages that will help identify the use of *voluntas* by Origen in a Christological context.

The first piece of the puzzle is found in a fragment of Origen's lost *Commentary on Ephesians*. In this passage he comments on the phrase "through the will of God" in Eph. 1:1. The use of this phrase raises a potential problem. The preposition διὰ indicates "what is subordinate" (τὸ ὑπηρετικὸν), referring to that which stands in the second position to something greater.[46] In light of this, Origen anticipates the puzzlement of some concerning Eph. 1:1. How could the "will of God" stand in second position to something greater? The puzzlement arises presumably because the thought seems blasphemous, suggesting that the divine will is subordinated to something else. Did Paul, then, misuse the preposition? According to Origen, the first step toward resolution is to recognize that "through God" (διὰ θεοῦ) is not the same as "through the will of God" (διὰ θελήματος θεοῦ). The former is clearly blasphemous, subordinating God to something greater. But it is not unreasonable to use "the will of God" to refer to something standing in second position since "what God uses is itself considered to have being."[47] The argument is that if "the will of God" can possess hypostasis in itself (ὑπόστασιν ἔχον αὐτόν), then it is possible to refer to it as "what is subordinate" (τὸ ὑπηρετικὸν), standing in a second position to God. But is it possible that the "will of God" possesses hypostasis in itself? Origen suggests that this is possible if this phrase is interpreted Christologically:

> And you will take note also if the phrase "will of God" can be applied to Christ so that as he is "the power of God and the wisdom of God" (1 Cor. 1:24), so he may also be his "will," himself having the hypostasis of God. But if someone should think it absurd to say that the "will of God" is invested with substance, let him note if the seeming absurdity is not about the same also in the case of the "Power of God," the "Wisdom of God," the "Word of God," "Truth," "Resurrection" and "Way." For it seems to me to be about the same concerning all of these, insofar as they are invested with substance in the only-begotten Word.
>
> ἐπιστήσεις δὲ καὶ περὶ τοῦ θελήματος τοῦ θεοῦ εἰ δύναται τάσσεσθαι ἐπὶ Χριστοῦ· ἵν' ὥσπερ ἐστὶ Θεοῦ δύναμις καὶ θεοῦ σοφία, οὕτως ᾖ καὶ θέλημα αὐτοῦ, Θεοῦ ὑπόστασιν ἔχον αὐτόν· ἐὰν δέ τινι ἀπεμφαῖνον φαίνηται οὐσιῶσθαι λέγειν τὸ τοῦ Θεοῦ θέλημα, ἐπιστησάτω εἰ μὴ ἡ δοκοῦσα ἀπέμφασις παραπλήσιός ἐστι καὶ ἐπὶ δυνάμεως Θεοῦ καὶ σοφίας Θεοῦ καὶ λόγος Θεοῦ, καὶ ἀληθείας καὶ ἀναστάσεως καὶ ὁδοῦ· παραπλήσιος γάρ μοι δοκεῖ τυγχάνειν περὶ πάντων τούτων, ὡς οὐσιωμένων ἐν τῷ μονογενεῖ Λόγῳ.[48]

If Scripture says that Christ *is* the power and wisdom of God among many other things, then it is not absurd to think that he is also the "will of God." In the same way that hypostasis is granted to the "power of God," the "wisdom of God," and many others titles, so is it possible to conceive of the "will of God" as a distinct hypostasis so long as the phrase is understood to refer to Christ himself. It is possible, then, to conceive of the Son as τὸ τοῦ Θεοῦ θέλημα. Consequently, this fragment highlights Origen's teaching that Christ is to be conceived of as the hypostasis of the very will of God.

But what is the "will of God" that has acquired hypostasis in Christ? Does θέλημα refer to the object of an act of willing, the act of willing itself, or the result of an act of willing? This is unclear from the fragment of *ComEp.* So another piece of the jigsaw is needed. In the *Commentary on John*, where Origen is commenting on John 4:34, we find another hint of his thinking on the Son as the will of God:

> For that is not the Father's will in its entirety—I mean that which comes to be extraneous to the one who wills, apart from the previously mentioned will. The complete will of the Father is done by the Son when *the willing of God that comes to be in the Son* does that which the will of God wishes.
>
> Ἐκεῖνο γάρ, λέγω δὲ τὸ ἔξω τοῦ θέλοντος γινόμενον χωρὶς τοῦ προειρημένου θελήματος οὐχ ὅλον μὲν τὸ θέλημα τοῦ πατρός. πᾶν δέ ἐστιν τὸ θέλημα τοῦ πατρὸς ὑπὸ τοῦ υἱοῦ γινόμενον ὅτε τὸ θέλειν τοῦ θεοῦ γενόμενον ἐν τῷ υἱῷ ποιεῖ ταῦτα ἅπερ βούλεται τὸ θέλημα τοῦ θεοῦ.[49]

In this passage Origen differentiates two senses according to which the Son does the Father's will. The Son could be doing the Father's will by performing his will apart from the Father. In other words, the Son does the will of the Father merely as a *separate* will. For Origen, this sense is insufficient to account for the profound sense of the Son's doing the will of the Father: the Son does the "complete will" of the Father.[50] The "complete will" of the Father is accomplished when "the willing of God that comes to be in the Son does that which the will of God wishes" (τὸ θέλειν τοῦ θεοῦ γενόμενον ἐν τῷ υἱῷ ποιεῖ ταῦτα ἅπερ βούλεται τοῦ πατρός). In the Greek, τὸ θέλειν τοῦ θεοῦ γενόμενον ἐν τῷ υἱῷ is the subject of the verb ποιεῖ. It is natural, then, to interpret τὸ θέλειν τοῦ θεοῦ γενόμενον ἐν τῷ υἱῷ as the act of willing of the Father that comes to be in the Son. It follows that the Son "does the complete will of the Father" by being the very hypostasis of the Father's act of willing, accomplishing everything that the Father wills. This observation further qualifies what we have seen in *ComEp*. For this passage suggests that Origen thinks what has acquired a hypostasis in the Son is the Father's *act of willing*, since τὸ θέλειν τοῦ θεοῦ γενόμενον ἐν τῷ υἱῷ is what does "that which the will of God wishes." It is through the Son, as a distinct hypostasis, that the Father wills what he wills into actuality. Putting the two pieces of the jigsaw together, Origen seems to have the *actus mentis* in mind when he teaches that the Son is the "will of God" acquiring hypostasis.

It remains unclear, though, how the Son as the "will of God" shed light on the idea of his generation from the Father. I shall now turn to establishing this connection. In the same section of the *Commentary on John* we examined above, Origen offers a clue as to how the language of the Son as the "will of God" clarifies the nature of his generation:

> Perhaps this is why he [the Son] is the image of the invisible God. For indeed the will that is in him is an image of the first will, and the divinity that is in him is an image of the true divinity. But even though he is an image of the Father's goodness, he says, "Why do you call me good?" *And indeed it is this will that is the distinctive food of the Son himself, food on account of which he is what he is.*
>
> Καὶ τάχα διὰ ταῦτα εἰκών ἐστιν τοῦ θεοῦ τοῦ ἀοράτου· καὶ γὰρ τὸ ἐν αὐτῷ θέλημα εἰκὼν τοῦ πρώτου θελήματος, καὶ ἡ ἐν αὐτῷ θεότης εἰκὼν τῆς ἀληθινῆς θεότητος· εἰκὼν δὲ καὶ τῆς ἀγαθότητος ὢν τοῦ πατρός φησι· Τί με λέγεις ἀγαθόν; καὶ τοῦτό γε τὸ θέλημα βρῶμά ἐστιν τοῦ υἱοῦ ἴδιον αὐτοῦ, δι' ὃ βρῶμα ἔστιν ὃ ἔστιν.[51]

The last sentence in this passage hints at Origen's understanding of the Son's generation from the Father in terms of "will." Here Origen identifies the food on account of which the Son is who he is (δι' ὃ βρῶμα ἔστιν ὃ ἔστιν) as the first will of which the Son is an image. The phrase δι' ὃ suggests that the Father's will, identified as the Son's food, constitutes the basis for the Son's existence. This brings us the final piece of the jigsaw. In *ComEp* the Son's hypostasis is identified as the very "will of God" (τὸ τοῦ Θεοῦ θέλημα). The first passage from *ComJn* clarifies that it is the Father's act of willing (τὸ θέλειν τοῦ θεοῦ) that acquires a distinct reality in the Son. What the final passage adds, then, is the claim that the Son's hypostasis is dependent for its existence upon the Father's act of willing. It is in this sense that the Father's will constitutes the food of the Son. It follows that Origen thinks that the language of the Son as the Father's will also expresses the dependence of the Son's existence on the Father's act of willing.

In light of these points, returning now to *PArch* I.2.6, *voluntas* in this passage should be read as referring to the Father's act of willing, not the result or object of this act.[52] The Son is generated as the Father's own act of will proceeds from himself, acquiring its own hypostasis. How, then, does *tanquam a mente voluntas* provide Origen the "exceptional process" that differs radically from Valentinian animal-like emissions? The model of the will proceeding from the mind does so by capturing how the divine mind operates in a radically different way than the human mind. In the human mind, different stages of its activity are emitted as separate existences because human mental activities suffer delay due to embodiment. But this cannot be the case for divine mental activities, as we have seen in *PArch* I.1.6: "That simple and wholly intellectual being can have no delay or hesitation in its movements or operations." Already in Irenaeus we have seen how a simple mind cannot generate something that exists separately. Hence, activities of God's mind—including his act of willing—cannot result in something generated separately (*partiliter*) from itself: "Rather, then, as an act of will proceeds from the mind, and neither cuts off any part nor is separated or divided from it, so in some similar fashion, is the Father to be supposed to have begotten the Son."[53] Like Irenaeus, then, Origen affirms that God's mental activity, including his act of will, cannot lead to the generation of entities that divide God. The Son's generation *tanquam a mente voluntas,* grounded in the nature of *divine* mental activities, is therefore unlike Valentinian *probolē* and hence, compatible with the simplicity of the Father.

But as Irenaeus has required, the Father's simplicity remains only if what he generates is in some sense identical to himself. Given Origen's anti-Monarchian sensibility, it is unlikely that he would follow Irenaeus to the further conclusion that the simple mind cannot generate something that exists distinctly. Yet a limited parallel may be found in *PArch* I.2.9. Commenting on Wis. 7:25–6, Origen writes:

> The breath, then, or if I may speak thus, the vigour of all this great and so immense power itself comes to have its own subsistence, for although it proceeds from the power itself as will from the mind, nevertheless even the will of God itself becomes the power of God. Another power, therefore, comes to be, subsisting in its own properties, a kind of breath, as the passage of Scripture affirms, of the first and unbegotten power of God, drawing from him whatever it is. There is no "when" when it did not exist.

> Huius ergo totius uirtutis tantae et tam inmensae vapor et, ut ita dixerim, vigor ipse in propria subsistentia effectus quamvis ex ipsa virtute velut voluntas ex mente procedat, tamen et ipsa voluntas dei nihilominus dei virtus efficitur. Efficitur ergo virtus altera in sua proprietate subsistens, ut ait sermo scripturae, vapor quidam primae et ingenitae virtutis dei, hoc quidem quod est inde trahens; non est autem quando non fuerit.

This passage interprets the sense in which the Son is "a breath of the power of God" according to Wis. 7:25–26. According to Origen, the breath proceeds from the power (i.e., the Father) as the will proceeds from the mind. He begins by affirming that the very strength of God's power is sufficient to secure the distinct hypostasis of the breath (i.e., the Son)—by now a familiar point from Origen's teaching of the Son as the "will of God." As we have seen, Origen sees the Son not as merely a separate will doing the Father's will but as the hypostasis of the Father's very act of willing. This sense of identity between the Father and the Son is elaborated further in the above passage: here Origen implicitly identifies the *voluntas dei* (i.e., τὸ θέλημα τοῦ θεοῦ) Christologically. It is on this basis that Origen further identifies the will of God as the power of God. The argument seems to be that the breath, proceeding from the power (i.e., the Father) and acquiring a distinct hypostasis, comes to be nothing less than being *another* power of God "subsisting in its own proper nature" (*in sua proprietate subsistens*).[54] This power has its existence from the source identified as the first and unbegotten power of God. What is remarkable, then, is that this passage, in reproducing the observations we have made so far, clarifies how Origen's account of the Son as the "will of God" leads to a limited sense in which the Son is identical to the Father: he is the Father's own act of will and power. The Son does not become a *separate* will or power of God, nor is he the effect of the will of the Father since there is only *one* will of God, namely, the Son himself.

It is then possible to pinpoint what is "exceptional" in the nature of divine mental activity that enables it to form the basis of Origen's preferred model of the Son's generation. Unlike in the case of human minds, where something may be generated with its own hypostasis through dividing the source and the generator, the simple mind (the Father) operates in such a way that his own act of will could acquire hypostasis without suffering divisions. It is this possibility, expressed by the language of *tanquam a mente voluntas*, that captures the mystery of the Son's generation and explains why this is an "exceptional process." Orbe summarizes this point beautifully:

> The mystery is that a *voluntas* in itself (at a human level) that is incapable of subsisting acquires in the divine procession of the *Logos* such a real subsistence (although of a superior nature) as that which animals acquire under *prolatio*. . . . In God, such a mystery cannot be a surprise, according to Origen, because of the singular nature of the procession, *tanquam a mente voluntas*. For the Son is not born as the simple effect of the divine will but proceeds as a volitional exercise (= *voluntas*) of the same Mind of God.[55]

Accordingly, the language of *tanquam a mente voluntas* safeguards the anti-Valentinian thesis. It follows, furthermore, that this mystery of divine mental activity also secures the anti-Monarchian thesis. Since the mystery lies in the fact that the very act of the divine will is sufficient to grant subsistent existence to itself, the model of the will proceeding from the mind guarantees the Son's possession of a distinct hypostasis.[56] Hence, for Origen generation *tanquam a mente voluntas* provides a via media that steers clear of both Valentinian *probolē* and Monarchianism.

The astute reader, though, might wonder: does not the identification of the Son as the Father's own act of will subsisting compromise the Father-Son distinction? That this would not be so is hinted at in *PArch* I.2.9, where Origen describes the Son as "another power subsisting in his own properties" (*virtus altera in sua proprietate subsistens*). Origen's sensitivity to the Monarchian danger permeates his thinking on this point, as illustrated, for instance, in his comment on John 5:19–20 in *ComJn* XIII.228: "When he [the Son] wills in himself what was also the Father's will, so that the will of God is in the will of the Son, and the will of the Son has become indistinguishable from the will of the Father . . . there are no longer two wills but one."[57] According to this passage, the Father's will and the Son's will are *two*. But the Son's will can be identified with the Father's very own will subsisting on the basis of the unity or harmony between the two wills. In *Contra Celsum*, Origen confirms this point: "We worship the Father of the truth and the Son who is the truth; they are two distinct existences, but one in mental unity, in agreement, and in identity of will" (δύο τῇ ὑποστάσει πράγματα, ἓν δὲ τῇ ὁμονοίᾳ καὶ τῇ συμφωνίᾳ καὶ τῇ ταυτότητι τοῦ βουλήματος).[58] So when Origen identifies the Son as the Father's own will, he does so on the basis of John 5:19–20, which affirms that the Son mirrors the Father perfectly at the level of act and willing—the Son "does the complete will of the Father." Putting this point differently, in the hypothetical scenario in which the Son is the Only Begotten who possesses his own hypostasis and yet does not do the complete will of the Father, the Son cannot in the same way be identified as the Father's act of will subsisting.[59] Origen's identification of the Son as the Father's act of will, then, does not in any way leads to Monarchianism. On the contrary, this account is built with a sharp anti-Monarchian orientation.[60]

The Son's generation *tanquam a mente voluntas* is the "exceptional process" Origen was searching for in *PArch* I.2.4. This language successfully avoids connotations associated with animal-like generation. Unlike Valentinian *probolē*, in this account the Father does not generate something separate from himself, hence subjecting himself to divisions. In this sense, Origen has successfully implemented the inseparability condition, securing the Son's generation in a manner compatible with the Father's simplicity. But Origen's anti-Monarchian concern has led to a more sophisticated consideration of the sense in which such a non-animal-like process may secure the distinct hypostasis of the generated. Unlike Irenaeus, who only affirms that divine simplicity is incompatible with any processes that result in something generated *efficabiliter et partiliter*, Origen resorts to divine mystery to further preserve the compatibility of an anti-Valentinian account of the Son's generation with anti-Monarchianism. The Son's generation *tanquam a mente voluntas*, as an "exceptional process," therefore preserves his distinct hypostasis without conceding any divisions in the Father. In this manner, the language of *tanquam a mente voluntas* resolves the problematic stated in *PArch* I.2.4.

Implementing Consubstantiality: The Son as Image and Mirror

According to Irenaeus, a simple God can generate only that which is "of one form, in every way equal and similar" to himself.[61] A mode of generation compatible with simplicity, then, could allow differences between generator and generated only by generation (*generatione*) or by size (*magnitudine*).[62] The first allows one to distinguish between two statuses: as source (e.g., sun) and as derivative (e.g., rays from the sun). The second allows one to distinguish two of the same kind (light) where one is greater (e.g., the brightness of the sun) and one is lesser (e.g. the brightness of the rays). The key point is that despite these differences, the generator and the generated are *one in nature*. Just as rays of the sun and the sun itself are both lights, so must the generator and the generated share the same nature. This condition is required in processes involving a simple source because, as we saw in chapters 1 and 2, that which is simple, which is always self-same, contains in itself nothing contrary to its own nature. Consequently, what a simple source generates could be only one in nature with itself.[63] This is what I have called the "consubstantiality condition." In Origen's account of the Son's generation, a similar condition is implemented, as I shall argue, albeit using a different language based on Col. 1:15 ("the image of the invisible God"), Heb. 1:3 ("the express image of his substance"), and Wis. 7:25–26 ("an unspotted mirror of the working or power of God and an image of his goodness"). Since the exact status of consubstantiality (ὁμοούσιος) in Origen is widely debated, in what follows my argument will not attempt to establish a conclusion regarding the status of the specific term in Origen.[64] Rather, my aim is more modest, namely, to suggest that Origen's use of the language of image fulfils requirements similar to those summed up by the language of consubstantiality in Irenaeus. Hence, whenever I use the term "consubstantiality" in the context of discussing Origen, I am referring to the sense of "perfect likeness" captured by this term in Irenaeus.

Drawing on the language of Col. 1:15, Origen suggests that the Son's relation to the Father is expressed by the term *image*.[65] In *PArch* I.2.6 Origen considers two senses in which one is an image of the other. In a material sense, a thing is called an image of an object if it is a realization of the object in material form (e.g., a wooden statue). However, in an immaterial sense, a thing is called an image if it reproduces faithfully every aspect of what is imaged. The second sense does not require a materialistic understanding of imaging because it is grounded in the idea of faithful reproduction. According to Origen, it is in this sense that Col. 1:15 describes the Son as "an image of the invisible God." He suggests that this sense is indicated by Gen. 5:3, where it is written that "Adam begat Seth after his own image and after his own kind." In Rufinus's Latin text, Origen's comment on this verse reads: "This image preserves the unity of nature and substance of a Father and of a Son" (*Quae imago etiam naturae ac substantiae patris et filii continent unitatem*). Given the language of *substantia* here, this phrase likely belongs to Rufinus, but Origen's point is clear: the sense of image in Gen. 5:3 illustrates the immaterial sense of imaging, namely, that the offspring possesses perfect likeness to the parent. This immaterial sense of imaging provides the language that reveals Origen's understanding of the "perfect likeness" between Father and Son.

Origen further elaborates how the Son is a perfect image of the Father: at the level of act and will. In Origen's thinking, the language of image is closely connected to the language of will we have considered previously. The Son is the perfect image of the Father because he does the complete will of the Father. The kind of unity between the Father and Son expressed by the language of image, then, is conceived by Origen primarily at the level of act.[66] An extant Greek text further confirms this point. In *ComJn* XIII.234 we read that the relation between the Son's will and the Father's will is like the relation between an image and what is imaged. Here, as in *PArch* I.2.6, the language of image is used to capture the content of John 5:19–20: the Son does the complete will of the Father. Given that the Son's will is not naïvely identified with the Father's will, as I have argued, the two wills are nevertheless one because of the perfect harmony between them.[67] The sense of perfect imaging in Origen's Christological use of the language of image must therefore be understood at the level of act and will. Hence, what was implemented by consubstantiality in Irenaeus is captured in Origen by the language of image, which is understood on the basis of reading Col. 1:15 in light of John 5:19–20.

The language of image in Col. 1:15, though, is not the only way Origen articulates a sense of perfect likeness between the Father and the Son. He makes a similar point when commenting on the phrase "flawless mirror of the energy [ἐνεργείας] or working of God" in Wis. 7:25. Although the language of image is absent from this verse, Origen's discussion of the language of "mirror" in Wis. 7:25 is closely related to his discussion of the language of image in Col. 1:15. In the first half of *PArch* I.2.12 Origen recalls what we know from his exegesis of the phrase "the breath of the power of God." He interprets the Son as the strength of the power of God subsisting, with himself *another* power of God (1 Cor. 1:24). In the second half Origen turns to considering the unity between the Father and the Son implied by Wis. 7:25. According to Origen, the phrase "flawless mirror . . . of the working of God" speaks of how the Son is one with the Father. When a person looks into a mirror, he sees the image moving and acting in perfect accord with how he himself moves and acts. This imagery offers another way to clarify the unity between Father and Son:

> As, then, the Son in no respect is separated or differs from the Father in the power of his works, nor is the work of the Son anything other than the Father's, but one and the same movement, so to speak, is in all things, he therefore called him a flawless mirror, that by this expression it might be understood that there is no dissimilarity whatsoever between the Son and the Father.
>
> Quoniam ergo in nullo prorsus filius a patre virtute operum inmutatur ac differt, nec aliud est opus filii quam patris, sed unus atque idem, ut ita dicam, etiam motus in omnibus est: idcirco speculum eum immaculatum nominavit, ut per hoc nulla omnino dissimilitudo filii intellegatur ad patrem.[68]

This passage clearly outlines how the anti-Valentinian condition of consubstantiality in Irenaeus is implemented in Origen's thinking. First, the Son is not generated separately from the Father, as Wis. 7:25 refers to a process radically distinct from Valentinian animal-like *probolē*. Second, Origen argues, on the basis of the phrase "flawless mirror" in Wis. 7:25, that there are no dissimilarities between the Son and the Father.[69] Once again, though, Origen understands the perfect likeness indicated by this phrase at the level of act (*opus*). Unlike Irenaeus—and, I would argue, characteristically—Origen turns away from affirming the perfect likeness between Father and Son using the language of substance. The language of mirror in Wis. 7:25, then, is also central to Origen's articulation of the sense of perfect likeness between the Father and the Son.

The sense of perfect likeness captured by consubstantiality in Irenaeus undoubtedly finds a different expression in Origen's thought. This sense of perfect likeness, in turn, rules out any possibility of understanding the Son's generation as an animal-like emission. But the language of image also enables Origen to maintain an anti-Monarchian affirmation of the Father-Son distinction that is compatible with the perfect likeness between the two. Here the parallel with Irenaeus is more striking, as Origen's account considers exactly the two ways Irenaeus allows for differentiation, namely, by generation and by size. In *PArch* I.2.8, commenting on how the Savior is "the image of God's subsistence" (Heb. 1:3), Origen proposes the (in)famous metaphor of the statues to describe the Father-Son relation:

> For example, suppose there were a statue of such magnitude as to fill the whole world and on that account could be seen by no one; but that another statue was made similar to it in every respect, in the shape of limbs and outline of countenance, in form and matter, but not in its immensity of size [*specie ac materia per omnia similis absque magnitudinis immensitate*] so that those who were unable to perceive and behold the immense one, on seeing the latter could be assured that they had seen the former, because it preserved every outline of limb and countenance, and even the form and matter, with an absolutely indistinguishable similarity; by some such likeness, the Son of God emptying himself of equality with the Father and showing us the way by which we may know him, becomes the "express figure of his substance."[70]

The metaphor of the statues shows clearly how the language of image enables reference to the same kind of difference highlighted by Irenaeus, namely, that by size (*magnitudione*). Of course, as Origen himself indicates, it would be absurd to take the materialistic connotation of size in this metaphor literally. But this passage confirms that in Origen's thinking there is a noted difference by size between the Father and the Son, differentiating the two in terms of knowability/accessibility in relation to creatures. This is important for Origen's insistence on the Son as mediator. It is precisely because the Son is lesser than the Father in the immensity of goodness, divinity, brightness, and so on that "we, who were unable to look upon the glory of the pure light while it remained in the magnitude of his divinity, may, by his becoming for us 'the splendour,' obtain the way of beholding the divine light through looking upon the splendour."[71] Origen, then, deems a difference "by size" between the Father and the Son to be compatible with the perfect likeness between the two.

Origen also allows a difference between the Father and the Son by generation (*generatione*). That is, he allows the possibility of differentiating the Father as source from the Son as derivative. Given that the Son-Father relation is analogous to the relation between an image and what is imaged, the language of image already contains within it this sense of differentiation. For the very language of image already supposes that the image is a reflection of some *actual* object other than itself. The language of image inevitably highlights the image's derivative, dependent nature, hence contrasting the image with the source of the image. As we saw in chapter 6, this aspect of Origen's thought manifests itself in his understanding of the Father as goodness itself and the Son as "the image of goodness" (Wis. 7:26). Origen's clarification of this point can be found in a few extant Greek passages we have already considered. In *ComJn* II.20 he speaks of the Father—the God and true God—as the *source* of divinity in relation to the Son, who is the image of his divinity. In *ComJn* XIII.234 Origen calls the Son "an image of the true divinity." He allows a similar differentiation with respect to goodness as well.[72] Thus, it is the language of source and image that allows Origen to differentiate "by generation" between the Father and the Son.

Origen's use of the language of image and mirror, then, accomplishes the work done by the term "consubstantiality" in Irenaeus. Since Origen, like Irenaeus, rejects Valentinian *probolē*, it is not surprising that the mode of generation he endorsed should also affirm the characteristic features of Irenaeus's account: the generator and the generated are "of one form, in every way equal and similar"[73] while allowing differences "by generation" and "by size." I have argued that Origen's use of the language of image and mirror preserves these conditions, but what is less clear, is whether his account also maintains a polemical edge against Monarchianism. I suggest that Origen's account may be envisaged as a via media in the following way. On the one hand, portraying the Son as the image and mirror of the Father establishes the perfect likeness between the two. This stands in sharp contrast to Valentinian *probolē*, which introduces radical dissimilarities between generator and generated, a point Irenaeus never hesitates to repeat. On the other hand, while the Son as image is perfectly one with the Father as source—at the level of act and will—nevertheless the image is to be distinguished from the source by generation and size. Origen's anti-Monarchian sensibility, therefore, explains why he replaces the language of consubstantiality (as found in Irenaeus) by the language of image to capture the perfect likeness between the Father and the Son. Since *ousia*, hypostasis, and *hypokeimenon* are all tainted with Monarchian connotations, as we have seen in Origen's critique of Monarchianism, any sense of consubstantiality will struggle to maintain an anti-Monarchian sense of the Father-Son distinction. It is precisely the ability to express together perfect likeness and differentiation by generation and size that makes the language of image perfectly suited to maintaining both anti-Valentinian and anti-Monarchian emphases. The language of image offers a coherent way to do so because, in Origen's understanding, perfect imaging in the context of the Father and the Son means perfect harmony in act and will—a point that in principle allows *two* distinct wills to be in play. This reading of Col. 1:15 with John 5:19–20 enables Origen to use the language of image to speak of the Son as a *distinct* reality, perfectly similar to the Father without becoming a *separate* reality that is totally dissimilar to and cut off from the Father. In this manner, the language of the Son as image captures Origen's transformation of Irenaeus's consubstantiality condition, a requirement from divine simplicity, into a perfectly balanced via media between Valentinian *probolē* and Monarchianism.

Implementing Contemporaneity: *Tanquam Splendor a Luce*

Origen's account of generation *tanquam a mente voluntas* is also committed to the contemporaneity condition. As we saw in chapter 3, Irenaeus's analysis of this theme is somewhat underdeveloped. He asserts that if God is simple, then what is generated from him—*qua* substance—cannot stand in a relative temporal ordering with respect to its source. For Irenaeus this suffices to reject Valentinian protology, according to which a precise ordering is postulated between different generated aeons. A more precise implementation of contemporaneity is encountered in Origen. Given the extensive literature on Origen's doctrine of eternal generation, in this section I shall focus on drawing out a less emphasized dimension of this teaching, namely, its connection with anti-Valentinian and anti-Monarchian polemics.

Origen's account of contemporaneity is explicitly shaped by his exegesis of Heb. 1:3 and Wis. 7:25–26, according to which the Son is "the brightness of God's glory" and "the brightness of eternal light." Origen draws on this Scriptural language to capture the sense in which the generated is inseparable from the generator. As brightness from light, the Son is generated *inseparabiliter* from the Father.[74] Hence, the anti-Valentinian thesis is built into Origen's interpretation of Heb. 1:3 and Wis. 7:25–26 from the start. Valentinian *probolē*, which suggests that the generated has a separate existence from that of the generator, is ruled out by the Scriptural depiction of the Father-Son relation as light in relation to its brightness. Origen, then, follows Irenaeus closely in utilizing light imagery as an anti-Valentinian emphasis to safeguard the simplicity of the Father.

Like Irenaeus, Origen is sensitive to the implication of the language of light regarding the temporal status of the Son's generation. He interprets the language of the Son's generation *tanquam splendor a luce* found in Heb. 1:3 and Wis. 7:25–26 as suggesting that the Son is *eternally* generated from the Father: "For this is the eternal and everlasting begetting, just as brightness is begotten from light."[75] For Origen, the contemporaneity between Father and Son, and hence the Son's eternal generation, follows directly from the two Scriptural texts. Origen's affirmation of eternal generation is explained, in great detail, in *PArch* I.2.11 when he is commenting on the phrase "splendor of the eternal light" in Wis. 7:25–26:

> That which neither had a beginning of existence, nor can ever cease to be what it is, is properly called everlasting or eternal. And this is pointed out by John when he says, "God is light." Now his Wisdom is the splendor of that light, not only in respect of its being light, but also in respect of its being everlasting light, so that his Wisdom is eternal and everlasting splendor. If this be fully understood, it clearly shows that the subsistence of the Son derives from the Father himself, yet not temporally nor from any other beginning except, as we have said, from God himself.

Rufinus's translation of this passage is contentious since he is generally unreliable when it comes to temporal language in Origen, as Tzamalikos has argued.[76] A more precise understanding of Origen's teaching must be sought in an extant Greek text, *HomJe* IX.4. In this passage Origen states that "the Father has not begotten the Son and then severed him from his generation, but always begets him" (οὐχὶ ἐγέννησεν ὁ πατὴρ τὸν υἱὸν καὶ ἀπέλυσεν αὐτὸν ὁ πατὴρ ἀπὸ τῆς γενέσεως αὐτοῦ, ἀλλ' ἀεὶ γεννᾷ αὐτόν).

A few lines later he turns to expanding on this statement by contrasting the present tense of the verb γεννάω with the perfect tense of the same verb:

> But let us consider who is our Savior: a reflection of glory. The brightness of glory (cf. Wis. 7:26) has not been begotten just once and no longer begotten [τὸ ἀπαύγασμα τῆς δόξης οὐχὶ ἅπαξ γεγέννηται καὶ οὐχὶ γεννᾶται]. But just as the light is an agent of reflection, in such a way the reflection of the glory of God is begotten. Our Savior is the wisdom of God. But the wisdom is the reflection of everlasting light. . . . The Savior is always begotten [ὁ σωτὴρ ἀεὶ γεννᾶται]—because of this he also says, "Before all the hills he begets me" (and not "Before all the hills he has begotten me [γεγέννηκεν]," but, "Before all of the hills he begets [γεννᾷ] me")—and the Savior is always begotten by the Father [καὶ ἀεὶ γεννᾶται ὁ σωτὴρ ὑπὸ τοῦ πατρός].

In this passage Origen argues that the Son, as "brightness" (ἀπαύγασμα), is not begotten once and then no longer begotten. Just as light begets brightness in a co-temporal manner, in the same way the Son is begotten from the Father. This text confirms that Origen's understanding of light imagery closely resembles what we have seen in Irenaeus. Origen thinks that light is, by nature, ceaselessly reflected by its brightness. The contrast between γεννᾶται/γεννᾷ (present) and γεγέννηται/γεγέννηκεν (perfect) in this passage offers a more precise formulation of this point. The Father (i.e., the light source) always begets the Son (i.e., the brightness) in the present tense, meaning that the Father never ceases (in time) to beget the Son. The implication of the present tense stands in contrast to the use of the perfect tense, which implies that the Father has begotten the Son at one point in time and subsequently, having completed this action, has ceased to beget the Son. Thus, eternal generation implies that the Father always (ἀεὶ) begets the Son without ceasing. It follows that the Son's begetting has no beginning in time and does not stand in a temporal ordering in relation to the Father.[77] *HomJe* IX.4, then, clarifies the reasoning behind Origen's use of Heb. 1:3 and Wis. 7:25–26 to secure the eternal generation of the Son. The very nature of light and its brightness captures, for Origen, the sense of when something is generated co-temporally with its source.

The polemical purpose of Origen's teaching on eternal generation is not explicitly stated. I have suggested that an anti-Valentinian emphasis is hinted at by Origen's comments on Heb. 1:3,[78] but, unlike in Irenaeus, Origen does not consider contemporaneity directly as a critique of Valentinian protology. I suggest that Monarchianism may have been one important polemical background underlying Origen's doctrine of eternal generation. According to the Monarchians, the divine Word does not possess his own hypostasis due to the fact that they reject the pre-existence of a divine Son *before* (temporally) the incarnation.[79] Consequently, in Monarchian theology the procession of the Word in creation (cf. Prov. 8:22–25, Ps. 44:2 LXX, John 1:3–5) refers not to an eternal generation of the divine Son endowed with individual hypostasis but rather to a Stoic λόγος προφόρικος—an uttered word that, like sound or voice, fades away. The Son of God came to be, as far as the Monarchians are concerned, at the time of the incarnation, when God's spirit (i.e., the Father himself) indwells the flesh of the man Jesus.[80] It becomes immediately clear that two things in the Monarchian account stand in direct opposition to Origen's doctrine of eternal generation: (1) there was no distinct hypostasis of a divine Son before the incarnation and (2) there was a time when the Son of God "came to be," potentially implying that there was a time when the Son was not (ἦν ποτε ὅτε οὐκ ἦν) or that the Son had a temporal origin in time. If this reconstruction is correct, then Origen's emphasis on eternal generation and his critique of the phrase "there was a time when he was not" could have been part of his anti-Monarchian polemic.[81] Eternal generation, on this reading, emerges as part of Origen's attempt to secure the individual hypostasis of the pre-existent Son (refuting 1), asserting, against the Monarchians, that the Son is without any temporal origin (refuting 2). Admittedly, this is conjectural, but in light of the anti-Monarchian undertones in *PArch* I.2 and indeed throughout the first two books of the *Commentary on John*, written during the same period, Origen certainly could have developed the contemporaneity condition required by divine simplicity into a fully anti-Monarchian account of eternal generation.

If my reading is correct, Origen integrates both anti-Valentinian and anti-Monarchian emphases into his consideration of the contemporaneity condition required by divine simplicity. Much of Origen's use of light imagery is in line with what we have seen in Irenaeus. Though less explicitly against Valentinian *probolē*, Origen uses the language of light and splendor in Heb. 1:3 and Wis. 7:25–26 to safeguard the Son's inseparability from the Father. But he offers a more developed account of their contemporaneity, which is expressed in the Son's eternal generation. The language of eternal generation, no doubt aimed at the temporal ordering between the generator and the generated in Valentinian *probolē*, perhaps also offers a polemical edge against Monarchianism. If the Son is eternally generated from the Father, then he clearly possesses individual hypostasis for eternity, refuting the Monarchian account that the Son was generated as an "uttered word" with a temporal beginning. In Origen, then, contemporaneity maintains an anti-Valentinian concern with safeguarding the simplicity of God; however, this condition has likely acquired an additional anti-Monarchian concern with the Alexandrian's more developed form of the condition entailed in his doctrine of the Son's eternal generation.

By the second century, Irenaeus had already recognized that the affirmation of divine simplicity leads to specific conditions as to how one speaks of the process of generation from God. Whenever an ante-Nicene theologian is engaged in polemic against Valentinian *probolē*, these conditions become important because they are taken to be characteristic marks of an alternative theory of generation vis-à-vis Valentinian *probolē*, polemically portrayed as materialistic and anthropomorphic. Origen was engaged in anti-Valentinian polemic in *PArch* I.2, which explains why his account of the Son's generation in this chapter continues to be concerned with the same conditions spelled out by Irenaeus. In Origen, then, divine simplicity undoubtedly functions as an anti-Valentinian principle that spells out the sense of unity between the Father and the Son. Here we find a second way divine simplicity has significantly shaped Origen's account of the Father-Son relation.

But, as I have argued throughout this chapter, *PArch* I.2 was written within a more crowded polemical landscape than Book 2 of Ireaneus's *Adversus Haereses*. As an anti-Monarchian, Origen had an additional concern with maintaining the Son's distinct individual existence. At the end of chapter 4, I characterized the ante-Nicene Trinitarian problematic as follows: Is it possible to maintain the anti-Valentinian emphasis on the Son's continuity with the Father's nature (ruling out Valentinian emissions) without falling into the Monarchian position that the Son and the Father are one and the same divine acting subject? Is it possible to maintain the anti-Monarchian emphasis on the Son's non-identity with the Father (such that there are two divine acting subjects in Scripture) without introducing Valentinian *probolē* that divides the Father? In this chapter I have put forward a case for framing Origen's reflection on the Son's generation in *PArch* I.2 as a solution to this problem. First, the Son is generated from the Father *tanquam a mente voluntas*. He acquires a distinct hypostasis without dividing the Father due to the mystery of the nature of divine mental activities. Second, the Son is the perfect image of the Father, who mirrors the Father in act and will. As such, the Son neither divides the Father nor is naïvely identified with the Father. Rather, the Son is distinct from the Father as any image is distinguished from its original. But the Son does the perfect will of the Father so that the Son's will (the image) and the Father's will (the original) are indistinguishable on the basis of the harmony between the two. Finally, the Son is generated from the Father *tanquam splendor a luce*. The Father always begets the Son, and his begetting never ceases. Consequently, the Son always exists with the Father and does not possess a temporal origin. Putting these themes together, I have argued that Origen's account of the Father-Son relation in *PArch* I.2 successfully implements the anti-Valentinian conditions required by divine simplicity while maintaining an anti-Monarchian emphasis throughout. The second function of divine simplicity in Origen's account of the Father-Son relation is therefore thoroughly shaped by the ante-Nicene Trinitarian problematic, one that requires the theologian to steer clear of Valentinian and Monarchian dangers.

Epilogue

Toward a Prospective Historiography

One of the significant implications of John Henry Newman's *Arians* is that "a sound dogmatic theology depends on honest doctrinal history."[1] Contemporary scholars have echoed this predicament. Khaled Anatolios has argued that the historical development of Trinitarian theology is key to its intelligibility.[2] The far-reaching implication of this claim is that doctrinal history is *indispensable* for understanding the meaning of doctrine. In this book I have sought to contribute to this enterprise of connecting doctrinal history and theological understanding. The upshot for contemporary theology is that pure doctrinal analysis of divine simplicity apart from historical understanding, whether theological or philosophical, is fraught with danger. Throughout I have hinted at a number of things that illustrate this danger. The task remains, however, for systematic and philosophical theologians to think through the implications of the fresh issues and nuances of divine simplicity arising from ante-Nicene doctrinal history set out in the preceding pages. In particular, the distinctive ante-Nicene developments I have charted have significant ramifications with regard to two central issues that have animated the crisis of divine simplicity in modern theology. The first concerns how divine simplicity should be understood, the second, the compatibility of divine simplicity and Trinitarian theology.

Regarding the first issue, in this book I have clarified that the understanding of divine simplicity operative in modern systematic and philosophical theology is overly narrow. The definition of divine simplicity is often spelled out metaphysically, but what is missed is that ethical considerations were also central to the ancient philosophical and early Christian accounts of divine simplicity. What I have uncovered through narrating the philosophical developments from Plato to Origen is that the intelligibility of the doctrine rests significantly on the integrity of the deep interconnection between the metaphysical and the ethical. This, in turn, grants the possibility that there is a much richer definition of divine simplicity. First and foremost—if *The Republic* is to be taken as the *locus classicus*—divine simplicity refers to God's perfect self-consistency. It is for the purpose of safeguarding this perfect self-consistency that Middle Platonists and early Christians affirmed the absence of multiplicity in God. When read in light of the Platonic theory of forms, these affirmations are statements of the total absence of contraries in God. What the doctrine of divine simplicity intends to rule out are only multiplicities that would violate God's perfect self-consistency. For instance, a simple God may not possess goodness and justice as opposing aspects—in this sense they are *one* and the *same*. If divine simplicity is understood this way, it becomes difficult to imagine it as a doctrine that obviously leads to conflict with divine freedom or violates the integrity of God's distinctive acts in salvation history. Thus, the puzzlement regarding God's simplicity among modern philosophers and theologians may have resulted from an overly accentuated disjunction between metaphysical and ethical doctrines of God. Further, it will be fruitful to rethink whether the seeds for a theologically rich doctrine of divine simplicity were already hidden in the Platonic frameworks inherited by early Christian theologians. Along these lines, further explorations on divine simplicity as a metaphysical-ethical synthesis promise to advance contemporary debates, especially for reinstating the theological integrity of divine simplicity in modern theology. For a starting point, this book recommends no better place to look than Origen's understanding of divine simplicity spelled out in chapter 5.

Regarding the second central issue that has animated the crisis of divine simplicity in modern theology, in this book I have highlighted further issues regarding the intuition central to the modern crisis, namely, that there is an incompatibility between divine simplicity and Trinitarian theology. By charting the distinctive shape of the ante-Nicene Trinitarian problematic, I have clarified why patristic theologians hardly ever noticed the logical incompatibility between divine simplicity and Trinitarian theology. In light of the ante-Nicene sources, it has become clear that it is too simplistic to suppose that divine simplicity collapses into Monarchianism. Divine simplicity does not entail this position, at least not in any obvious sense, because the historical Monarchian position was not treated simply as a thesis about logical identity. Thus, the analysis underlying the "logical problem" frequently offered by modern philosophers today makes little sense for patristic theologians who had the historical form of Monarchianism in mind. Moreover, for the purpose of constructive theology, it will be fruitful to attend to a different theological issue that was indeed noticed by patristic theologians concerning the implication of divine simplicity for Trinitarian theology: how to conceive of the generation of the Son while safeguarding the simplicity of God the Father, the generator? As I have argued, this was *the* theological location where early Christian theologians first recognized a potential incompatibility between divine simplicity and the anti-Monarchian emphasis on the Father-Son distinction. This issue may turn out to be a fruitful site for contemporary theological and philosophical reflections. This book thus challenges the commonplace intuition that divine simplicity and Trinitarian theology are logically incompatible; in fact, historically, divine simplicity played an indispensable role in shaping Trinitarian reflections in the ante-Nicene period.

In these ways I have offered the ante-Nicene developments charted in this book as fresh resources for advancing the contemporary debate on divine simplicity and its relation to Trinitarian theology. But why should these developments be privileged? Why should the theological issues before Nicaea be considered *foundational* for a Christian doctrine of God? These questions reveal a final aspect of my argument that has hitherto remained hidden beneath the surface. This concerns how the distinctive shape of the ante-Nicene doctrinal ecology surrounding the doctrine of divine simplicity relate to the overall development of patristic Trinitarian theology between the time of Origen and the fourth century.

It is well known that adherence to divine simplicity was a core commitment in fourth-century Christian theology. Pro-Nicene writers—East and West—possessed what Lewis Ayres has called a shared *habitus* in which we find the language of divine simplicity serving a variety of theological purposes.[3] Athanasius, in his anti-Arian polemical writings, employed the language of simplicity to establish the centrality of "Father" as a theological term.[4] Moreover, he also turned to simplicity to sever the association between human and divine generation.[5] The centrality of divine simplicity was prevalent in the West as well. Hilary of Poitiers, like Athanasius, employed the doctrine of divine simplicity to safeguard the nature of the Son's begetting from anthropomorphism.[6] Hilary thought that the simplicity of God not only calls for devotion, reverence, and worship; it also indicates the supreme efficacy of divine action.[7] Divine simplicity became firmly established as a key category for pro-Nicene theologians in the second half of the fourth century. Most notably, the anti-Eunomian polemic of the Cappadocians Basil of Caesarea and Gregory of Nyssa revolved around the understanding of divine simplicity and its implications for theological epistemology.[8] Basil and Gregory thought that divine simplicity need not force the theologian to choose between radical apophaticism, according to which God is absolutely unknowable, and radical knowledge of God's essence (*ousia*), which is to be gained through a single divine name, "unbegotten" (*agennētos*).[9] Hence Basil and Gregory's anti-Eunomian writings reimagined God's simplicity such that it enables the *possibility* of knowing God without claiming too much or too little. The Cappadocians' understanding sits alongside that of another theological giant in the fourth century, Augustine, who famously stated: "We say it [i.e., the Trinity] is simple because it is what it has, with the exception of the relation of the persons to one another."[10] According to Augustine, God's simplicity entails that all the divine names such as "great," "good," "wise," and many others must be identical to each other, as he explains in *De Trinitate*.[11] *De Trinitate* V–VII spell out an account of the predication of divine names that allows us to make sense of the distinctions between Father, Son, and Holy Spirit without compromising the simplicity of God. Our fourth-century sources, then, suggest that it is perhaps not too much of an exaggeration to identify divine simplicity as omnipresent in pro-Nicene theological discourse, functioning as a key "grammatical" principle shaping pro-Nicene theological language.[12]

Far from being exclusively a pro-Nicene strategy, divine simplicity was also a crucial piece of anti-Nicene theology of the fourth century. We find that Arius was already concerned with models of the generation of the Son that would potentially endanger the simplicity of God.[13]

This concern with safeguarding God's simplicity in speaking of divine generation was not unique to Arius.[14] But he thought that absolute divine primacy is attributed to the Father, implying, along with Origen, that the Father is the *only* purely simple and immutable being who possesses divinity absolutely.[15] Whatever the Son's divine status is, he does not possess the kind of divinity found only in the Father.[16] Simplicity, functioning in this context, already serves a "subordinating" purpose to differentiate the Father's divine status from the Son's. This use of divine simplicity as a theological strategy continued to occupy a unique place in anti-Nicene theology beyond Arius, most notably in the works of Aetius and Eunomius of Cyzicus. According to Lionel Wickham, ". . . the concept of God is, for Aetius and Eunomius, the concept of the absolute and metaphysically simple."[17] Eunomius, following Aetius, argued that the simplicity of God implies that only a single name could be absolutely attributable to the divine essence, namely, "unbegotten" (*agennētos*).[18] Like Origen and Arius before him, Eunomius employed divine simplicity to differentiate the Father from the Son, reserving primacy in relation to divinity only to the former. A closer look at the variety of theological sources in the fourth century, then, reveals that divine simplicity was a central theological strategy, albeit used in radically different and even opposing ways, for both pro-Nicenes and anti-Nicenes.

This is a puzzling phenomenon. The commitment to divine simplicity seems to have led to two radically divergent visions of the Trinity in the fourth century. These two visions, in turn, were built upon two divergent interpretations of divine simplicity. Accounting for this phenomenon, I suggest, is a crucial task for deepening our understanding of how the debates in the early fourth century emerged in the first place. In my view, we still lack an adequate historical account of this phenomenon framed in terms of the theological developments after Origen.[19] While I do not pretend to have resolved the puzzle in this book, the ante-Nicene doctrinal development charted in the preceding chapters opens up a fresh perspective for doing so. The decisive insight that has emerged from my argument is that before Nicaea, divine simplicity assumed two roles in the context of the Father-Son relation. As we have seen, it is possible to utilize simplicity—as Origen did—to frame both the distinction and the unity between the Father and the Son. This dual function of simplicity offers a new lens through which to narrate the transition from third- to fourth-century Trinitarian thought *prospectively.* In contrast to a *retrospective* narrative that narrates the transition in terms of issues that became central only later in the fourth century, a *prospective* narrative describes the transition in terms of issues that were central *before* Nicaea. Whereas a retrospective narration measures doctrinal developments by looking back, a prospective narration measures doctrinal developments by looking forward. In what follows I shall briefly explain how the bifurcation of the function of divine simplicity in Origen offers a fresh way of mapping the transition from third- to fourth-century Trinitarian theology.[20]

As I have argued elsewhere, Valentinian emission and Monarchianism marked out the key erroneous positions on the Father-Son relation in Origen's own representation of his third-century polemical landscape.[21] Origen's heresiology offers a window into the *ante-Nicene* polemical landscape associated with the question of the Father-Son relation before the outbreak of controversy between Arius and Alexander and well before Athanasius's polemical attempt to reshape the landscape in terms of "Arianism." Building a narrative of the transition from third- to fourth-century Trinitarian theology in light of Origen's own heresiological categories has the advantage over a general categorization of post-Origenian trajectories into those stressing unity and others stressing distinction between the Father and the Son. This is because "anti-Valentinian" and "anti-Monarchian" situate theological emphases of unity or distinction within specific polemical contexts found in the ante-Nicene period.

By tracking the fate of the anti-Valentinian and anti-Monarchian emphases, which sit alongside each other in Origen's via media, as I have argued in this book, we can take a fresh look at the emergence of rival accounts of the Trinity in post-Origenian developments. For after Origen, the tight integration of the anti-Monarchian and anti-Valentinian functions of simplicity in Origen's Trinitarian theology seems to have fallen apart. The anti-Monarchian function was the contentious one.[22] Some, like Arius, can be read as stretching the anti-Monarchian move to emphasizing the Father's transcendence over the Son in a more radical way than Origen probably would allow.[23] This tendency was continued by those with "subordinationist" tendencies, such as Aetius and Eunomius. Others, like Alexander of Alexandria and Athanasius, instead emphasized the Father and the Son as equal (perhaps in a return to Irenaeus's emphasis?),[24] thus drifting toward a dissolution of the Origenian point that the Father, as the absolute simple source of divinity, is *greater* than the Son, who is the derived image.[25] Needless to say, both trajectories are problematic from the viewpoint of Origenian theology. The second trajectory is problematic because it disrupts the anti-Monarchian component of Origen's synthesis. Origen construes monotheism as the idea that there is only one purely simple source of divinity, the Father himself. This is how Origen refutes the Monarchian objection that he has fallen into polytheism. It is easy, then, to imagine why some (like Arius and those sympathetic to his concerns) might find the theology of Alexander and Athanasius problematic: this trajectory threatens to compromise monotheism (construed in the Origenian manner in terms of the absolute transcendence of the Father).

But the first trajectory is also problematic from the Origenian viewpoint because the understanding of the Son as the perfect image of the Father in act and will is already at the breaking point when it comes to holding together the anti-Monarchian emphasis on the transcendence of the Father and the anti-Valentinian requirements on the Son's generation. Further stress on the transcendence of the Father over the Son disrupts the balance, with the risk of leading back toward the Valentinian notion of emission in which the Father is said to generate that which is (1) separate from himself, (2) contrary in nature to himself, and (3) related to himself in a relative temporal order. It is also easy, then, to imagine why many in the fourth century found the "Arian" position problematic: this trajectory threatens to violate the required continuity between the Father and the Son, thus bringing back a Valentinian kind of separation between the two.[26]

The shape of the post-Origenian landscape, therefore, may be framed in light of the fact that divine simplicity as a principle of differentiation between the Father and the Son (originally an anti-Monarchian emphasis) gradually acquired a polemical overtone after Origen. On the other hand, the anti-Valentinian function of divine simplicity—its requirements regarding the Son's generation—seems to have been universally accepted and explicitly stressed by theologians after Origen. From Arius to Athanasius, Eusebius of Caesarea to Hilary of Poitiers, all maintained the anti-Valentinian point as crucial to Trinitarian theology.[27] This suggests that while the anti-Monarchian function of simplicity became a central issue of contention at the end of the third century and the beginning of the fourth, the anti-Valentinian function remained indisputable. In light of this, the disintegration of Origen's synthesis between the anti-Monarchian and anti-Valentinian functions of divine simplicity can be seen as a key theological dimension of the fourth-century dispute.

The foregoing sketch, given its brevity, naturally invites further examination. But it suffices to illustrate the promising questions made available when we attempt to narrate the development of patristic Trinitarian theology from Origen to the fourth century *prospectively*. In particular, new conceptual clarity is available on two issues concerning the *status quaestionis* of Trinitarian theology at the beginning of the fourth century.

First, in chapter 6 I emphasized that Origen's "subordinationist" tendency actually reflects primarily his anti-Monarchianism when read in his ante-Nicene context. If my argument is correct, then it opens up the possibility of rethinking the "subordinationist" trajectory in post-Origenian theology as the result of a persistent anti-Monarchian concern that originated in the late second or early third century and passed through to later "Arian" and "Eusebian"[28] theologies of the fourth century. This opens up a further set of illuminating questions for interrogating more deeply the nature of disagreements between various participants of the controversy in the fourth century: how did an anti-Monarchian theological tendency (i.e., what is commonly termed "subordinationism") come to be read and understood out of this context in the case of Arius and those sympathetic to him? Did Arius and his supporters think of themselves as simply "anti-Monarchian" in the sense that Origen thought of his own "hierarchical" understanding of the Father-Son relation? The reinterpretation of "subordinationism" in ante-Nicene, rather than post-Nicene, terms leads to the first set of new questions emerging from a prospective narration.

Furthermore, as we have seen in Origen, divine simplicity was primarily attributed to the *Father*. In the fourth century, however, divine simplicity was attributed primarily to the divine essence (*ousia*) shared by the Father, the Son, and the Holy Spirit.[29] This is the state of affairs we find in fourth-century pro-Nicene theology. If one narrates the development of patristic Trinitarian theology *retrospectively*, the ante-Nicene use of simplicity seems "heretical." This perspective, once again, has the potential to mislead, not least because it misses the fact that one of the reasons divine simplicity emerged as central in patristic Trinitarian discourse at all was certainly its usefulness in an anti-Monarchian context, as I have argued. The simple-composite distinction offers third-century anti-Monarchians like Origen a strategy for affirming an emphasis on the distinction between the Father and the Son in terms of "order of priority."[30] When viewed *prospectively*, then, it is the emergence of the idea of the simplicity of the divine essence, which seems innovative and requires explanation. This might perhaps explain why the "Arians" or "Eusebians" found what Anatolios calls the "reconstruction of divine transcendence" in Athanasius odd and perhaps even dangerous because simplicity of the Father was probably taken by these theologians as a given if one wanted to safeguard Trinitarian discourse against the threat of Monarchianism.[31] A prospective narrative therefore turns the question upside down. It is the emergence of the idea of the simplicity of the divine *ousia* in pro-Nicene theology that becomes the puzzle, not the "subordinationist" (in fact, anti-Monarchian) attribution of simplicity to the Father in anti-Nicene theology. This transformation of perspective leads to fresh questions: How did divine simplicity evolve from being attributed to the Father to being attributed to the divine essence? Might we understand this transition in terms of the dissociation between divine simplicity as a principle of differentiation between Father and Son and its anti-Monarchian polemical function? The transition from the simplicity of the Father to the simplicity of the divine *ousia* highlights a second set of new questions emerging from a prospective narration of the developments of patristic Trinitarian theology.

To sum up then, my suggestion is that the dual functions of divine simplicity before Nicaea charted in this book offers a promising starting point from which to narrate the emergence of rival Trinitarian visions after Origen. By tracking the fate of divine simplicity in later divergent visions of the Trinity, we will be better placed to understand how later fourth-century developments have their origins in the disintegration of Origen's via media that can be understood only in terms of ante-Nicene heresiological categories. For Origen, the key errors in connection with the Father-Son relation were Valentinian emission and Monarchianism. Did these contexts remain shared markers of doctrinal errors on the Father-Son relation among key participants in the fourth-century controversies? If doctrinal-polemical contexts indeed shifted in the transition from Origen to the post-Origenian theological landscape, how should our historiography map this shift from ante-Nicene doctrinal categories ("Valentinian emission" and "Monarchianism") to ones emerging in the fourth century ("Arian," "Nicene," "Eusebian," "Eunomian")? I have argued that these questions arise naturally when the historian considers doctrinal developments *prospectively*. It is my hope that what I have offered in this epilogue will spark further work exploring the potential of this approach, leading to a more compelling account of the transition from Origen to the beginning of the fourth-century Trinitarian controversies.

In the introduction I framed my project in this book as a "Newmanian" exercise, seeking to resource doctrinal analysis in and through the medium of doctrinal history. It is well known that Newman in his later life famously turned to the task of setting out the general principles of doctrinal development.[32] No doubt his studies on the development of Trinitarian orthodoxy inspired him to search more formally for a way to make sense of the development of doctrine. It has been argued that, while in *Arians* Newman had a "romantic" perception of ante-Nicene theology as displaying a reverent simplicity for mystery in its refusal to formulate orthodoxy in a single formula, the central axis of his panoramic view of the development of patristic theology shifted from the ante-Nicenes to Athanasius. Subsequently, for Newman Athanasius and "Nicene orthodoxy" eclipsed Origen and ante-Nicene theology as the key to understanding the doctrinal development in the early centuries.[33] Given this crucial trajectory in Newman's thinking, the final aspect of my argument in this book takes an "anti-Newmanian" turn. For, as I have argued in this epilogue, a careful study of the ante-Nicene doctrinal ecology should urge us to seek a *prospective* rather than *retrospective* account of the development of doctrine. The burden of explaining the discrepancies between ante-Nicene theology and later established "Nicene orthodoxy" could potentially lead to a distorted understanding of doctrinal developments. Origen is a case in point. Might it not be more fruitful to shift the burden of explanation to a different question, namely, how can we make sense of the emergence of "Nicene orthodoxy" out of ante-Nicene doctrinal contexts? In other words, why did doctrinal markers shift from those found in the ante-Nicene period to a more complex set found in the fourth century? Posing these questions is to call for a reverse movement to the one found in Newman's own development. What I have suggested in the epilogue is a fresh narration of the development of patristic Trinitarian theology by returning to the distinctive *ante*-Nicene doctrinal ecology as the starting point. It is in light of this historiographical orientation that I offer the historical developments charted in this book as *foundational* for a better understanding of how divine simplicity became established as a crucial part of Christian doctrine after Origen.

NOTES

INTRODUCTION

1. *Civ. Dei* XI.10: *Et haec trinitas unus est Deus; nec ideo non simplex, quia trinitas.*

2. An extensive coverage of the state of scholarship can be found in Steven J. Duby, *Divine Simplicity: A Dogmatic Account* (London: Bloomsbury, 2015), 34–53, 179–234; Jordan P. Barrett, *Divine Simplicity: A Biblical and Trinitarian Account* (Minneapolis: Fortress, 2017), 3–34; Jonathan M. Platter, *Divine Simplicity and the Triune Identity* (Berlin: Walter de Gruyter, 2021), 9–30. In what follows, I offer a more focused review of the debate, stressing specific points discussed by systematic and philosophical theologians I wish to engage with through the historical account offered in this book.

3. I should clarify that here I have in mind Protestant theologians reacting against "classical theology" from Dorner onward. It is evident that Protestant theologians from an earlier period ("Protestant scholastics") were chief proponents of divine simplicity in their own right. See Duby, *Divine Simplicity.*

4. Isaak A. Dorner, *A System of Christian Doctrine*, trans. Alfred Cave and John S. Banks, vol. 1 (Edinburgh: T&T Clark, 1883), 195.

5. Ibid., 197.

6. Wolfhart Pannenberg, *Systematic Theology*, trans. Geoffrey W. Bromiley, vol. 1 (Grand Rapids, MI: Eerdmans, 2010), 283.

7. Robert W. Jenson, *Systematic Theology: The Triune God*, vol. 1 (Oxford: Oxford University Press, 1997), 111. It is worth emphasizing that Jenson's approach to the subject is much more complex, as is evident from the discussion by Platter in *Divine Simplicity and the Triune Identity*, 104–35. Platter argues that the "logic of divine simplicity" is actually operative in Jenson's own Trinitarian theology, despite his critical remarks on the "classical" form of the doctrine.

8. Dorner, *A System of Christian Doctrine*, 195.

9. Pannenberg, *Systematic Theology*, 283.

10. Jenson, *Systematic Theology*, 111.

11. My review of philosophical criticisms of divine simplicity here should be supplemented by the more extensive discussion in Duby, *Divine Simplicity*, 42–53, 186–93.

12. For instance, see William Hasker, *Metaphysics and the Tri-Personal God* (Oxford: Oxford University Press, 2013), 55–61. On the incompatibility between the Trinity and divine simplicity more generally, see James E. Dolezal, "Trinity, Simplicity and the Status of God's Personal Relations," *International Journal of Systematic Theology* 16, no. 1 (January 1, 2014): 79–98; Duby, *Divine Simplicity*, 40–41, 207–11.

13. "But . . . it would appear that the concept of divine simplicity was adopted too readily by some Christian writers who did not pause to consider its implications. Thus we find Athanasius arguing that God, being perfectly simple, cannot possess a multiplicity of accidents; but it is not clear why the same argument should not be used to exclude a diversity of divine characteristics (which Athanasius upheld), or even a trinity of persons." G. C. Stead, *Divine Substance* (Oxford: Clarendon, 1977), 187. Stead captures the heart of the worry shared by modern theologians: If divine simplicity is used to rule out the proper distinct realities of the attributes, then why not the distinction between the Trinitarian persons as well?

14. G. C. Stead, "Divine Simplicity as a Problem for Orthodoxy," in *The Making of Orthodoxy: Essays in Honour of Henry Chadwick*, ed. Rowan D. Williams, 255–69 (Cambridge: Cambridge University Press, 1989), 266.

15. A lot of ink has been spilled recently defending the "classical" doctrine. In addition to the works of Duby and Barrett mentioned above, see also James E. Dolezal, *God without Parts: Divine Simplicity and the Metaphysics of God's Absoluteness* (Eugene, OR: Pickwick, 2011); D. Stephen Long, *The Perfectly Simple Triune God: Aquinas and His Legacy* (Minneapolis: Fortress, 2016); Christopher A. Franks, "The Simplicity of the Living God: Aquinas, Barth, and Some Philosophers," *Modern Theology* 21, no. 2 (2005): 275–300; Stephen R. Holmes, "'Something Much Too Plain to Say': Towards a Defence of the Doctrine of Divine Simplicity," *Neue Zeitschrift für Systematische Theologie und Religionsphilosophie* 43, no. 1 (2008): 137–54; Thomas Joseph White, "Divine Simplicity and the Holy Trinity," *International Journal of Systematic Theology* 18, no. 1 (January 1, 2016): 66–93; Pui Him Ip, "Re-imagining Divine Simplicity in Trinitarian Theology," *International Journal of Systematic Theology* 18, no. 3 (2016): 274–89. On the other side, besides the systematic theologies discussed in my brief reception history, many are adamant that the "classical doctrine" is untenable today. See R. T. Mullins, "Simply Impossible: A Case against Divine Simplicity," *Journal of Reformed Theology* 7, no. 2 (January 1, 2013): 181–203; Paul R. Hinlicky, *Divine Simplicity: Christ the Crisis of Metaphysics* (Grand Rapids, MI: Baker Academic, 2016).

16. On this front, Gavin Ortlund has made a helpful contribution drawing on Pseudo-Dionysius the Areopagite and John of Damascus. See Gavin Ortlund, "Divine Simplicity in Historical Perspective: Resourcing a Contemporary Discussion," *International Journal of Systematic Theology* 16, no. 4 (2014): 436–53.

17. Rowan D. Williams, "Newman's Arians and the Question of Method in Doctrinal History," in *Newman after a Hundred Years*, ed. I. T. Ker and Alan G. Hill, 263–85 (Oxford: Clarendon, 1990), 265.

18. The term "doctrinal ecology" was coined by Williams to describe what Newman was doing in the book on Arianism. See ibid., 284–85. See also Williams's elaboration on this term in his introduction to Newman's discussion on ante-Nicene Trinitarian language in the Arians of the fourth century in John Henry Newman, *The Arians of the Fourth Century*, ed. Rowan D. Williams (Notre Dame, IN: Gracewing, 2001), xli–xlii.

19. Williams, "Newman's Arians," 283.

20. Hence I am not claiming that modern scholarship has failed to engage with divine simplicity's doctrinal history. In fact, plenty of scholars have done so, engaging with the sources in the patristic (Barrett, Ortlund, Stead, and Platter), medieval (Dolezal and Long), and early modern periods (Duby). My claim in this book, however, is that knowledge of the specific ante-Nicene developments charted in this book, which hitherto have received little attention, is crucial for making sense of later developments well documented in previous scholarship.

21. Barth and Pannenberg were right to sense that it is possible to conceive a richer notion of simplicity and immutability theologically. See Karl Barth, *Church Dogmatics*, trans. G. W. Bromiley and Thomas F. Torrance, vol. 2, Part 1 (Edinburgh: T&T Clark, 1957), 458, 460–61; Wolfhart Pannenberg, "The Appropriation of the Philosophical Concept of God as a Dogmatic Problem of Early Christian Theology," in *Basic Questions in Theology*, vol. 2, 119–83 (Minneapolis: Fortress, 1971), 180. But in my view, they did not appreciate that such a view is possible within the Platonic framework of patristic theology. This idea is what I go on to develop in this book.

22. This term is frequently used in the modern literature on divine simplicity. Throughout this book, I prefer the term "Monarchianism" in order to sidestep some of the complex historical questions regarding the relationship between different groups in the ante-Nicene period that had been identified as displaying tendencies to oppose affirmations of "Trinitarian" distinctions. See chapter 4 for further details on this point.

23. Hasker, *Metaphysics and the Tri-Personal God*, 59–60.

24. A persuasive case on prosopological exegesis as the original context for Trinitarian thought has been made recently by Matthew W. Bates in *The Birth of the Trinity* (Oxford: Oxford University Press, 2016).

25. Stead, *Divine Substance*, 90–97, 180–89; G. C. Stead, *Philosophy in Christian Antiquity* (Cambridge: Cambridge University Press, 1994), 120–35; Stead, "Divine Simplicity as a Problem for Orthodoxy"; Pannenberg, "Philosophical Concept of God."

26. Lewis Ayres, *Nicaea and Its Legacy: An Approach to Fourth-Century Trinitarian Theology* (Oxford: Oxford University Press, 2006), 273–301; Andrew Radde-Gallwitz, *Basil of Caesarea, Gregory of Nyssa, and the Transformation of*

Divine Simplicity (Oxford ; New York: Oxford University Press, 2009); Andrew Radde-Gallwitz, "Gregory of Nyssa and Divine Simplicity: A Conceptualist Reading," *Modern Theology* 35, no. 3 (July 2019): 452–66.

27. Elsewhere I have argued that the emergence of divine simplicity in Christian theology might be best understood as part of the emergence of Christian theological arguments. See Pui Him Ip, "Athenagoras of Athens and the Genesis of Divine Simplicity in Christian Theology," in *Studia Patristica C*, ed. Hugh A. G. Houghton, Megan L. Davies, and Markus Vinzent, 61–70 (Leuven, Belgium: Peeters, 2020).

28. Lewis Ayres and Andrew Radde-Gallwitz, "Doctrine of God," in *The Oxford Handbook of Early Christian Studies*, ed. Susan Ashbrook Harvey and David G. Hunter, 864–85 (Oxford: Oxford University Press, 2010), 874–75.

29. Cited in Christoph Bruns, *Trinität und Kosmos: Zur Gotteslehre des Origenes* (Munster: Aschendorf, 2013), 19.

30. *ComJn* II.75; *CCels.* VIII.12; *PArch* I.2.2.

31. *ComJn* XIII.228–34; *PArch* I.2.6; *CCels.* VIII.12.

32. *ComJn* I.283; *ComMt* XV.10; *PArch* I.2.6, I.2.12–13.

33. *ComJn* II.12–18; XIII.151–53. See also Origen's highly suggestive inquiry into whether God the Father is glorified in a greater manner in his self-contemplation than in the Son. *ComJn* XXXII.350.

34. *PArch* I.2.11, IV.4.1; *HomJe* IX.4.

35. *ComHe*, quoted in Pamphilus's *Apol.* 99. This point is controversial since we have the text only in Rufinus's Latin translation. See R.P.C. Hanson, "Did Origen Apply the Word 'Homoousios' to the Son?" in *Épektasis: Mélanges patristiques offerts au cardinal Daniélou*, ed. C. Kannengiesser and J. Fontaine, 293–303 (Paris: Beauchesne, 1975). Against Hanson, Mark Edwards has defended the use of the term *homoousios* in these fragments as genuine. See Mark J. Edwards, "Did Origen Apply the Word Homoousios to the Son?," *Journal of Theological Studies* 49, no. 2 (October 1, 1998): 658–70. For a review of the wider debate on the term *homoousios*, see Pier Franco Beatrice, "The Word 'Homoousios' from Hellenism to Christianity," *Church History* 71, no. 2 (June 2002): 243–72, 251–52.

36. Simonetti spoke of the development in Trinitarian theology after Origen simply as "50 anni di controversie origeniane." Manlio Simonetti, *La crisi ariana nel IV secolo* (Rome: Institutum Patristicum Augustinianum, 1975), 11–24. See also the insightful analysis in Rowan D. Williams, *Arius: Heresy and Tradition*, rev. ed. (Grand Rapids, MI: Eerdmans, 2002), 131–48.

37. Bruns, *Trinität und Kosmos*, 17–18 (my translation).

38. Ibid., 19–20. On Ramelli's argument, see Ilaria L. E. Ramelli, "Origen's Anti-Subordinationism and Its Heritage in the Nicene and Cappadocian Line," *Vigiliae Christianae* 65, no. 1 (2011): 21–49. Elsewhere I have discussed critically Athanasius's claim that Origen anticipates Nicene "anti-Arianism" in Pui Him Ip, "'Arianism' *Ante-Litteram* in Origen's *Peri Archōn* 4.4.1," *Journal of Theological Studies* 72, no.1 (April 2021): 247–78.

39. Mark J. Edwards, review of *Trinität und Kosmos. Zur Gotteslehre des Origenes*, by Christoph Bruns, *Journal of Ecclesiastical History* 66, no. 2 (April 2015): 390–91.

40. See R.P.C. Hanson, *The Search for the Christian Doctrine of God: The Arian Controversy*, 318–81 (Grand Rapids, MI: Baker Academic, 2006), 361–70, for a summary.

41. Though the work by Samuel Fernández has gone a long way toward addressing this. See Samuel Fernández, "La generación del Logos como solución al problema monarquiano, según Orígenes," in *Multifariam: Homenaje a Los Profesores Anneliese Meis, Antonio Bentué y Sergio Silva*, edited by Samuel Fernández, J. Noemi, and R. Polanco, 193–229 (Santiago, Chile: Pontificia Universidad Católica de Chile, 2010). Bruns's *Trinität und Kosmos* also situates Origen in his third-century context despite regarding the Alexandrian as forefather of Nicene theology.

42. See *ComJn* II.16, XXXII.183–97; *ComTt*, quoted in Pamphilus, *Apol.* 33; *ComRm* VIII.5.9.

43. Though Origen should not be naïvely identified as a "Platonist." See Mark J. Edwards, *Origen against Plato* (London: Routledge, 2017).

CHAPTER 1

1. Stead, "Divine Simplicity as a Problem for Orthodoxy," 256.

2. "The doctrine of divine simplicity became conventionalised; attempts were still made to define and defend it, but in the main it was protected from attack by the elusive character of the term 'simple,' which could mean either 'excluding all differentiation' or 'comprehending all differentiation' or merely 'not composite,' 'not constructed out of parts.'" Ibid., 93–94.

3. The argument is summarized in Stead, "Divine Simplicity as a Problem for Orthodoxy." The detailed analysis is found in Stead, *Divine Substance*, 90–97, 180–89; see also Stead, *Philosophy in Christian Antiquity*, 120–35.

4. See ἁπλοῦς in G.W.H. Lampe's *A Patristic Greek Lexicon* (Oxford: Clarendon, 1961), 187. See also the useful survey of the use of the term from the Septuagint to post-Apostolic Christian literature in Joseph Amstutz, *ΑΠΛΟΤΗΣ: Eine Begriffsgeschichtliche Studie zum jüdisch-christlichen Griechisch* (Bonn: Peter Hanstein, 1968).

5. Stead, *Philosophy in Christian Antiquity*, 132.

6. As far as I know, Amstutz is the only one who has taken note of the significance of this passage for understanding the philosophical origin of divine simplicity. He calls this passage "die maßgebende Stelle." See Amstutz, *ΑΠΛΟΤΗΣ*, 54, n. 76.

7. Plato's attitude toward traditional mythology is complex. For a helpful discussion of the gods in traditional Greek religion that forms the background to this passage, see Gerd van Riel, *Plato's Gods* (Farnham, UK: Ashgate, 2013), 25–30. As

Rick Benitez has argued, Plato's discussion about the gods may not be straightforwardly read as a "demythologization" exercise. In fact, Plato could well be crafting a "philosophical mythology." See Rick Benitez, "Plato and the Secularisation of Greek Theology," in *Theologies of Ancient Greek Religion*, ed. Esther Eidinow, Julia Kindt, and Robin Osborne (Cambridge: Cambridge University Press, 2016), 301–16.

8. *Rep.* 379a: Οἷος τυγχάνει ὁ θεὸς ὤν, ἀεὶ δήπου ἀποδοτέον, ἐαν τέ τις αὐτὸν ἐω ἔπεσι ποιῇ ἐάν τε ἐω μέλεσιν ἐάν τε ἐω τραγῳδίᾳ.

9. *Rep.* 379a–b: Οὐκοῦν ἀγαθὸς ὅ γε θεὸς τῷ ὄντι τε καὶ λεκτέον οὕτως.

10. *Rep.* 380a–b.

11. *Rep.* 380d: Ἆρα γόητα τὸν θεὸν οἴει εἶναι καὶ οἷον ἐξ ἐπιβουλῆς φαντάζεσθαι ἄλλοτε ἐν ἄλλαις ἰδέαις, τοτὲ μὲν αὐτὸν γιγνόμενον καὶ ἀλλάττοντα τὸ αὑτοῦ εἶδος εἰς πολλὰς μορφάς, τοτὲ δὲ ἡμᾶς ἀπατῶντα καὶ ποιοῦντα περὶ αὑτοῦ τοιαῦτα δοκεῖν, ἢ ἁπλοῦν τε εἶναι καὶ πάντων ἥκιστα τῆς ἑαυτοῦ ἰδέας ἐκβαίνειν. Translations from LCL 237, slightly modified.

12. See the commentary on Proteus and Thetis in James Adam, ed., *The Republic of Plato*, edited with critical notes, commentary and appendices, vol. 1 (Cambridge: Cambridge University Press, 1902), 120.

13. *Rep.* 380d.

14. On Plato's relation with traditional mythologies, see the complexities mentioned in note 7 above.

15. Apart from the works of Ayres and Radde-Gallwitz, which I shall discuss below, see also Mark Sheridan, *Language for God in Patristic Tradition: Wrestling with Biblical Anthropomorphism* (Downers Grove, IL: InterVarsity Press, 2015), for an account of how early Christian language of God functions in this manner.

16. Ayres, *Nicaea and Its Legacy*, 279.

17. Ibid., 14.

18. See Ibid., 281, 286–87, for some examples. A particularly important case is the generation of the Son, which must be understood "within the bounds of the divine simplicity." This point will play a significant part in this book.

19. Ibid., 287.

20. Radde-Gallwitz, *Basil of Caesarea*, 19–37.

21. Ibid., 20.

22. Ibid., 6.

23. This is to take up a suggestion by Sheridan in *Language for God*, 59.

24. This is made clear in the concluding statement of the argument for premise 6. *Rep.* 381c: Ἀδύνατον ἄρα, ἔφην, καὶ θεῷ ἐθέλειν αὑτὸν ἀλλοιοῦν, ἀλλ', ὡς ἔοικε, κάλλιστος καὶ ἄριστος ὢν εἰς τὸ δυνατὸν ἕκαστος αὐτῶν μένει ἀεὶ ἁπλῶς ἐν τῇ αὑτοῦ μορφῇ. It is impossible for a god to *wish* to alter himself; this is not to say a god *could* not change himself.

25. This has potential ramification for the contemporary debate on the incompatibility between divine simplicity and divine freedom. According to Socrates, a simple god is perfectly *free* to choose to be different than to remain self-same.

But such a god *would* not do so because it would be absurd for a divine being to choose to be greater or lesser than themself. Divine immutability, connected to simplicity, is therefore not as incompatible with the "infinite plenitude of ever new possibilities" that is entailed by divine freedom, as Pannenberg requires (Pannenberg, "Philosophical Concept of God," 161) so long as the "ever new possibilities" we are speaking of that are opened to the divine are understood to be possibilities that are perfectly consistent with who the god is. From this consideration, one could develop a response to the critique against divine simplicity developed in Mullins, "Simply Impossible."

26. The alert reader will have noticed that this supposes that a god has a soul. This highlights an idiosyncrasy of Platonic theology in which "deities" are likely to be perfect souls. See van Riel, *Plato's Gods*, chap. 3.

27. *Rep.* 382d–e.

28. *Rep.* 382e: Κομιδῇ ἄρα ὁ θεὸς ἁπλοῦν καὶ ἀληθὲς ἔν τε ἔργῳ καὶ ἐν λόγῳ, καὶ οὔτε αὐτὸς μεθίσταται οὔτε ἄλλους ἐξαπατᾷ, οὔτε κατὰ φαντασίας οὔτε κατὰ λόγους, οὔτε κατὰ σημείων πομπάς, οὔθ' ὕπαρ οὔτ' ὄναρ.

29. James Adam, in a perceptive comment, also reinforces this conclusion. Ἁπλοῦν is "one of the watchwords of Plato's state (370b and c, 374a–d, et al.)" in that every ideal citizen is supposed to focus on a single task according to each individual's nature, that is, becoming ἁπλοῖ. The parallel between divine simplicity and the simplicity of the citizens reflects in Plato a kind of theology that is concerned to make "the gods a reflection of the type of human character he [i.e., Plato] desired to foster." Adam, *The Republic*, 1:119, n. 27. This observation is apt because, as many scholars have pointed out, Plato's theology in Book 2 of *The Republic* is no doubt concerned with the effect of theology on the formation of the guardians. See David Sedley, "Plato's Theology," in *The Oxford Handbook of Plato*, ed. Gail Fine, 2nd ed. (Oxford: Oxford University Press, 2019), 627–44 (especially 627–28). I shall return to the intrinsic connection in ancient thought between God's simplicity and the simplicity that characterizes the perfect human life when I turn to Philo (chapter 2) and Origen (chapter 5).

30. For a summary, see van Riel, *Plato's Gods*, 119–21. For the literature on this topic, see 61–64.

31. "It is true that in the earlier stages of the theory of Forms theological concerns are mostly irrelevant to the metaphysical exigencies of the arguments. Nevertheless, once Plato begins to engage in natural theology seriously, it quickly becomes clear that the metaphysical and the theological paths merge." Lloyd P. Gerson, *God and Greek Philosophy: Studies in the Early History of Natural Theology* (London: Routledge, 1990), 62.

32. Van Riel writes: "Plato's metaphysical principles (the Good and the Forms) may be termed 'divine,' but they are not 'gods.' Plato's gods are individuals, meaning individual souls, who are bound to their position by the fate-like laws imposed by his metaphysical principles." Van Riel, *Plato's Gods*, 119. Van Riel argues throughout

that it could well be an anachronistic reading of Plato, first suggested by Aristotle, that led to the identification.

33. *Rep.* 476a–b: Καὶ περὶ δικαίου καὶ ἀδίκου καὶ ἀγαθοῦ καὶ κακοῦ καὶ πάντων τῶν εἰδῶν πέρι ὁ αὐτὸς λόγος, αὐτὸ μὲν ἓν ἕκαστον εἶναι, τῇ δὲ τῶν πράξεων καὶ σωμάτων καὶ ἀλλήλων κοινωνίᾳ πανταχοῦ φανταζόμενα πολλὰ φαίνεσθαι ἕκαστον.

34. *Rep.* 479e.

35. Constance C. Meinwald, *Plato* (London: Routledge, 2016), 233.

36. This connection between the simplicity of God and the requirement for the forms explains why "the functions of calling God simple and of saying that one should not attribute contradictory statements to (the same) God got mapped onto one another," as highlighted by Radde–Gallwitz, *Basil of Caesarea*, 20–22. If the language of simplicity was conceived as integrally connected to the nature of forms, then it makes sense that ancient writers recognize the same impossibility for contrary states to arise in God, as in the case of forms. Theologically, it seems to me that the language of God's "uncontradictable Life" is on track to capture the essence of the idea of simplicity. See Franks, "The Simplicity of the Living God."

37. See Gerson, *God and Greek Philosophy*, 57–65. Gerson also maps out how later Platonists utilized the latent possibility for the connection between the Form of the Good and God. See Lloyd P. Gerson, "From Plato's Good to Platonic God," *International Journal of the Platonic Tradition* 2, no. 2 (January 1, 2008): 93–112.

CHAPTER 2

1. Pannenberg, "Philosophical Concept of God," 131.

2. Scholars of ancient philosophy dispute the usefulness of the label "Middle Platonism." Here I follow the minimalistic interpretation of Zambon by taking the label to specify the period of development in Platonism between the end of the Academy to Plotinus. See Marco Zambon, "Middle Platonism," in *A Companion to Ancient Philosophy*, ed. Mary Louise Gill and Pierre Pellegrin, 561–76 (Oxford: Wiley-Blackwell, 2009), 561–62.

3. For Pannenberg, the sense of divine immutability due to God's trustworthiness, faithfulness, and constancy is to be found only in the language of Scripture and does not come from the philosophical doctrine of immutability. See Pannenberg, "'Philosophical Concept of God,'" 161–62, 180. Despite this negative judgment, Pannenberg does not fall into an uncritical wholesale acceptance of the "Hellenization thesis" commonly accepted by Protestant writers. He actually offers a sophisticated analysis as to why the philosophical concept of God had to be appropriated by Christian theologians in the early centuries. His technical term for this appropriation is "linkage," intending to contrast it with the classical "Hellenization" model in the wake of Adolf von Harnack (see especially 134–40).

4. In the Middle Platonic period, Platonists had various schemes to relate different first principles in their system. To avoid confusion, unless otherwise stated, whenever I use the term "first principle" in this chapter I am speaking of the *highest* principle. My claim is that it is the identification of the simple deity as the highest first principle that led to the rise of further metaphysical qualifications of divine simplicity in this period.

5. John M. Dillon, trans, *Alcinous: The Handbook of Platonism* (Oxford: Clarendon Press, 1993), xiii–xiv. The identity of the author of this text has been subjected to scholarly speculations. Some scholars in the past have identified the author as "Albinus," following the suggestion of J. Freudenthal, but most scholars today accept the conclusion of John Whittaker, who argues for Alcinous as the author of the treatise. See Dillon, ix–xiii, for a review of this matter. But as a result of this scholarly dispute, in what follows some of the older literature cited will still retain the name "Albinus."

6. See Ilsetraut Hadot, *Arts libéraux et philosophie dans la pensée antique* (Paris: Études augustiniennes, 1984); Pierre Hadot, "Les divisions des parties de la philosophie dans l'Antiquité," *Museum Helveticum* 36, no. 4 (1979): 201–23.

7. Boys-Stones has helpfully supplied a schema that situates Alcinous's position alongside those of other Middle Platonists. See George R. Boys-Stones, *Platonist Philosophy 80 BC to AD 250: An Introduction and Collection of Sources in Translation* (Cambridge: Cambridge University Press, 2018), 150–59. See also Henny Fiskå Hägg, *Clement of Alexandria and the Beginnings of Christian Apophaticism: Knowing the Unknowable* (Oxford: Oxford University Press, 2006), 71–133, for a helpful comparison of Alcinous's theology with that of two other Platonists from this period, Atticus and Numenius.

8. I do not cover the Aristotelian background here since it is well known. The relevant Aristotelian discussions related to the concept of divine simplicity are found in *Phys.* VIII.10 (on the nature of the unmoved mover), *Met.* Δ (on mereology), and *Met.* Λ (esp. Λ.7–8, on the simplicity of the supreme first principle). A detailed discussion of Aristotelian theology in these texts is found in Gerson, *God and Greek Philosophy*, 82–141. See also Paul L. Gavrilyuk, "Plotinus on Divine Simplicity," *Modern Theology* 35, no. 3 (2019): 442–51, for a helpful discussion of the importance of Aristotelian considerations in this period. On Aristotelian mereology in *Met.* Δ, see Kathrin Koslicki, *The Structure of Objects* (Oxford: Oxford University Press, 2008), 122–64.

9. On this term, see André-Jean Festugière, *La Révélation d'Hermès Trismégiste IV: Le Dieu inconnu et la gnose* (Paris: Lecoffre, 1944), 95, n. 5.

10. Here it seems that Alcinous takes himself to be simply supposing the Platonic commitment to the existence of forms.

11. Dillon, *Alcinous*, 102.

12. See the parallels with Aristotle's argument for the nature of the unmoved mover in *Met.* Λ, 1071b3ff up to the concluding statement at 1073a13.

13. What is at play here is likely to be a hierarchy of deities in which the primal god, or "God," is identified as the supreme deity. See Dillon, *Alcinous*, 102–3. On the general issue regarding counting gods in Platonism in this period, see the bibliography in Boys-Stones, *Platonist Philosophy*, 161–62.

14. *Did.* 10,164.39–41.

15. Scholars have debated whether Alcinous identifies the primal God as the principle even higher than the first intellect. See Jaap Mansfeld, "Three Notes on Albinus," in *Studies in Later Greek Philosophy and Gnosticism* (London: Variorum Reprints, 1989), 6: 61–80 at 61–67. Mansfeld persuasively argues that Alcinous did not admit a higher principle superior to the first intellect. But he is surely right in saying that Alcinous's conception of the highest principle in his hierarchy of entities is not without its problems.

16. The question concerning the status of the intellect in the Platonic systems of this period is extremely complex. A sense of this can be gleaned from the variety of positions encountered in the bibliographical essay in Boys-Stones, *Platonist Philosophy*, 160–68. Thus Alcinous's position on God's relation to the intellect reflects his peculiar brand of systematic Platonism and so cannot be regarded as reflecting a "representative" position in the Middle Platonic period. Platonists like Numenius of Apamea can differentiate the first god from a second intellect (see ibid., 156–57).

17. I make no claim to interpret Alcinous as a monotheist. Alcinous could have conceived of multiple deities (see note 13 above). But the conclusion I am drawing from Alcinous's *Did.* 10 about divine simplicity is, strictly speaking, the conclusion he draws only for his primal God.

18. Dillon, *Alcinous*, xxvii–xxviii.

19. My translation.

20. Radde-Gallwitz, *Basil of Caesarea*, 5–6.

21. The exact mechanics of how Alcinous's God can be the single, simple, unifying principle of all forms remains unclear. In the Middle Platonic period, there were many proposals by Platonists as to how God should be related to the forms. See Boys-Stones, *Platonist Philosophy*, 150–59. But Alcinous's statement was surely due to the fact that he held God to be what Boys-Stones has called the "form of all paradigmaticism." For a speculative interpretation of Alcinous as referring to the One, thus anticipating Plotinus, see Knut Kleve, "Albinus on God and the One," *Symbolae Osloenses* 47, no. 1 (January 1, 1972): 66–69. See, however, the critique of Pierre Louis and John Whittaker, trans., *Alcinoos: Enseignement des doctrines de Platon* (Paris: Belles Lettres, 1990), 103–4, n. 188. Louis and Whittaker are unconvinced by Kleve's argument.

22. Dörrie et al. suggest a similar conclusion. According to them, here Alcinous is warning against interpreting the multiple divine attributes as possessing independent existence, requiring God to participate in them in order to possess these qualities. This would invalidate Alcinous's position that God is the supreme first principle, who is self-grounding. Dörrie et al. conclude that for Alcinous, the

multiple attributes "mit Gott selbst eins sind," which entails that they are not "real" (in the sense that they do not possess independent existence apart from God: "Alles in Gott ist Gott"). Heinrich Dörrie et al., *Der Platonismus in der Antike: Grundlagen, System, Entwicklung; Die philosophische Lehre des Platonismus: Theologia Platonica. Bausteine 182–205: Text, Übersetzung, Kommentar*, vol. 7.1 (Stuttgart–Bad Cannstatt: Frommann-Holzboog, 2008), 332.

23. As many scholars have highlighted, it is not obvious how to interpret the significance of Alcinous's divine attributes, both positive and negative, given his strong commitment to the claim that God is beyond opposite pairs. For my purpose here, which is to illustrate the philosophical considerations underlying the connections between simplicity and its neighboring ideas, I shall not go into this debate even though it is relevant to the question of divine simplicity and its implications for theological epistemology. For a masterful account that helps one to make sense of Alcinous's theory of divine attributes, see Jaap Mansfeld, "Compatible Alternatives: Middle Platonist Theology and the Xenophanes Reception," in *Knowledge of God in the Graeco-Roman World*, ed. R. van den Broek, Tjitze Baarda, and Jaap Mansfeld, 92–117 (Leiden: Brill, 1988).

24. As Dillon has noted, Alcinous is probably following a trend of giving an "ontological interpretation" to the logical exercises in Plato's *Parmenides*. See Dillon, *Alcinous*, 109.

25. On the argument based on geometry, see Michel René Barnes, "'Shining in the Light of Your Glory': Finding the Simple Reading of Scripture," *Modern Theology* 35, no. 3 (2019): 418–27, 420, n. 4.

26. *Phae.* 78c (translation from LCL 36, slightly modified).

27. Ibid. 92b-c.

28. Ibid. 92e–93b.

29. Alcinous's application of the term ἀκίνητος to God alludes to Aristotle's *Met.* Λ. But given the parallels here, it seems likely that Alcinous saw the term as grounded on the argument found in *The Republic*.

30. Harry Austryn Wolfson, *Philo: Foundations of Religious Philosophy in Judaism, Christianity, and Islam*, vol. 2 (Cambridge, MA: Harvard University Press, 1962), 94–164; Francesca Calabi, *God's Acting, Man's Acting: Tradition and Philosophy in Philo of Alexandria* (Leiden: Brill, 2008), 13–16, 17–38.

31. For a more detailed discussion of Philo's doctrine of divine immutability in this work, see Wilhelm Maas, *Unveränderlichkeit Gottes: Zum Verhältnis von griech-philosophischer und christlicher Gotteslehre* (Munich: Ferdinand Schöningh, 1974), 87–124.

32. Philo's Greek text of this passage is found in *Deus* 20. English translation from LCL 247.

33. Nikiprowetzky helpfully suggests that *Deus* 20–50 is primarily concerned with the question of God's repentance, whereas *Deus* 51–69 is concerned with the question of God's anger. See V. Nikiprowetzky, "L'exégèse de Philon d'Alexandrie

dans le *De Gigantibus* et le *Quod Deus*," in *Two Treatises of Philo of Alexandria: A Commentary on De Gigantibus and Quod Deus Sit Immutabilis*, ed. David Winston and John M. Dillon, 5–75 (Chico, CA: Scholars Press, 1983), at 27. My division of Philo's two theological discussions follows this outline.

34. David Winston and John M. Dillon, *Two Treatises of Philo of Alexandria: A Commentary on De Gigantibus and Quod Deus sit Immutabilis* (Chico, California: Scholars Press, 1983), 284. This does not mean, however, that Philo never disagrees with how this pattern is to be applied to ancient literature. See Howard Jacobson, "A Philonic Rejection of Plato," *Mnemosyne* 57, no. 4 (January 1, 2004): 488.

35. *Deus* 22. This argument has a Stoic background. See ibid., *Two Treatises of Philo of Alexandria*, 284.

36. See the discussion on *Gig.* 49, where Philo also comments on this Scriptural passage, in Winston and Dillon, *Two Treatises of Philo of Alexandria*, 261–62. This rendering of Deut. 5:31 captures Philo's meaning (see Dillon and Winston, 287).

37. *Deus* 24–25.

38. Ibid. 26–27.

39. Philo's Greek text of this passage is found in *Deus* 51. English translation from LCL 247.

40. Ibid. 52.

41. Ibid. 55.

42. Ibid. 56. The question of how to interpret Philo's claim that God has no needs of "properties" is complex. For a detailed discussion, see Calabi, *God's Acting, Man's Acting*, 17–38.

43. *Leg. All.* 2.1: Ὁ θεὸς μόνος ἐστὶ καὶ ἕν, οὐ σύγκριμα, φύσις ἁπλῆ, ἡμῶν δ'ἕκαστος καὶ τῶν ἄλλων ὅσα γέγονε πολλά· οἷον ἐγὼ πολλά εἰμι, ψυχὴ σῶμα, καὶ ψυχῆς ἄλογον λογικόν, πάλιν σῶματος θερμὸν ψυχρὸν βαρὺ κοῦφον ξηρὸν ὑγρόν· ὁ δὲ θεὸς οὐ σύγκριμα οὐδὲ ἐκ πολλῶν συνεστώς, ἀλλ' ἀμιγὴς ἄλλῳ.

44. *Deus* 56–57: οἱ δέ συμβάσεις και σπονδὰς πρὸς σῶμα θέμενοι Οὐ λογισάμενοι ὅτι τῷ μὲν ἐκ πλειόνων συνόδου δυνάμεων γενομένῳ πλειόνων ἔδει μερῶν πρὸς τὴν τῶν καθ' ἕκαστον χρειῶν ὑπηρεσίαν, ὁ δὲ θεὸς ἅτε ἀγὲνητος ὢν καὶ τὰ ἄλλα ἀγαγὼν εἰς γένεσιν οὐδενὸς ἐδεήθη τῶν τοῖς γεννήμασι προσόντων.

45. The synthesis between the self-consistent simple deity of *The Republic* and the simple first principle of metaphysics might also have something to do with the identification of the Good and the One in Middle Platonism. I have not treated this topic, but see Hägg, *Clement of Alexandria*, 90–93; Zambon, "Middle Platonism," 569–70.

46. These two aspects are, of course, one in God, following the logic already set out by Alcinous, because God is the supreme first principle in whom there can be no contraries. In Philo we thus gain greater clarity than in Alcinous concerning the relationship between the metaphysical and the ethical sense of simplicity in the case of God.

47. "Dieser Aspekt der Gotteslehre [= ἁπλότης Gottes] ist schließlich für Philon nicht eine bloße metaphysische Randbemerkung, sondern ein wesentliches Element seiner geistlichen Lehre." Amstutz, *ΑΠΛΟΤΗΣ*, 54 (my translation).

CHAPTER 3

1. There is no doubt that divine simplicity has a central place in Irenaeus's theology. See Anthony Briggman, *God and Christ in Irenaeus* (Oxford: Oxford University Press, 2018), 90–99. In what follows, my exposition of Irenaeus's account largely focuses on its polemical dimension. But as John Behr has argued recently, Irenaeus's approach goes much deeper than simply affirming divine simplicity as a metaphysical principle. For Irenaeus, God's simplicity is perfectly reflected in the one divine economy as "a symphony of salvation." See John Behr, "Synchronic and Diachronic Harmony: St. Irenaeus on Divine Simplicity," *Modern Theology* 35, no. 3 (2019): 428–41.

2. Stead, *Philosophy in Christian Antiquity*, 108, 131–32; Stead, *Divine Substance*, 109, 163–64, 187–89. For a recent account, see Briggman, *God and Christ in Irenaeus*, 95–97.

3. To my knowledge, only a few scholars have taken note of this, mostly in recent Irenaeus scholarship. See Pannenberg, "Philosophical Concept of God," 166–68; Jackson Lashier, *Irenaeus on the Trinity* (Leiden: Brill, 2014), 86–89, 92–148 (esp. 130–47); Briggman, *God and Christ in Irenaeus*, 121–36 (esp. 127ff). My conclusions are largely in agreement with Lashier and Briggman.

4. The most detailed account of Valentinianism to date is Einar Thomassen, *The Spiritual Seed: The Church of the "Valentinians"* (Leiden: Brill, 2008). Following Joel Kalvesmaki, I find the term "protology" helpful as it indicates how in their theories Valentinians sought to account for everything beginning from a πρῶτος. See Joel Kalvesmaki, *The Theology of Arithmetic: Number Symbolism in Platonism and Early Christianity* (Washington, DC: Harvard University Press, 2013), 4.

5. The term "Valentinian" refers to what Irenaeus conceived to be a follower of Valentinus, a second-century Christian teacher whose teachings may not agree with those of the followers. The discrepancy between the Valentinians and Valentinus himself on doctrine is well established. As Thomassen has remarked, it is important to remember that this is a "heresiological" term, as the "Valentinians" would never have referred to themselves by the term. See Thomassen, *The Spiritual Seed*, 4–5. In *Adversus haereses*, Book 1, Irenaeus himself recognizes that there are variations among the teachings of the "Valentinians." For the purpose of our study, "Valentinianism" remains a good term because it reflects how certain doctrines—especially the emission of the aeons from God the Father—were associated by subsequent Christian theologians with the followers of Valentinus. So in what follows,

I speak of the "Valentinians" not as a term referring to the genuine teachings of the Valentinians but to capture the "heresiological" perspective of the authors examined in this book (i.e., Irenaeus, Tertullian, and Origen) who considered the teaching of emission (*prolatio*) to be "Valentinian."

6. *Haer.* II.13 and II.17.

7. *Grande notice* refers to the opening chapters of the work (*Haer.* I.1–8). See François M. M. Sagnard, *La gnose valentinienne et le témoignage de Saint Irénée*, Études de philosophie médiévale 36 (Paris, 1947), 31–50, 140–232.

8. *Haer.* I.1. It is worth noting that there are internal debates among Valentinians on whether at the head of the emission of aeons is a monad or a dyad. Moreover, it is also debated whether the First Father is gendered or not. See Kalvesmaki, *The Theology of Arithmetic*, 52–60. Once again, I present the dyadic version because it is the one that is criticized by Irenaeus in *Haer.* II.13 and II.17.

9. This account is based on Irenaeus's report in *Haer.* I.1–2, 4–5. For an account drawing on all available sources, see Thomassen's and Kalvesmaki's works cited above.

10. For the Pythagorean background, see Kalvesmaki, *The Theology of Arithmetic*, 50–51.

11. "Irenaeus believes the principle of divine simplicity bears on the question of the emission or production of aeons." Briggman, *God and Christ in Irenaeus*, 118.

12. In *Haer.* II.13 Irenaeus argues against the first stage of Valentinian protology, namely, the emission of the aeons in the primary ogdoad. In II.17 he then turns to argue against the second stage, namely, the emissions of the rest of the aeons in the *Pleroma*. His argument in both chapters, however, retains the same shape.

13. On the philosophical background of Irenaeus's definition of simplicity, see Briggman, *God and Christ in Irenaeus*, 92.

14. My analysis thus agrees with Lashier, who, in his more comprehensive study on Irenaeus's Logos theology, also highlights these points. See Lashier, *Irenaeus on the Trinity*, 136–42 on (contemporaneity), 142–45 (on inseparability), and 145–47 (on consubstantiality).

15. For the justification of translating the Latin *efficabiliter* as "distinctly," see Briggman, *God and Christ in Irenaeus*, 128, n. 76. As Briggman notes, following the suggestion of Adelin Rousseau, this Latin term likely corresponds to the Greek term ἀποτελεστικῶς.

16. *Haer.* II.17.3.

17. As Barnes has highlighted, Irenaeus's critique of spatiality is based on his understanding of God as Spirit since Irenaeus's conception of "spiritual" reality seems to be characterized by intellectuality and simplicity. See Michel René Barnes, "Irenaeus's Trinitarian Theology," *Nova et Vetera* 7 (2009): 67–106, at 76–78. Barnes's point is further developed in greater detail and situated within Irenaeus's anti-Valentinian polemic by Lashier, *Irenaeus on the Trinity*, 86–90. See also a recent defense of the connection between spirituality and simplicity in Briggman,

God and Christ in Irenaeus, 99–101. This sets Irenaeus on a trajectory against the attribution of corporeal qualities to God similar to that we have seen in Philo and Alcinous. However, there are also significant differences between Irenaeus and the Middle Platonic theology inherited by Christian writers such as Justin. On this point, see Jackson Lashier, "Irenaeus as Logos Theologian," *Vigiliae Christianae* 66, no. 4 (January 1, 2012): 341–61.

18. This association is presupposed by Irenaeus throughout Book 2. See *Haer.* II.3.2 (composite = changeable and transitory), II.7.6 (composite = earthly and perishable things vis-à-vis spiritual things), II.13.3 (composite = made up of body and soul), II.13.5 (composite = corporeal), and II.17.7 (composite = ensouled, i.e., made up of body and soul).

19. In this argument Irenaeus is determined to interpret the Valentinian language of emission uncharitably. But as Antonio Orbe has suggested, the Valentinians were unlikely to fall into such basic errors, namely, to associate animal-like generation to God. Given the philosophical sophistication of their systems, it is more probable that they would be as keen as Irenaeus to prevent the application of animal-like generations to the divine Pleroma. See Antonio Orbe, *Hacia la primera teología de la procesión del Verbo*, 2 vols. (Rome: Aedes Universitatis Gregorianae, 1958), 1:389, 2:648–49. In light of Orbe's comment, we must be careful to take Irenaeus's argument at face value to conclude that the Valentinians themselves understood *prolatio* in a corporeal sense. However, what is significant to note about Irenaeus's argument is that it provides a standard response to rule out the theological plausibility of Valentinian protology. As we shall see, exactly the same kind of anti-Valentinian argument is rehearsed by Origen.

20. *Haer.* II.13.1–4.

21. Irenaeus's analysis of emission based on the analogy of the human mind is by no means unique, as it is a constant theme among Christian writers (including Gnostics) in the early centuries. Moreover, different writers draw on the analysis of the human mind for opposite reasons. Irenaeus uses the analysis to highlight the discontinuity between the activities of the divine mind and those of the human mind, whereas Justin (*Dial.* 61) and Tertullian (*APrax.* 5–6) draw on the same analysis to stress instead the analogy between the two. See Orbe, *Hacia*, 1:363–86.

22. *Haer.* II.13.1: *de aliquo in cogitatu dispositae qualeslibet motiones . . . et in cogitationem conterminatae.* We shall see what Irenaeus means by this phrase in the detailed breakdown of the different stages of mental activities below.

23. Ibid., II.13.2.

24. Ibid., II.13.1.

25. Ibid. II.13.2: *Vnum autem et idem est omnia quae praedicta sunt, a no initium accipientia et secundum augmentum adsumentia appellationes.*

26. Ibid. Irenaeus also accuses the Valentinians of getting the order of mental activities wrong. See ibid., II.13.1. Again, Irenaeus is perhaps reading the Valentinians' account uncharitably to suggest that their aeons are emitted as though there

was a separation between the stages of mental activities in a sense appropriate only to animal generation *secundum corporis amissionem.*

27. Ibid., II.13.2.

28. Ibid., II.28.4. See also II.13.3–4.

29. Irenaeus is not often considered a "negative" theologian, but here we have a clear instance of his negative theology. For Irenaeus, divine transcendence is best preserved by making a clear distinction between the divine Mind and human minds.

30. *Haer.* II.17.4: *eiusdem . . . substantiae cum sint cum principe emissionis ipsorum.*

31. Irenaeus did not analyze the metaphor of rays from the sun in relation to consubstantiality. Instead, he relates this metaphor to the necessity of a receptacle in emission (ibid., II.13.5). But here I simply offer a plausible reconstruction of Irenaeus's reasoning for consubstantiality, a point made clear from this chapter.

32. Ibid., II.13.3–4, II.17.3, 5–6 (rejecting the possibility of passion arising in the Pleroma), II.17.5, 8–11 (rejecting the possibility of ignorance arising in the Pleroma).

33. Ibid., II.17.4 (emphasis added).

34. "Because the source and product are constituted of the same simple substance, a substance not subject to temporal differentiation, the substance of the product cannot be said to come to be in any temporally defined way." Briggman, *God and Christ in Irenaeus*, 134.

35. There is, however, one way Irenaeus thinks we can differentiate the relative temporal status of the generated lights after their recombination: with respect to the process of lighting. When the lights are recombined, the only difference marker left between them is that some had been lit before others. It is difficult to determine what Irenaeus means precisely. But perhaps he is thinking of something like this: if two lights, A and B, are recombined, they are no longer two lights *qua* lights. This is because they are consubstantial. As a result, there will be no relative temporal ordering between them *qua* lights once they are recombined. However, A and B retain one way in which they can be distinguished as two: with respect to their relative order of generation. Given that (say) A is generated before B, after recombination we can still identify A as generated temporally before B even though they have now become one light (and so it is impossible to differentiate their relative temporal status *qua* lights). It is unclear what Irenaeus means by this, but perhaps we can speculate. If we turn to the recombined light, we cannot point to one part and say that it is generated earlier than another part. This is because, *qua* light, the recombined light is one and the same. However, what we can say is that this recombined light is lit *now*, whereas the lights used in the recombination were lit *earlier.* In other words, it is still possible to analyze the relative temporal status not of the various lights used in the recombination but of those and the newly recombined light. Perhaps this is what Irenaeus wishes to suggest by insisting that the only way

to distinguish between A and B when they are recombined is with respect to their order of generation.

36. "For how can one aeon be called younger or older among them, since the light of the whole Fullness is one?" *Haer.* II.17.5.

37. *Haer.* II.13.3: *simplex et non compositus et similimembrius et totus ipse sibimetipsi similis et aequalis est, totus cum sit sensus et totus spiritus et totus sensuabilitas et totus ennoia et totus ratio et totus auditus et totus oculus et totus lumen et totus fons omnium honorum, quemadmodum adest religiosis ac piis dicere de Deo.* Scholars have noted that Irenaeus's language of divine simplicity echoes that of the pre-Socratic philosopher Xenophanes. See Robert M. Grant, *Gods and the One God* (Philadelphia: Westminster John Knox Press, 1988), 89–90; Eric F. Osborn, *Irenaeus of Lyons* (Cambridge: Cambridge University Press, 2001), 38–43; Briggman, *God and Christ in Irenaeus*, 92–94; Mansfeld, "Compatible Alternatives," 112–14.

38. *Haer.* II.13.9: *Et neque sensum uita antiquiorem aliquis potest dicere, ipse enim sensus uita est; neque uitam posteriorem a sensu, uti non fiat aliquando sine uita is qui est omnium sensus, hoc est Deus.*

39. Ibid. II.13.9.

40. This is not to deny that there are also significant dissimilarities between Irenaeus and Middle Platonic theology, as Lashier has highlighted. See note 17 above.

41. *Haer.* II.28.2–3. If Mansfeld is correct, then Irenaeus might even have considered God as beyond positive qualification such as simplicity. See Mansfeld, "Compatible Alternatives," 113–14.

42. For a discussion of this, see Barnes, "Irenaeus's Trinitarian Theology," 74–75.

43. Lashier has pointed out that Irenaeus's affirmation of divine simplicity in *Haer.* II is primarily a reaction against the Valentinian affirmation of the emitted aeons as "distinct entities." Lashier, *Irenaeus on the Trinity*, 86–87. If this is right, then it is possible to argue that Irenaeus's theology better aligns with the so-called "Monarchian" theology since Irenaeus's understanding of divine simplicity implies the possibility of dissolving the distinction between the Son and the Father through a process of reunion into a single being, a process analogous to Irenaeus's account of lights recombined into one light. From this perspective, reading Irenaeus as a "proto-Trinitarian" (as I do here) amounts to doing great violence to his original intentions. In Reinhard M. Hübner (with Markus Vinzent), *Der Paradox Eine: Antignostischer Monarchianismus im zweiten Jahrhundert* (Leiden: Brill, 1999), 197–98, Hübner set out such an interpretation: "Er [Irenaeus] bestreitet, daß er [Logos] als ein aliud neben dem Vater existiert." Lashier is unconvinced, however, that Irenaeus can be interpreted in this manner. See Lashier, *Irenaeus on the Trinity*, 145–46. In my view, Irenaeus is ambiguous on this point so that a "Monarchian" reading such as Hübner's is equally forced as claiming that Irenaeus conceives of the Logos as a distinctive "second person."

CHAPTER 4

1. Hübner (with Vinzent), *Der Paradox Eine*, 198 (my translation).

2. For a brief history of Monarchianism, see Gustave Bardy, "Monarchianisme," in *Dictionnaire de Théologie Catholique*, ed. Alfred Vacant, E. Mangenot, and Emile Amann (Paris: Letouzey et Ané, 1929), vol. 10.2: 2193–2209. Bardy offers a helpful historical narrative as well as engaging with most of the critical questions surrounding Monarchianism. The Monarchian controversy stood at the center of the doctrinal context in the third-century Roman Church. This is because two popes—Zephyrinus and Callistus—were both Monarchianis of some sort. See Ronald E. Heine, "The Christology of Callistus," *Journal of Theological Studies* 49, no. 1 (1998): 56–91. Heine's essay offers an excellent reconstruction of Callistus's theology that is representative of the state of Roman theology in the third century. Heine also provides an insightful reconstruction of the Stoic philosophical background of Monarchianism, as well as a helpful characterization of third-century Monarchian contexts (both Asian and Roman). On Roman Monarchian theology more generally, see the reconstruction in Markus Vinzent, "From Zephyrinus to Damasus: What Did Roman Bishops Believe?," in *Studia Patristica LXIII*, ed. Markus Vinzent, 273–86 (Leuven, Belgium: Peeters, 2013).

3. On the problem caused by the notion of "identity" for Trinitarian theology, see Hasker, *Metaphysics and the Tri-Personal God*, 59.

4. What I am concerned about here is not whether the modern worry is theologically or philosophically warranted. My concern is rather with showing that the modern formulation of the problem is unhelpful for appreciating the historical shape of the problem in the ante-Nicene period. For my attempt to address the modern problem theologically, see Ip, "Re-Imagining Divine Simplicity in Trinitarian Theology."

5. I have taken this term from Matthew W. Bates, who in turn borrowed it from Marie-Josèphe Rondeau. The term refers to the exegetical task of identifying the *prosopa*—roles or persons—in a dramatic setting. In a given Scriptural passage, can we identify correctly the distinct roles or persons in play so as to make sense of the passage? Throughout this section, I characterize the Monarchian controversy as a debate about prosopological exegesis in this sense. See Bates, *The Birth of the Trinity*, especially 31–34. Prosopology as a technique is firmly rooted in classical philology. See Bernhard Neuschäfer, *Origenes als Philologe*, 2 vols. (Basel: Reinhardt, 1987), 1:263–76. See also Peter W. Martens, *Origen and Scripture: The Contours of the Exegetical Life* (Oxford: Oxford University Press, 2014), 58–59. For examples of ante-Nicene usage, see Lewis Ayres, "Irenaeus vs. the Valentinians: Toward a Rethinking of Patristic Exegetical Origins," *Journal of Early Christian Studies* 25, no. 2 (Summer 2015): 153–87.

6. Gen. 1:26, 18–19, 21:12; Ps. 44:2, 7–9 (LXX); Ps. 109:1 (LXX).

7. See Michael Slusser, "The Exegetical Roots of Trinitarian Theology," *Theological Studies* 29 (1988): 461–76. Slusser shows (466–68) that the issues related

to prosopological exegesis in the Monarchian controversy were anticipated by Justin Martyr in the *Dialogue with Trypho*. My perspective on Monarchianism offered here is significantly in debt to the article by Slusser, who writes: "It was a method of literary and grammatical analysis of Scripture that provided the early Christian thinkers with a way to talk about God in a Trinitarian fashion" (475).

8. Adolf von Harnack, *History of Dogma*, trans. Neil Buchanan, vol. 3 (Boston: Little, Brown, 1907), 1–118. On the historiography of this distinction and its problems, see Xavier Morales, "'Modalism'—Critical Assessment of a Modern Interpretative Paradigm," in *Studia Patristica* CXXIII, ed. Markus Vinzent (Leuven: Peeters, 2021), 237–48.

9. I have argued that this distinction, while terminologically unhelpful, does indeed refer to the heresiological construct found among anti-Monarchians in the early third century. The division is present, for instance, in the heresiological schema found in a fragment of Origen's *Commentary on Titus*, reproduced in Pamphilus's *Apol.* 33. See Ip, "'Arianism' *Ante-Litteram*."

10. See Heine, "The Christology of Callistus."

11. Bardy, "Monarchianisme," 2194–95.

12. In doing so, I exclude the psilanthropists and adoptionists, who are traditionally referred to as "monarchians" of some sort. See Samuel Fernández, "Verso la teologia Trinitaria di Origene: Metafora e linguaggio teologico," in *Origeniana Decima: Origen as Writer*, ed. Sylwia Kaczmarek and Henryk Pietras (Leuven, Belgium: Peeters, 2011), 457–73. In my view, a major reconstruction of the categories that clarify the historical interrelation(s) among the three groups specified by Fernández remains urgently needed.

13. *CN* 2.3.

14. *APrax.* 2.

15. *CN* 2.

16. By the time Hippolytus wrote *Contra Noetum*, this term was already controversial (see Justin Martyr, *Dial.* 55–62). While Hippolytus did not explicitly attribute a technical use of the term ἕτερος to Noetus, from the key passages (Ex. 3:6, 20:3; Bar. 3:36–38) used by Noetus we can learn that the term was central to his conception of monotheism. The fact that the use of ἕτερος was under question is further supported by the careful explanation offered by Hippolytus in *CN* 11.1. According to Hippolytus, when he uses the term ἕτερος, he does not mean two gods. This clarification suggests that Hippolytus anticipates that Noetus would object to the term due to its violation of monotheism.

17. *CN* 3.2.

18. In all but one of our contemporary sources, these two passages were mentioned and received a full treatment from anti-Monarchians. See *CN* 7; *APrax.* 20; *Trin.* (Novatian) 27.1, 28.2. The only source that did not mention these passages, namely, Pseudo-Hippolytus's *Refutatio omnium haeresium*, deliberately withholds the exegetical character of Monarchianism in order to portray the teaching as

originated from the philosophy of Heraclitus. See Heine, "The Christology of Callistus," 60.

19. *CN* 7.1; *APrax*. 22; *Trin.* (Novatian) 27.1–2.

20. *CN* 7.4; *APrax*. 24; *Trin.* (Novatian) 28.2–30.

21. A good illustration of this is John 2:19: "Destroy this temple, and in three days I will raise it up." Origen reports a Monarchian interpretation that attempts to read this passage in conjunction with 1 Cor. 15:15, a passage that suggests God was the one who raised Christ, in order to conclude that the *prosopon* speaking in John 2.19 is the Father himself. See *ComJn* X.246. This example illustrates how Monarchians will look for possibilities to interpret a given passage so that the meaning is compatible with the presupposition that there is only one divine acting and speaking subject in Scripture.

22. I do not deal with the Holy Spirit here because it lies outside the scope of this study, which is primarily concerned with the Father-Son relation.

23. Mark DelCogliano, "The Interpretation of John 10:30 in the Third Century: Anti-Monarchian Polemics and the Rise of Grammatical Reading Techniques," *Journal of Theological Interpretation* 6 (2012): 117–38.

24. This is by no means the only exegetical technique the anti-Monarchians used to refute Monarchianism. See Ibid., 125–32, for other examples.

25. *APrax*. 12; *Trin.* (Novatian) 27.

26. *APrax*. 12.

27. *CN* 7; *APrax*. 22; *Trin.* (Novatian) 27.

28. *CN* 7.1.

29. Ibid. 7.2–3. Here we have a problematic usage of "substance" that lies beyond the scope of this chapter. But it reveals one of the most crucial yet trickiest issues in Trinitarian theology: Does the affirmation of "one substance" deny any distinction between the Father and the Son, ending up with the Monarchian position? Hippolytus's statement here seems to suggest that this is the case, whereas Tertullian is happy to use, to denote the unity between the Father and the Son, *una substantia*, which will respect the distinction between the two (*APrax*. 2, 12). See Ernest Evans, ed., *Tertullian's Treatise against Praxeas: The Text Edited, with an Introduction, Translation, and Commentary* (London: S.P.C.K, 1948), 39–45.

30. *APrax*. 22.

31. *Trin.* (Novatian) 27.2.

32. Ibid., 27.4.

33. Ibid., 27.5.

34. The Son as *persona* is the sense of his distinct existence that Tertullian needs to preserve in his account of generation. See *APrax*. 7: "Whatever therefore the substance of the Word was, that I call a Person, and for it I claim the name of Son; and while I acknowledge him as Son I maintain he is another beside the Father (*secundum a patre*)." Thus *persona* for Tertullian captures his anti-Monarchianism, as indicated by the phrase *secumdum a patre* in the last sentence.

35. *APrax.* 8.

36. Hübner, of course, argues that Irenaeus's rejection of Valentinian emissions obviously leads to a commitment to Monarchianism. See Hübner (with Vinzent), *Der Paradox Eine*, 197–98. But I prefer to interpret Irenaeus as ambiguous on this point because Hübner's interpretation requires a huge amount of speculative redating of second-century documents, on which much doubt has been cast by scholars. See the reviews of Hübner's *Der Paradox Eine* by Mark J. Edwards in *Journal of Theological Studies* 52.1 (2001): 354–56; by Michael Slusser in *Journal of Early Christian Studies* 9.3 (2001): 407–8; by Allen Brent in *Journal of Ecclesiastical History* 53, no. 1 (2002): 114–17; and by Wolfram Kinzig in *Theologische Literaturzeitung* 131, no. 9 (2006): 1015–18.

37. *APrax.* 8.

38. See the fascinating exploration in Orbe, *Hacia*, 2:584–603. Orbe argues that this distinction is equivalent to the distinction between κατὰ μερισμόν and κατὰ ἀποκοπὴν in Tatian, *Orat.* V. While Orbe's thesis is conjectural, what seems clear is that in the ante-Nicene period there is a theological awareness of two kinds of "distinctions" that could result from the process of generation: one that preserves unity between the generator and the generated and another that compromises this unity.

39. *APrax.* 9.

40. Ibid., 8.

41. Ibid.

42. In fact, it is hardly probable that Tertullian was committed to divine simplicity along the lines of Middle Platonic theology. This is indicated by his lack of use of *simplicitas/simplex* in relation to God. The only entries on these terms in René Braun, *Deus Christianorum: Recherches sur le vocabulaire doctrinal de Tertullien*, 2nd ed. (Paris: Études augustiniennes, 1977), is found in the context of the soul (147, n. 2) and the simplistic interpretation of Scripture (261, 266).

43. *Monarchia* is Tertullian's primary way of speaking about the lack of divisions in God. See *APrax.* 3–4, 8.

CHAPTER 5

1. See Robert M. Berchman, *From Philo to Origen: Middle Platonism in Transition*, Brown Judaic Studies 69 (Chico, CA: Scholars Press, 1984), 123–27; Peter Widdicombe, *The Fatherhood of God from Origen to Athanasius* (Oxford: Oxford University Press, 2001), 22–25. While he does not recognize the ethical sense of simplicity, Widdicombe rightly highlights the close connection in Origen between God as the good and the metaphysical notion of God as "he who is" (ὁ ὤν) (26).

2. As in Philo, as I noted at the end of chapter 2.

3. This synthesis is so striking that Alfons Fürst has recently called it "das metaphysisch-ethische Einheitsdenken des Origenes" (Origen's metaphysical-ethical

doctrine of oneness). See *Die Homilien zum Ersten Buch Samuel*, trans. Alfons Fürst (Berlin: Walter de Gruyter, 2014), 31–59.

4. See Berchman, *From Philo to Origen*, 113–64, for a detailed analysis of Origen's doctrine of the first principles.

5. Identifying Origen as a Platonist is controversial. See Edwards, *Origen against Plato*, for an argument against calling Origen a Platonist. But, for a different perspective on the question, see Ilaria L. E. Ramelli, "Origen and the Platonic Tradition," *Religions* 8, no. 2 (February 2017): 1–20. My perspective is more aligned with Ramelli's than with that of Edwards here, although, of course, by using the label "Christian Platonist" I am indicating that Origen is not exactly the same sort of "Platonist" as pagan Platonists, a point stressed by Edwards. Scholars also debate whether Origen's philosophical theology is to be aligned with Middle Platonic or Neo-Platonic tendencies. See Berchman, *From Philo to Origen*, 113–17, for a review of the debate. In my view, Berchman's situation of Origen as "Middle Platonic" is helpful. Among many things, this approach sheds light on Origen's insistence on God as a simple intellectual existence. Further, Origen's early philosophical theology as set out in *PArch* I.1 seems to align with Middle Platonic theology as found, for example, in Alcinous (*Did.* 10). Nonetheless, as we shall see in the next chapter, there is an anti-Monarchian strand of Origen's exegetical theology that stresses the differentiation between the Father and the Son in a way that resembles the Neo-Pythagorean (e.g., *Numenius*, fr. 11 [des Places]) hierarchical understanding of the *archai*. This strand of Origen's theology bears resemblance to Neo-Platonism.

6. See George E. Karamanolis, *The Philosophy of Early Christianity* (London: Routledge, 2014), 60–116.

7. Origen expresses uncertainty as to whether God is to be identified as mind or whether he transcends mind (e.g., *CCels.* VII.38). See Widdicombe, *The Fatherhood of God*, 34–43, for a discussion of this problem.

8. As Boys-Stones has highlighted, Platonists at Origen's time conceived of God as the "same sort of thing as a form," hence obviously incorporeal. See Boys-Stones, *Platonist Philosophy*, 147.

9. The solution is found in *PArch* I.1, where Origen identifies the term "invisible" (ἀόρατον) in Scripture as equivalent to ἀσώματον. See also *PArch* II.3.6. The conclusion of his inquiry on this problem is given in *PArch* IV.3.15.

10. Guy Stroumsa argues that while the latter appear frequently in Origen's corpus for their literal reading of Scripture, including language that applies physical properties or motions to God, the former are more likely to be Origen's target. See G. Stroumsa, "The Incorporeality of God," *Religion* 13, no. 4 (1983): 346–47. This identification is also made by Berchman, *From Philo to Origen*, 259, 276–80, and Edwards, *Origen against Plato*, 57.

11. For a good summary of the principles in Stoic physics, see A. A. Long and D. N. Sedley, eds., *The Hellenistic Philosophers*, vol. 1: *Translations of the Principal*

Sources with Philosophical Commentary (Cambridge: Cambridge University Press, 1987), 270–72. See, for instance, the report of Stoic physics found in Alexander of Aphrodisias's *On Mixture* in Brad Inwood, *Stoics Reader: Selected Writings and Testimonia*, trans. Lloyd P. Gerson (Indianapolis: Hackett, 2008), 95 (Text 67).

12. For an overview of this issue, see Ricardo Salles, ed., *God and Cosmos in Stoicism* (Oxford: Oxford University Press, 2009), 6.

13. Michael J. White, "Stoic Natural Philosophy (Physics and Cosmology)," in *The Cambridge Companion to the Stoics*, ed. Brad Inwood (Cambridge: Cambridge University Press, 1999), 130.

14. *CCels.* I.21 (translation from Chadwick, slightly modified).

15. *CCels.* VI.69.

16. Berchman, *From Philo to Origen*, 276–77; White, "Stoic Natural Philosophy," 133–38.

17. *CCels.* VI.71: "Because Celsus has not comprehended the doctrine about the Spirit of God . . . he takes into his head the notion that when we say 'God is spirit,' there is in this respect no difference between us and the Stoics among the Greeks who affirm that God is spirit that has permeated all things and contains all things within itself."

18. On the Stoic interpretation of "spirit" (*pneuma*), see Inwood, *Stoics Reader*, 93–96.

19. *CCels.* VI.71.

20. Ibid., I.21, III.75.

21. Ibid., IV.14.

22. Ibid., I.21. See also *PEuch* XXI.2.

23. "Let us grant, again, that we turn away others from Stoic physicians because they think that God is corruptible [φθαρτὸν], and affirm that His essence is a material substance [τὴν οὐσίαν αὐτοῦ λεγόντων σῶμα], which is entirely changeable and subject to alteration and transformation [τρεπτὸν δι' ὅλων καὶ ἀλλοιωτὸν καὶ μεταβλητὸν], and believe that at some times everything is destroyed and God alone left (Chadwick).

24. *Rep.* 380d.

25. Ibid., 380d–386c.

26. *CCels.* IV.14. This strategy of interpreting anthropomorphic language in Scripture as divine pedagogy closely resembles what we find in Philo's *Deus*. See, for example, *Deus* 60–69.

27. *CCels.* IV.12. The verb Origen uses to describe the Christian interpretation is τροπολογέω, a key verb in the Origenian vocabulary that is closely related to ἀλληγορέω. See Lorenzo Perrone, ed., *Origenes: Die neuen Psalmenhomilien; Eine kritische Edition des Codex Monacensis Graecus 314*, trans. Lorenzo Perrone (Berlin: Walter de Gruyter, 2015), 11 (esp. n. 28). As Robert Lamberton has noted, the verb τροπολογέω appears extensively in Origen's corpus but "has virtually no existence in Greek outside the literature of Hellenizing Judaism and of Christianity."

Robert Lamberton, *Homer the Theologian: Neoplatonist Allegorical Reading and the Growth of the Epic Tradition* (Berkeley: University of California Press, 1989), 62.

28. See also *PEuch.* XXIII.

29. *CCels.* I.21. As we shall see, these passages will also be important in Origen's discussion of the ethical sense of divine simplicity.

30. Ibid., IV.14.

31. Ibid., VII.38.

32. *PArch* I.1.6 (translation from Behr, slightly modified): "Now mind, to move and operate, needs no bodily space, nor sensible magnitude, nor bodily shape or colour, nor does it need anything else whatever of things proper to bodies or matter."

33. E.g., Alcinous, *Did.* 10.165,16–19; Clement of Alexandria, *Str.* V.11–12.

34. On the method of abstraction, see Raoul Mortley, "The Fundamentals of the Via Negativa," *American Journal of Philology* 103, no. 4 (1982): 429–39. See especially Henny Fiskå Hägg, *Clement of Alexandria and the Beginnings of Christian Apophaticism: Knowing the Unknowable* (Oxford: Oxford University Press, 2006), 71–133, for a helpful survey of Middle Platonic negative theology.

35. *PArch* I.1.6 (translation from Behr, slightly modified).

36. Ibid.

37. According to Origen, only the divine nature has the privilege to exist entirely without bodies and association with material substance. See *PArch* I.6.4, I.7.1, II.2.2, II.9.1, IV.3.15, IV.4.8.

38. Ibid., IV.3.15.

39. Ibid., I.1.8.

40. Ibid., II.4.3.

41. This two-step process reflects the explicit methodological approach in this work, stated in *PArch* praef. 10.

42. In my view, Origen's basic understanding on this topic remains consistent throughout his works. The examples discussed in this part of the chapter will provide evidence for this claim, since I draw on a variety of writings across genres and times of composition.

43. *SelGn* (PG 12: 112), my translation.

44. *Philoc.* V.2–3.

45. The term θεώρημα in this context refers to the multiple Scriptural titles of Christ discussed in detail in Books 1 and 2 of Origen's *Commentary on John.* See *ComJn* I.244.

46. *Philoc.* V.4, 13–16 (translation from FoC 80, slightly modified).

47. *Philoc.* V.4, 16–20.

48. John 5:39.

49. Origen makes this point on the basis of his reading of Ps. 39:7 (LXX) as spoken by Jesus himself: "In the volume of the Book it is written of me." Origen provides numerous other examples to argue that Scripture itself utilizes the sense of the one book that goes beyond its literal meaning of numerical oneness. See *Philoc.* V.5.

50. Dan. 7:10. See *Philoc.* V.5–7 for Origen's full argument on the point that one can find in Scripture the opposition between the one and many, understood in the ethical sense.

51. *HomEz* 9.1.

52. Ibid., 9.2.

53. *Philoc.* VIII.2.

54. Ibid., VIII.3, 1–9.

55. *HomlS* I.4, 8–14: Nos, qui adhuc peccatores sumus, non possumus istum titulum laudis acquirere, quia unusquisque nostrum non est unus, sed multi. Intuere namque mihi illius uultum nunc irati, nunc iterum tristis, paulo post rursum gaudentis et iterum turbati et rursum lenis, in alio tempore de rebus diuinis et uitae aeternae actibus consulentis, paulo post uero, uel quae ad auaritiam uel quae ad gloriam saeculi pertinent, molientis. Vides, quomodo ille, qui putatur unus esse, non est unus, sed tot in eo personae uidentur esse, quot mores, quia et secundum scripturas "insipiens sicut luna mutatur" (translation from Christian Hengstermann, made available to the author through private communication, slightly modified).

56. *HomlS* I.4.

57. *HomLv* V.12.9, 127–29.

58. *PEuch* XXI.2 (italics mine).

59. The view of corporeality espoused by Origen's contemporary Numenius of Apamea. See Numenius, fr. 4a and 4b (des Places).

CHAPTER 6

1. *ComJn* I.119.

2. According to G. C. Stead, the differentiation between an absolute simple first God and a "second" God who is one-many became necessary due to the need to explain how the simple God could govern the world of change and multiplicity. Such a differentiation subsequently gained support from a particular reading of Plato's *Parmenides* and was eventually passed down to the Christian writers. See Stead, *Divine Substance*, 93–94, 164, 186–87; Stead, "Divine Simplicity as a Problem for Orthodoxy," 262.

3. *Numenius*, fr. 11 (des Places).

4. Eric F. Osborn, *The Emergence of Christian Theology* (Cambridge: Cambridge University Press, 1993), 53.

5. Stead, *Divine Substance*, 187.

6. See *Pan.* 64.4, 2–4.

7. Ilaria L. E. Ramelli exemplifies this trajectory of interpretation. See Ramelli, "Origen's Anti-Subordinationism"; Ilaria L. E. Ramelli, "Origen, Greek Philosophy, and the Birth of the Trinitarian Meaning of Hypostasis," *Harvard Theological Review* 105, no. 3 (2012): 302–50. The most recent comprehensive treatment

of Origen's Trinitarian theology, Bruns, *Trinität und Kosmos*, recognizes Origen's own third-century contexts, but the agenda of the author is still set by the "retrospective" question, as pointed out by Mark Edwards in his review of the book in the *Journal of Ecclesiastical History*, 66, no. 2 (2015): 390–91.

8. Here I am following a trajectory dominant in Spanish and Italian scholarship. See Orbe, *Hacia*, 1:387–452; Simonetti, *La crisi ariana nel IV secolo*, 11–15; Fernández, "La generación del Logos"; Fernández, "Verso la teologia trinitaria di Origene." This point is also made by Henri Crouzel, *Théologie de l'image de Dieu chez Origène* (Paris: Aubier, 1956), 111–12, but Crouzel does not develop it further. In English scholarship, the only one to my knowledge who has developed the thesis of an anti-Monarchian function in Origen's doctrine of the three hypostases is Alastair H. B. Logan, in "Origen and the Development of Trinitarian Theology," in *Origeniana Quarta*, ed. Lothar Lies (Innsbruck: Tyrolia, 1987), 424–29. Williams briefly mentions Origen's anti-Monarchianism in passing. See Williams, *Arius*, 143.

9. *ComJn* II.16 (ET: Heine, slightly modified).

10. *ComTi* apud Pamphilus, *Apol.* 33 [7], 40–50.

11. *ComRm* VIII.5.9.

12. The exact identities of Origen's opponents in these reports are difficult to determine. Several possible known targets could be associated with these reports. First, Origen could have in mind Beryllus of Bostra since his teaching, summarized by Eusebius in *HE* VI.33.1, resembles a Monarchian position. Second, Origen could be thinking of the unknown Monarchian group attacked in *Dialogue with Heraclides*. On this group, see Henry Chadwick and J.E.L. Oulton, eds., *Alexandrian Christianity* (Philadelphia: Westminster John Knox Press, 2006), 430–34. Third, Origen could be thinking of the Roman Monarchians he met during his visit to Rome. The most detailed modern treatment with respect to the Roman side of the question is Heine, "The Christology of Callistus." Origen could be referring to Callistus's theology or to Sabellian theology, which utilizes more technical terminologies. See also Stephen E. Waers, "Wisdom Christology and Monarchianism in Origen's Commentary on John," *Greek Orthodox Theological Review* 60, nos. 3–4 (2015): 96–98. Waers offers a clear introduction and a detailed survey of the literature, once again with respect to the more restricted question on the relation between Origen and Roman Monarchianism. On the difficult but important question concerning Origen's historical relation with Monarchianism, see Fernández, "La Generación Del Logos" especially 194–98. For a more detailed argument for identifying these two groups as Origen's most likely polemical targets in his Trinitarian thought, see Ip, "'Arianism' *Ante-Litteram*."

13. This group consistently appears in Origen's heresiological reports. See also *ComJn* XXXII.193 and *DialHe* 4.

14. I am convinced that this is a crucial doctrinal detail that unites the two groups in Origen's mind. This is supported by Ronald Heine's detailed work, too. See Heine, "The Christology of Callistus," 71. As Heine points out here, the difference

between modalist ("Monarchian" in my terms) and adoptionist ("psilanthopist" in my terms) tendencies likely lies in the manner in which the historic Christ "became" (in time) divine. The Monarchians saw the divine and the human as having come together at Jesus's conception, the psilanthropists at Jesus's baptism. However, both positions share the common denial of a pre-existent Son of God before the historic Christ. Wishing to avoid ditheism, Monarchians argue that before the incarnation there was only one divine ὑπόστασις, the Father himself. There was no pre-existent divine Son because the Son *became* divine through conjoining with the Father's divine Spirit in the incarnation. Wishing to avoid ditheism, too, psilanthropists agree with the first group concerning the existence of only one divine ὑπόστασις. But for them, there was no pre-existent divine Son because it was during his baptism that the divine Spirit of the Father entered into the man Jesus.

15. Origen's "subordinationism," most evident in his *Commentary on John*, has received a detailed treatment by Giovanni Hermanin de Reichenfeld. This author calls what I term Origen's hierarchical understanding of the Father-Son relation an "ontological subordinationism of priority," indicating that differentiating between the divine persons in no way indicates an ordering of perfection; that is, when Origen affirms one divine person is "greater than" another, he simply indicates the ontological dependence of one on the other and in no way implies a difference in divine perfection. See Giovanni Hermanin de Reichenfeld, *The Spirit, the World and the Trinity: Origen's and Augustine's Understanding of the Gospel of John* (Leuven: Brepols, 2021), 39–59 (on the Father-Son relation), 59–71 (on the Holy Spirit). In what follows, I largely agree with Hermanin de Reichenfeld's thesis, though I prefer to avoid the terminology "subordinationism" and emphasize more than Hermanin de Reichenfeld does the "anti-Monarchian" context of Origen's approach. These differences aside, my analysis in this chapter (and the next) should be read in conjunction with de Reichenfeld's work since he completes the picture I offer by discussing the Holy Spirit's relation with the Father and the Son.

16. It will become apparent that my argument has been significantly shaped by the speculative yet illuminating analyses in Orbe, *Hacia*, 1:437–48. While following Orbe's analysis of Origen's anti-Monarchian commitments (1:431–37), nevertheless my analysis of the ἐπίνοιαι in the main body of this chapter set out an alternative approach to the speculative philosophical approach offered by Orbe to fill in the content of Origen's hierarchical account of the Father-Son relationship.

17. For a more comprehensive analysis of Origen's anti-Monarchian passages, see Antonio Orbe, "Origenes y los Monarquianos," *Gregorianum* 72, no. 1 (1991): 39–72. It will become clear, though, that I judge Origen's anti-Monarchianism to be a far more important factor in his Trinitarian theology than Orbe would allow.

18. On the doctrine of three *hypostases*, see also *ComJn* II.75; *HomLv* XIII.4. As we shall see in the next chapter, Origen also prefers to steer clear of Monarchianism by speaking of the unity between the Father and the Son in terms of their harmony of mind and will, a key emphasis in *CCels.* VIII.12. See Orbe, *Hacia*, 1:438.

On this theme, see *ComJn* XIII.228–34; *PArch* I.2.6. It makes sense that this theme assumes prominence in Origen since this model of unity grounded in harmony of mind, will, and act is clearly an anti-Monarchian strategy, as seen in Hippolytus (*CN* 14), Tertullian (*APrax.* 3) and Novatian (*Trin.* XXVII.4).

19. This debate between Monarchians and anti-Monarchians concerning the mode of reference of divine names has had an enduring significance in the development of patristic Trinitarian theology. In the fourth century it evolved into the debate between the Cappadocians and the Eunomians. On this debate, see Mark DelCogliano, *Basil of Caesarea's Anti-Eunomian Theory of Names: Christian Theology and Late-Antique Philosophy in the Fourth Century Trinitarian Controversy* (Leiden: Brill, 2010).

20. Καὶ τὸ πολλούς φιλοθέους εἶναι εὐχομένους παράσσον, εὐλαβουμένους δύο ἀναγορεῦσαι θεούς καὶ παρὰ τοῦτο περιπίπτοντας ψευδέσι καὶ ἀσεβέσι δόγμασιν, ἤτοι ἀρνουμένους ἰδιότητα υἱοῦ ἑτέραν παρὰ τὴν τοῦ πατρὸς ὁμολογοῦντας θεὸν εἶναι τὸν μέχρι ὀνόματος παρ'αὐτοῖς υἱὸν προσαγορευόμενον, ἢ ἀρνουμένους τὴν θεότητα τοῦ υἱοῦ τιθέντας δὲ αὐτοῦ τὴν ἰδιότητα καὶ τὴν οὐσίαν κατὰ περιγραφὴν τυγχάνουσαν ἑτέραν τοῦ πατρός, ἐντεῦθεν λύεσθαι δύναται. From ἢ ἀρνουμένους τὴν θεότητα τοῦ υἱοῦ. Origen describes a second position.

21. *ComJn* II.149.

22. Orbe, *Hacia*, 1:431–32. Subsequently, Orbe draws the connection between Origen's anti-Monarchianism and the theology of Eunomius. If Origen indeed had the Father-Son distinction κατ' οὐσίαν in mind in his polemic against the Monarchians, then by emphasizing that the Son's essence (οὐσία) is other than that of the Father, the Eunomian logic is somewhat "Origenian." For Eunomius's theology, see Richard Paul Vaggione, *Eunomius of Cyzicus and the Nicene Revolution* (Oxford: Oxford University Press, 2001). As shall become clear, I am not entirely convinced about Orbe's claim here.

23. *ComJn* II.150–54.

24. Ibid., X. 246 (Heine translation slightly modified).

25. See the suggestive conjectures in Orbe, "Origenes y los Monarquianos," 45–48; Orbe, *Hacia*, 1:436–37.

26. Unfortunately, we have little evidence beyond the heresiological reports that the Monarchians themselves indeed formulated their position in these technical terms. As Le Boulluec and Nautin have argued, Origen often presents an abstract and oversystematized account of heresy that might not reflect the true positions of his opponents. *ComJn* X.246 might simply reflect an instance of this at work. See Alain Le Boulluec, *La notion d'hérésie dans la littérature grecque, IIe-IIIe siècles*, vol. 2: *Clément d'Alexandrie et Origène* (Paris: Études augustiniennes, 1985), 519–42; Pierre Nautin, *Lettres et écrivains chrétiens des IIe et IIIe siècles*, Collana patristica e del pensiero cristiano 2 (Paris: Cerf, 1961), 216.

27. In *PEuch* XV.1 we have another testimony to the use of ὑποκείμενον in the context of Origen's anti-Monarchian critique: "For if, as is shown elsewhere,

the Son is different from the Father in person and in subject (ἕτερος . . . κατ' οὐσίαν καὶ ὑποκείμενόν ἐστιν ὁ υἱὸς τοῦ πατρὸς), we must pray either to the Son and not to the Father, or to both, or to the Father alone." See also *ComMt* XVII.14. When commenting on Matt. 21:46, Origen attempts to safeguard this verse from οἱ συγχέοντες πατρὸς καὶ υἱοῦ ἔννοιαν καὶ τῇ ὑποστάσει ἕνα διδόντες εἶναι τὸν πατέρα καὶ τὸν υἱόν. Here Origen is likely referring to the Monarchians, who took this verse to support the claim that there was no pre-existing divine Son of God who possessed a distinct individual existence. He then qualifies the Monarchian view further with reference to ὑποκείμενον: τῇ ἐπινοίᾳ μόνῃ καὶ τοῖς ὀνόμασι <μόνοις> διαιροῦντες τὸ ἓν ὑποκείμενον (GCS 40, 623, 15–16). It seems safe to conjecture that there must be some intrinsic connection between the affirmation of one ὑπόστασις and one ὑποκείμενον either in the original Monarchian view or in Origen's polemical portrayal of this view.

28. The most illuminating attempts remain the ones offered by Orbe and Simonetti. Orbe suggests that Origen thinks the term "Spirit" (πνεῦμα) was conceived as the first generic ὑποκείμενον common between the Father and the Son. This ὑποκείμενον is, in turn, was individualized by different properties (ἰδίοτητες), which is how Origen differentiates the Father and Son. This position was developed in Orbe, *Hacia*, 1:431–48. Simonetti is of the opinion that Orbe's position is a bit overly speculative. His own position is that Origen did not rely on postulating a common ὑποκείμενον that was then individuated differently in order to differentiate the Father and the Son. Rather, Simonetti argues that Origen thinks it is the distinct properties that serve to identify and characterize a particular individual being. Hence, the Father and the Son are distinguished by the unique properties each possesses, and they are two ὑποστάσεις and (perhaps) οὐσίαι. See Manlio Simonetti, *Studi sulla cristologia del II e III secolo* (Rome: Institutum Patristicum Augustinianum, 1993), 109–23. Both Orbe and Simonetti attempt to arrive at a systematic understanding of Origen's use of these terms. These analyses are suggestive and illuminating, but in what follows I shall take a less speculative approach since, in my view, while Origen was no doubt a systematic writer, he was nowhere as systematic as the accounts of Orbe and Simonetti suggest. It will become clear that my understanding is somewhat closer to that of Simonetti than to that of Orbe.

29. *ComJn* XIII.151.

30. *CCels.* VIII.14.

31. *ComMt* XV.10.

32. *ComJn* XIII.152.

33. Ibid., II.123.

34. See Heb. 2:9.

35. John 14:6.

36. *ComJn* II.163.

37. Ibid., II.167–70.

38. Ibid., II.166.

39. Ibid., II.11–12. For a detailed analysis of Origen's anti-Monarchian approach to these verses, see Ronald E. Heine, "Stoic Logic as Handmaid to Exegesis and Theology in Origen's Commentary on the Gospel of John," *Journal of Theological Studies* 44, no. 1 (1993): 90–117.

40. *ComJn* II.12.

41. Origen is perhaps following Philo in making this distinction between God and "The God" since this is already found in *Somn.* I.229–30.

42. *ComJn* II.14.

43. Ibid., II.14–5.

44. Ibid., II.12, 18.

45. Ibid., II.17.

46. One possible schema to capture the precision of Origen's understanding here is provided by Hermanin de Reichenfeld, *The Spirit, the World and the Trinity*, 45–46. According to de Reichenfeld, we can say that Origen possesses an ontological "subordinationism of priority." What this phrase indicates is that Origen thinks the Father and the Son are two distinct ontological entities, yet both of them share the same set of attributes "at the same level, but the attribute of the second are completely derived from the first." Ontological subordinationism of priority, in this schema, does not necessarily imply "ontological subordinationism of superiority," which implies that the Father possesses the same set of attributes (e.g., goodness) as the Son but in a more perfect way. De Reichenfeld's schema offers systematic clarity, but I have doubts that within Origen's Platonic framework it is possible to make the differentiation between superiority and priority in the way de Reichenfeld intends. For it seems that in Platonic philosophy that which is prior with respect to an attribute (hence, the source and form of it) already entails a sense of possessing the attribute in the most perfect way. For it is the precise purpose of the theory of forms to identify the difference between perfect instances of something (e.g., the form of goodness) and an imperfect instance of something (e.g., particular goods). It is thus unclear to me whether de Reichenfeld's schema would be intelligible in Origen's philosophical understanding.

47. Origen has in mind the mention of "gods" in Ps. 50:1 (LXX): "The God of gods, the Lord has spoken."

48. Origen is not systematic when it comes to the description of the Son's possession of the absolute patrological titles. Sometimes, as in the case of divinity, he speaks of the Son participating in the Father. Other times, as in the case of goodness, he speaks of the Son as the image of the Father (*ComMt* XV.10; *ComJn* XIII.234). What is clear, however, is that with respect to the absolute patrological titles, the Son's possession of these qualities is derived from their source, namely, the Father himself.

49. *Otras, solo virtualmente (tanquam in causa) contenidas en la substancia del Padre* (Orbe, *Hacia*, 1:442).

50. See *ComJn* I.104–5, II.20.

51. The most detailed discussion of this distinction is found in *ComJn* I.247–51, II.125–26.

52. *ComJn* II.125: "We must know, however, that the Savior has some things not for himself, but for others, and that he has some things for himself and for others. And we must inquire if he has some things for himself and for no one else" (Χρὴ μέντοι γε εἰδίναι ὅτι τινὰ ὁ σωτὴρ οὐχ αὐτῷ ἐστιν ἀλλ' ἑτέροις, τινὰ δὲ αὐτῷ καὶ ἑτέροις· ζητητέον δὲ εἴ τινα ἑαυτῷ καὶ οὐδενί).

53. See *ComJn* I.120–24.

54. Ibid., XXXII.322.

55. See also ibid., XXVIII.157–70. Ibid., XXVIII.159: "And since he who dies is a man, but the truth, and wisdom, and peace, and justice, and him of whom it is written, 'The Word was God,' were not man, the Word which was God, and the truth, and wisdom, and justice did not die, for the Image of the invisible God, the Firstborn of all creation does not admit of death."

56. On this point, see also *ComMt* XV.10. See also Origen's discussion of the formal causation in *ComJn* I.104–5, where he elaborates on this analogy based on the language of "image."

57. Ibid., I.243–46.

58. Ibid., I.244.

59. Ibid., I.246.

60. Ibid., II.21–31.

61. Ibid., II.20.

62. Ibid., II.28–31.

63. This is a common charge made by Origen against the Epicureans and even the Aristotelians. See *CCels.* III.75.

64. *ComJn* II.32–33.

65. Ibid., VI.37–39.

66. Ibid., VI.38.

67. Ibid., VI.40.

68. Ibid., I.241–42.

69. Ibid., XX.239: "But I wonder whether to have stood in the truth is something single and simple, and not to have stood in it is something complex and manifold" (Ἀλλ' ἐφίστημι μήποτε ἓν μέν τι καὶ μονοειδές ἐστιν τὸ ἑστηκέναι ἐν τῇ ἀληθείᾳ, ποικίλον δέ τι καὶ πολύτροπον τὸ μὴ ἑστηκέναι ἐν αὐτῇ).

70. *ComJn* II.40.

71. Thus Origen already anticipates the idea that some aspect of Christ will come to an end in the eschaton. This idea was developed more fully by Marcellus of Ancyra in the fourth century. See Joseph T. Lienhard, *Contra Marcellum: Marcellus of Ancyra and Fourth-Century Theology* (Washington, DC: Catholic University of America Press, 1999), 64–66.

72. *ComJn* I.120–24.

73. Ibid., I.120

74. Ibid., I.121

75. Ibid., I.122

76. P. Tzamalikos argues that of all Christological titles, only "Wisdom" and "Word" are not subject to becoming. See P. Tzamalikos, *Origen: Cosmology and Ontology of Time* (Leiden: Brill, 2006), 37. Tzamalikos's position is based on a careful analysis of the sense in which Wisdom and Word were always (and thus did not become) in God. Tzamalikos's analysis is illuminating, but in my view, further analyses are needed to substantiate a further differentiation between Wisdom and Word from the rest of what I have called "absolute Sonship titles" (truth, justice, and power). It seems clear to me that Origen also considers these titles as free from "becoming."

77. *ComJn* I.123.

78. It seems clear that Origen's intuition is that while the absolute titles will remain, the soteriological titles assumed "for us" will not.

79. *ComJn* II.112–32.

80. Ibid., II.128: "If indeed 'life' and 'light of men' are the same—for the Scripture says, 'What was made in him was life, and the life was the light of men'—and the light of men is the light of some, and not of all spiritual beings, but is the light 'of men' insofar as the light 'of men' is specified, he would be also the life of those men of whom he is also the light. And, insofar as he is life, the Savior would be said to be life not for himself, but for those others of whom he is also the light."

81. *ComJn* II.129.

82. Ibid., VI.103–8

83. This diagram is an expansion of the one found in Orbe, *Hacia*, 1:443. Orbe's diagram focuses mainly on a strict comparison between the Father and the Son at the level of essence (οὐσία). I have added a third category of titles that will become important in my critical engagement with Orbe's view.

84. *ComJn* I.62, VI.105. The Father is the one who is immutable and unchangeable (*ComJn* VI.193).

85. Ibid., VI.193, 295.

86. Ibid., II.17–18.

87. Hence, Origen seems to accept that "the gods" refers to the heavenly bodies—the sun, moon, and stars, and so on. In *ComJn* II.25 Origen argues from Deut. 4:19–20 that when God "assigned to all the nations" the host of heavens as their gods, he did so on the one hand to indicate that the Israelites should worship the greater god, namely, "The God" himself. On the other hand, however, God assigned the heavenly bodies for the nations to worship because, according to Origen, this is still better than for them to worship idols made by the hands of men. Origen thought that the sense in which the heavenly bodies are "more divine" than idols made by men justifies the application of "god" to them as the third order in the hierarchy of divinity. On the heavenly bodies as "rational beings," see Alan Scott, *Origen and the Life of the Stars: A History of an Idea* (Oxford: Oxford University Press, 1991).

88. "God the Word is the minister of deity to all the other gods." *ComJn* II.19.

89. *ComJn* II.27.

90. Ibid., II.20–21.

91. John 17:3.

92. It is important to emphasize that figure 6.1 offers only a partial account of Origen's hierarchical understanding of divinity given that the Holy Spirit is missing. The Holy Spirit will fit into figure 6.1 as the third item on the list below the Son. Moreover, there should also be an additional line dividing the Father, the Son, and the Holy Spirit from the remaining items on the list. Properly speaking, in Origen's system the Holy Spirit is both divine and created. On the one hand, the Holy Spirit is perfectly divine as he eternally participates in the paternal source of divinity through the Son. On the other hand, the Holy Spirit belongs to "all things" that were created through the Logos (cf. John 1:3; *ComJn* II.72f.). It is therefore the Holy Spirit who sits at the boundary between God and creation. See Hermanin de Reichenfeld, *The Spirit, the World and the Trinity*, 59–71, 111–51.

93. Orbe, *Hacia*, 1:446.

94. *ComJn* I.119.

95. An ontological characterization of the Father-Son distinction is one that is grounded in the strict comparison between these characteristics of the Father's οὐσία and the characteristics of the Son's οὐσία.

96. *ComJn* I.52.

97. "And it is not extraordinary if, *as we have said before*, the Savior being many good things has conceived in himself things which are first and second and third" (*ComJn* I.112, italics mine). Here Origen is clearly referring to the discussion in *ComJn* I.51–62.

98. *ComJn* I.119.

99. On this point see *ComJn* I.246, 251 (on wisdom), *ComJn* II.22–23, 28–31, 33 (on Word), *ComJn* VI.38–39 (on truth).

100. *Philoc.* V.4. See my discussion in chapter 5.

101. See *CN* 3.2. This is also Tertullian's charge against the Monarchians throughout *Adversus Praxean Liber.*

102. My conclusion, then, resonates with the one made by Crouzel long ago, namely, that "he [Origen] seems to reduce the Logos-God to his role as mediator." Crouzel, *Théologie de l'image*, 127 (my translation).

103. In fact, in my view there are a number of further plausible conjectures we can make on the basis of the data we have examined in the schema above. First, Orbe's point can be construed not as an interpretation of how the Father's simplicity is contrasted with the Son's complexity in *ComJn* I.119, but as a reconstruction of the sense in which Origen holds that the Father and the Son are distinct κατ'οὐσίαν. This distinction is set out such that whereas the Father's οὐσία possesses only one kind of property, the Son's οὐσία possesses two kinds. Interpreted this way, Orbe's argument is quite plausible. Further, the same argument can be used to elaborate on the

content of what it means for "Fatherhood" to be a distinct ἰδίοτης from "Sonship." For the details of Orbe's reconstruction, see Orbe, *Hacia*, 1:440–48.

CHAPTER 7

1. Crouzel, *Théologie de l'image*, 83–98 focuses on image; Widdicombe, *The Fatherhood of God*, chap. 3, focuses on Fatherhood. The analysis that is most sensitive to the polemical contexts surrounding Origen's account is found in Orbe, *Hacia*, 1:431–52, and Orbe, *Hacia*, 2:674–92. In my opinion, though, Orbe's discussion is overly concerned with the connection between Origen and Arianism.

2. Ayres, *Nicaea and Its Legacy*, 20–30; Williams, *Arius*, 131–48; Hanson, *The Search for the Christian Doctrine of God*, 61–70.

3. Many have analyzed the polemical contexts of Origen's Wisdom Christology based on John 1:1–2 in *ComJn*. See Ronald E. Heine, *Origen: Scholarship in the Service of the Church* (Oxford: Oxford University Press, 2010), 89–103; Waers, "Wisdom Christology." Though as far as I know, we do not have a sustained analysis of *PArch* I.2 interpreted primarily in the light of Origen's third-century contexts. This is unfortunate because it is in this chapter of *PArch* that we find Origen's most detailed analysis of Wis. 7:25–26. My perspective has been anticipated by Alastair H. B. Logan in "Origen and Alexandrian Wisdom Christology," in *Origeniana Tertia*, ed. Richard Hanson and Henri Crouzel (Rome: Edizione dell'Ateneo, 1985), 123–29, where he writes: "The question then arises: was this all simply Origen's own theologizing on the basis of Sap [= Wis.] 7, 25–6 regarded by him as Scripture or as complementing the more acceptable scriptural text like He[b]. 1,3, developed to answer threats from Gnostics and Modalists?" (128). Logan's second option is the possibility explored in this chapter.

4. *PArch* I.2.6, IV.4.1.

5. I find persuasive Tzamalikos's argument concerning Rufinus's lack of understanding concerning Origen's use of temporal language with respect to the Son. See P. Tzamalikos, *Origen: Cosmology and Ontology of Time* (Leiden: Brill, 2006), 9–18. Further evidence of Rufinus's lack of reliability when it comes to the Son's generation is discussed in R. P. C. Hanson, "Did Origen Teach That the Son Is *ek tēs ousias* of the Father?," in *Origeniana Quarta*, ed. Lothar Lies (Innsbruck: Tyrolia, 1987), 201–2; and Rowan D. Williams, "Damnosa Haereditas: Pamphilus' Apology and the Reputation of Origen," in *Logos: Festschrift für Luise Abramowski zum 8. Juli 1993*, ed. Christoph Markschies, Hanns Christof Brennecke, and Ernst Ludwig Grasmück, 151–69 (Berlin: De Gruyter, 1993), at 164–66.

6. The dating of Origen's encounter with Roman Monarchianism locates it well within his Alexandrian period. See Waers, "Wisdom Christology," 96–98.

7. This is the conclusion reached by scholars such as Nautin and Heine after careful evaluation of the evidence. See Ronald E. Heine, trans., *Origen: Homilies on*

Genesis and Exodus (Washington, DC: Catholic University of America Press, 2002), 30–39.

8. Tzamalikos, *Origen*, 10–11.

9. In this sense, Tzamalikos suggests that one should treat the *PArch* as an "ancillary" source. Tzamalikos, 14.

10. *PArch* IV.4.1.

11. Ibid., I.2.6; *ComJn* XX.157–9.

12. Orbe, *Hacia*, 2:674–5.

13. Samuel Fernández, ed., *Orígenes: Sobre los principios* (Madrid: Editorial Ciudad Nueva, 2015), 185, n. 41; Cécile Blanc, ed., *Origène: Commentaire sur saint Jean* (Paris: Cerf, 1982), 233–34, n. 4.

14. *CRuf.* II.19 (emphasis added).

15. On the background of Jerome's anti-Origenist sentiments more generally, see Elizabeth A. Clark, *The Origenist Controversy: The Cultural Construction of an Early Christian Debate* (Princeton, NJ: Princeton University Press, 1992), 121–51.

16. *PArch* IV.4.1 (translation from Butterworth, emphasis added). The Greek text is given by Fr. 31 (Koetschau) *apud* Eusebius, *CM* I.4.

17. *PArch* I.2.6 (translation from Behr, slightly modified).

18. As Orbe has noted, it is necessary to distinguish between the Valentinians' actual account of *probolē* and the ones that were summarized and critiqued by the "eclesiasticos." This is because the heresiological accounts are often not accurate. See Orbe, *Hacia*, 2:677.

19. *PArch* I.2.6, IV.4.1.

20. Pierre Nautin, *Origène: Sa vie et son oeuvre* (Paris: Beauchesne, 1977), 170. Nautin believes that the dialogue with Candidus occurred before the composition of *PArch* due to the fact that *PArch* witnesses the topics discussed in the dialogue. This order of composition, of course, must be taken as conjectural and hence taken with caution. But the evidence suggests that it is perfectly plausible that the discussion in *PArch* on *probolē* is connected to Origen's dialogue with Candidus.

21. Ibid., 370–71.

22. Further evidence of this is available. The language of Origen's critique of materialistic generation in *PArch* also resembles the one in which Tertullian identified as "Valentinian." Tertullian actually identifies this view as belonging to Valentinus himself. Again, it is important to be cautious about the accuracy of the heresiological report. As many scholars have pointed out, the views of Valentinus and the Valentinians bear a complex relationship that goes far beyond the simple reality of the followers reciting the views of the founder of a school. See Thomassen, *The Spiritual Seed.* Nevertheless, according to Tertullian, the Valentinian view "secludes" (*discernit*) and "separates" (*separat*) the projections (προβολὰς) from their originator (*ab auctore*). See *AProx.* 8. The language in Tertullian's report agrees well with that of one found in Origen's *PArch* I.2.6 and IV.4.1.

23. *ComJn* XX.157–9.

24. This phrase is from Orbe, *Hacia*, 2:677.

25. *ComJn* XX.157.

26. Thus I share the view of Hanson in "Did Origen teach that the Son is *ek tēs ousias* of the Father?"

27. In drawing a parallel between Jerome's report and Origen's teaching in *ComJn*, I have made the assumption that the Latin *substantia* corresponds to the Greek *ousia*. It is worth noting that *substantia* could also be translated as hypostasis, as suggested by Pamphilus, *Apol.* 100, where we find the expression *ex substantia dei* in the context of discussing Origen's comment on Heb. 1:3, a passage in which we find hypostasis instead of *ousia* in the Greek. Tertullian, in *APrax*. 7, also uses *substantia* to refer to that which individuates a *person* of the Trinity. So there is a possibility that *substantia* in the discussion of the Son's generation in *PArch* can be translated as hypostasis instead of *ousia*. But given that Origen clearly rejects the phrase ἐκ τῆς οὐσίας in *ComJn* XX in the context of the Son's generation from the Father, and given that we do not find any instances in Origen's writings in which he rejects an analogous phrase involving hypostasis instead of *ousia* in the context of generation, in my view it is not unreasonable to make the assumption that *substantia* indeed translates *ousia* in the context of Origen's anti-Valentinian polemic.

28. That is, after 233–34, when Origen left Alexandria for Caesarea. For the dating of Origen's *ComJn* XIII–XXXII, see Ronald E. Heine, ed., *Origen: Commentary on the Gospel According to John, Books 13–32* (Washington, DC: Catholic University of America Press, 1993), 4–19.

29. Orbe argues that even though we do not possess any evidence that this is indeed a Valentinian interpretation of John 8:42b, given that Origen was engaging in a close critique of a Valentinian exegesis of John 8:42a in *ComJn* XX.135–51, it seems that "undoubtedly he speaks against the Valentinians." Orbe points to a further piece of evidence in Tertullian's *APrax*. 22, where he seems to allude to the Valentinian interpretation of John 8:42b: "'If God were your father you would have loved me, for I came forth and have come from God' (John 8:42b) (howbeit they [the Father and the Son] are not separated, though he said he was come forth, as some [Valentinians?] seize upon the chance that this saying gives them)." The phrase *et tamen non separantur* suggests that Tertullian indeed has the Valentinians in mind given that he has used similar terms to describe the Valentinian views in *APrax*. 8. I think Orbe's argument is convincing in the absence of further evidence. Orbe, *Hacia*, 2:677.

30. To be precise, in Origen's case it is the Father's simplicity that is in question.

31. See Heine, "The Christology of Callistus" and the references therein. Though it is necessary to point out that the account provided here, following Heine, might simply represent a polemical portrayal of Monarchian theology on the part of the "Logos-theologians" such as Origen and the author of the *Refutatio* (Pseudo-Hippolytus).

32. Ps. 44:2 (LXX). Heine illuminatingly suggests that this tradition is not restricted to the Monarchians because some "orthodox" Logos-theologians also utilize

Ps. 44:2 (LXX) in their accounts of the Son's generation. See Heine, "The Christology of Callistus," 64–65, for the references. In an illuminating essay Rowan Williams has written on how Origen was "misread" by both defenders and attackers in the fourth century. See Rowan D. Williams, "Christological Exegesis of Psalm 45," in *Meditations of the Heart: The Psalms in Early Christian Thought and Practice; Essays in Honour of Andrew Louth*, ed. A. Andreopoulos, Carol Harrison, and Augustine Casiday, 17–32 (Turnhout, Belgium: Brepols, 2011). Williams develops this point further in a recent essay, arguing that Origen intends to "correct" some of his orthodox predecessors' readings of the psalm in the discussion of the passage in *ComJn* I.280–88. See Rowan D. Williams, "On Not Misreading Origen," *Modern Theology*, "Re-thinking Origen" special issue, forthcoming 2022.

33. *ComJn* I.151.

34. Heine, "The Christology of Callistus," 64. According to Heine, this disagreement, in turn, is based upon two different philosophical frameworks on the Logos (Middle Platonic and Stoic). Heine convincingly shows that the Monarchians follow the Stoics by treating "Logos" as a category of speech, not ontology (66). The anti-Monarchians, following the Middle Platonists, treat "Logos" as the "second God," thus endowing it with independent existence (67).

35. *APrax*. 7. Tertullian himself also draws on Ps. 44:2 (LXX), but he does not consider the verse to imply what the Monarchians believe, that the Son was generated from the Father as an "uttered word."

36. *ComJn* I.280–88. For a detailed discussion, see Ronald E. Heine, "Origen on the Christological Significance of Psalm 45 (44)," *Consensus* 23, no. 1 (1997): 21–37 (especially 28–31). It is well known that the first two books of Origen's *ComJn* are largely structured by anti-Monarchian concerns. Origen's argument against the exegesis of Ps. 44 (LXX) forms part of this overall anti-Monarchian argument. See Heine, "Stoic Logic as Handmaid to Exegesis and Theology in Origen's Commentary on the Gospel of John," 92–100.

37. While I believe that Origen's thought in this section is modified by Rufinus to a point beyond repair, once again, I see no reason to think that these similarities are inauthentic.

38. See *ComJn* I.123, 153, 266. This point is convincingly argued in Waers, "Wisdom Christology." By "de-centering" Waers refers to the fact that in *ComJn* I Origen de-emphasizes "Logos" as the pre-eminent title of Christ, and stresses "Wisdom" instead as the supreme title of Christ.

39. *PArch* I.2.2: *Nemo tamen putet aliquid nos insubstantiuum dicere, cum eum dei sapientiam nominamus.*

40. Translation from Butterworth.

41. Here I do not wish to get into the scholarly debate on whether Origen made explicit use of the key term ὁμοούσιος for the following reasons. There is no doubt that "consubstantiality" invokes the crucial Greek term. According to Pier Franco Beatrice, in Gnostic literature the Greek term has three important senses:

"(1) identity of substance between generating and generated; (2) identity of substance between things generated of the same substance; (3) identity of substance between the partners of a syzygy." See Pier Franco Beatrice, "The Word 'Homoousios' from Hellenism to Christianity," 249. In chapter 3 we saw senses (1) and (2) in Irenaeus. Currently we find no scholarly consensus as to whether Origen used the term himself or in what sense he had a notion of consubstantiality. It is well known that Pamphilus's *Apology* preserves for us fragments of Origen's lost *Commentary on Hebrews*, which, according to Rufinus's Latin translation, made use of the term ὁμοούσιος. Few other texts exist to provide further evidence that Origen used the term in a Trinitarian context: (1) a fragment on the Psalms (see Lampe's *Patristic Lexicon* under ὁμοούσιος), (2) two recent fragments edited and translated by Tzamalikos (see Appendix II in P. Tzamalikos, *Anaxagoras, Origen and Neoplatonism: The Legacy of Anaxagoras to Classical and Late Antiquity*, 2 vols., Arbeiten zur Kirchengeschichte 128 (Berlin: Walter De Gruyter, 2016).) Scholars, however, are divided as to whether our sources provide solid evidence that (1) ὁμοούσιος was a part of Origen's Trinitarian terminology and (2) ὁμοούσιος was used in a way similar to its Nicene and post-Nicene usages. See the introduction.

For the purposes of my argument, what I shall demonstrate is that Origen had a notion of consubstantiality in the sense of *equality of nature* between generating and generated (e.g., Beatrice's first sense). In this precise sense, I suggest that there is a parallel in Origen's Trinitarian discussion of the generation of the Son to Irenaeus's discussion of generation in Book 2 of *Adversus haereses*. This parallel provides evidence for my overall claim in this chapter that divine simplicity serves as a principle of unity that shapes the "grammar" of generation, as seen first in Irenaeus's "proto-Trinitarian" discussion and also in a more explicitly Trinitarian discussion in Origen. Thus, in my view, and for the purpose of my argument, whether Origen used the Greek term ὁμοούσιος is not as important as the fact that he had a notion of consubstantiality as an equality of nature between generating and generated in his account of the Son's generation. This is because the claim that Origen had a notion of consubstantiality can be more securely established from the texts, as I shall demonstrate in this chapter, than the terminological claim that he made explicit use of the term ὁμοούσιος.

42. *Haer.* II.13.8.

43. The interpretation offered in what follows on the meaning of this phrase further develops the position first articulated by Orbe, *Hacia*, 1:398–407. Whereas Orbe sees Origen's account of the Son's generation *tanquam a mente voluntas* as attempting to find a via media between Valentinian emissions and Arianism *ante litteram* (according to which the Son is the product of the Father's will), I argue that the second target of Origen's account is better identified as Monarchians. For a detailed treatment of this identification, see Ip, "'Arianism' *Ante-Litteram* in Origen's *Peri Archōn* 4.4.1."

44. See the entry on θέλημα in Lampe, *Patristic Lexicon*, 620.

45. Arius taught that the Son came into being by the Father's will, thus treating the Son as the effect of the Father's will. See Williams, *Arius*, 101–2, lines 20–30.

46. Origen elaborates on this use of the διὰ in *ComJn* II.70–2 when he explains that John 1:3 ("All things were made through him") makes clear that the Word is an instrumental cause of "all things," standing in the second position to the Father, who is the primary and greater cause. Hence, "all things" are made by (ὑπὸ) the Father (cause in the first position), not by the Word, but through (διὰ) the Word (cause in the second position).

47. *ComEp*. Fr. 1, 10–11.

48. Ibid., Fr. 1, 12–18.

49. *ComJn* XIII.230 (emphasis added).

50. John 5:19–20.

51. *ComJn* XIII.234 (translation from FoC 89, slightly modified and emphasis added).

52. Thus Origen is not saying here that the Son's subsistence is guaranteed by the efficacy of the will of his Father. If this were the case, then we would have an "Arian" doctrine whereby the Son's subsistence is the result or effect of the Father's will, akin to how creatures were caused *ex nihilo* by the efficacy of the divine will. Rather, as Orbe has insightfully commented, Origen's point is that there is something in the simple nature of the divine mind that means that the very act of the Father's will in his mind acquires, in the specific case of the procession of the Son, a subsistent reality so real that humanly, speaking, it is normally possible only in the case of *probolē*. The point Origen wishes to highlight is not the efficacy of the divine will in ensuring the subsistence of the Son but rather the mysterious nature of the act of will (*voluntas*) in a simple being where it can acquire a distinct subsistence on its own that does not divide the mind. See Orbe, *Hacia*, 1:402–4.

53. *PArch* I.2.6 (translation from Behr, slightly modified).

54. As the next paragraph indicates, Origen is thinking of 1 Cor. 1:24, where Christ is said to be a power of God. This is why he turns to making the case that besides being "the breath of the power of God," the Son of God is a subsisting power of God in his own right—"a power proceeding from the power" (*PArch* I.2.9).

55. "El misterio está en que una «voluntas» en sí (humanamente) incapaz de subsistir, adquiera en la processión divina del Logos una subsistencia tan real (aunque de superior índole) como la que adquieren los animales en virtud de la prolatio. . . . En Dios tal misterio no puede extrañar, según Orígenes, por la índole singular de la procesión «tanquam a mente voluntas». Pues el Hijo no nace por simple efecto de la voluntad divina, sino que proviene como ejercicio volitivo (= «voluntas») de la Mente misma de Dios." Orbe, *Hacia*, 1:402 (my translation).

56. For an illuminating analysis of the mechanism of divine production, see Michel René Barnes, *The Power of God: Δύναμις in Gregory of Nyssa's Trinitarian Theology* (Washington, DC: Catholic University of America Press, 2001), 115–20.

57. *ComJn* XIII.228.

58. *CCels.* VIII.12 and *ComJn* XIII.228 highlight that Origen's account of the Son as identical to the Father's will is an *anti-Monarchian* move, as is clear from the fact that he utilizes the identity of wills to interpret the two key Monarchian texts, namely, John 10:30 and John 12:45.

59. I offer this as a hypothetical consideration that would be impossible, strictly speaking, if the Father were simple. This is because the simple Father could generate only that which is perfectly one in nature with himself, as we have seen in *Haer.* II.17.2. As a result, if God did indeed generate a Son who did not do the complete will of God, then the Son once again would have a separate existence from that of the Father. Consequently, the generation of such a Son would divide the Father and violate his simplicity. Given the commitment to the Father's simplicity, it would be quite impossible for Origen to imagine the Father generating a Son who would not do the complete will of the Father.

60. "Indeed, not only the Father comes first, but he is the only one who performs the acts of will in-himself and according-to-himself. So, while the Father acts in the Son and the Son needs the Father to be God, the Father does not need the Son to be God. But the Son is the only means through which the will of the Father is active in the world, for the perfection of the Father does not allow him to deal with the multiplicity. Therefore, the Son does not lack the attributes of the Father. The majesty of the Father towards the Son is to be found in the Father's will and power. As a matter of fact the Father acts in the Son, but the Son does not act in the Father; equally, while the will of the Father is the will of the God, the will of the Son is the will of the Father. The Son acts, wants and does what the Father acts, wants and does for necessity, for the Son's actions and will are completely derived from the Father." Hermanin de Reichenfeld, *The Spirit, the World and the Trinity*, 57. It is clear that de Reichenfeld and my foregoing analysis are largely in agreement up to the sentence "The Son acts, wants and does what the Father acts, wants and does for necessity." It seems to me, however, that despite Origen's wish to emphasize the utter dependence of the Son's will on the Father's will, by saying that the Son "by necessity" does the Father's will misses Origen's anti-Monarchian emphasis that the Son through the Father comes to be a free hypostasis willing the "complete will of the Father."

61. *Haer.* II.17.2.

62. Ibid., II.17.4.

63. In other words, pure goodness cannot give rise to evil, pure justice to injustice, etc.

64. See note 41 above.

65. The classic study that offers comprehensive coverage of this theme in Origen remains Crouzel, *Théologie de l'image*.

66. The link between language about image and will in Origen offers a key reason to suspect that the introduction of language about nature and substance in the Latin text came from Rufinus's editorial hand. It suggests that Rufinus might not have properly grasped that the purpose of Origen's use of language about will is

to avoid the Monarchian connotations associated with language about unity of substance (cf. *ComJn* X.246).

67. Ibid., XIII.228.

68. *PArch* I.2.12.

69. According to Irenaeus, what is simple must generate that which is "of one form, in every way equal and similar" to itself (*Haer.* II.17.2). Once again, in light of passages such as *ComJn* XIII.152–54, the language of *nulla omnino dissimilitudo* perhaps belongs to Rufinus and not to Origen. But Origen's point is not unrecoverable because, in the line before, Origen explains what he means by the unity between the Father and the Son: "there is one and same movement . . . in all they do." The unity at the level of act is clearly witnessed in Origen's Greek writings, as I have shown.

70. *PArch* I.2.8. This metaphor forms part of Jerome's case against the orthodoxy of Origen's teaching in *Epistle* 124.

71. *PArch* I.2.8. The Son as the accessible image of the Father who is inaccessible to creatures is a persistent theme from the rest of Origen's extant Greek writings. The crucial passage is *ComJn* XIX.34–39. According to Origen, "The Father is not seen otherwise than by seeing the Son . . . it is impossible, however, to behold God apart from the Word" (XIX.35). Similarly, "It is impossible, however, for the God of Wisdom to be apprehended apart from the leading of Wisdom" (XIX.36). In other words, Origen thinks the Father's greatness is such that creatures could approach him only *through* the image and mediator, the Son. We find other similar passages in *ComJn*: the Son is the way to the Father (VI.103–8); one is to come after him so that we might come to the Father (VI.191–2); it is through the Son that the Apostles came to see God (XIII.153).

72. *ComJn* VI.295, XIII.151–53; XIII. 234; *ComMt* XV.10.

73. *Haer.* II.17.4.

74. *PArch* I.2.7: Deus lex est secundum Iohannem. Splendor ergo huius lucis est unigenitus filius, ex ipso inseparabiliter velut splendor ex luce procedens et inluminans universam creaturam.

75. Ibid., I.2.4.

76. Tzamalikos, *Origen*, 10–2. For specific points at which Tzamalikos points out the issues in Rufinus's translation, see the entries on Rufinus in the index.

77. On this point, see also *ComJn* I.204. Origen thinks it is inappropriate to use the term "come to be" to describe the Son's being "in the beginning" (cf. wisdom) and his being *with* the Father (John 1:1). Rather, John uses the verb ἦν in his Gospel in order to indicate that "he [the Son-Logos] does not come to be 'in the beginning' from not being 'in the beginning,' nor does he pass from not being 'with God' to coming to be 'with God,' for before all time and eternity 'the Word was in the beginning,' and 'the Word was with God'" (*ComJn* II.9). This stands in contrast with "life" (John 1:4), "which comes into existence after the Word" (*ComJn* II.129). This is clarified by the fact that life "was made" in the Word (*ComJn* II.130–31).

Origen thinks that John 1:4 describes a logical ordering between "life" and "Word" that does not exist between "Word" and "in the beginning," as well as between "Word" and "with God."

78. In *PArch* I.2.7.

79. "All monarchians, i.e. modalists as well as adoptianists . . . have seen the 'Son' only in the historical Christ." Heine, "The Christology of Callistus," 71.

80. Heine, "The Christology of Callistus," 66–68.

81. We find this formula in *ComRm* I.5.1 and *PArch* IV.4.1. One of the biggest questions concerning Origen's theology remains whether he did in fact give theological weight to this expression, which clearly teaches the opposite of what was supposedly Arius's teaching. In my view, by treating "Arian-like" opponents of Origen as Monarchians, the conjecture set out here could potentially lead to a new resolution of this question (and whether there were indeed already any "Arians" *ante litteram* in the third century opposed by Origen, as postulated by Orbe, *Hacia*, 1:398–407). I have argued elsewhere that Origen's teaching on eternal generation can be situated in light of his anti-Monarchian and anti-psilanthropist polemics. See Ip, "'Arianism' *Ante-Litteram* in Origen's *Peri Archōn* 4.4.1," for an exploration of this line of inquiry.

EPILOGUE

1. Williams, "Newman's Arians," 283.

2. See Khaled Anatolios, *Retrieving Nicaea: The Development and Meaning of Trinitarian Doctrine* (Grand Rapids, M: Baker Academic, 2011), 1–13.

3. Ayres, *Nicaea and Its Legacy*, 274–78.

4. *Decr.* 23.

5. *CAr.* I.28: "It is not necessary to compare the generation of God with the nature of men, or to think that his Son is part of God, or that generation signifies any passion. . . . Having an unsettled nature, men beget passionately, waiting for the right time because of the weakness of their own nature. It is impossible to say this about God, for he is not composed of parts but is impassible and simple; he is without passion and indivisibly Father of the Son."

6. *Trin.* (Hilary), VIII.43: "Afterwards He [Christ] had said that 'as the Father had life in Himself, so He had given the Son to have life in Himself' (John 5:26), wherein He signified that by virtue of the mystery of the birth he possessed the unity of the same nature. For when He says that He has what the Father has, He means that He has the Father's self. For that God is not after human fashion of a composite being, so that in Him there is a difference of kind between Possessor and Possessed; but all that He is is life, a nature, that is, complete, absolute and infinite, not composed of dissimilar elements but with one life permeating the whole." See also ibid., IX.61.

7. Ibid., IX.72: "In God is no variability, no parts, as of a composite divinity, that in Him will should follow inaction, speech silence, or work rest, or that He should not will, without passing from some other mental state to volition, or speak, without breaking the silence with His voice, or act, without going forth to labour."

8. Basil, *Eun.* II.29; Gregory of Nyssa, *Eun.* II.359–86, 445–560.

9. Radde-Gallwitz, *Basil of Caesarea.* Radde-Gallwitz's reading, however, has been criticized by Richard Cross, "Divine Simplicity and the Doctrine of the Trinity: Gregory of Nyssa and Augustine," in *Philosophical Theology and the Christian Tradition: Russian and Western Perspectives*, ed. David Bradshaw, 53–65 (Washington, DC: Council for Research in Values and Philosophy, 2012). Radde-Gallwitz's earlier work needs to be read in light of the revision recently made by the author. See Radde-Gallwitz, "Gregory of Nyssa and Divine Simplicity."

10. *Civ. Dei* XI.10.

11. "God however is indeed called in multiple ways great, good, wise, blessed, true, and anything else that seems not to be unworthy of him; but his greatness is identical with his wisdom (he is not great in mass but in might), and his goodness is identical with his wisdom and greatness, and his truth is identical with them all; and with him being blessed is not one thing, and being great or wise or true or good, or just simply being, another." *Trin.* (Augustine), VI.8.

12. Ayres, *Nicaea and Its Legacy*, 278–301.

13. *Urk.* 1.3, 6.3.

14. Athanasius: *Decr.* 11, *CAr.* I.28, *Syn.* 52; Hilary: *Trin.* II.11, VIII.43, IX.61; Eusebius: *DE* IV.3, V.1, *ET* I.6.1–5, II.14.3–8; Gregory Thaumaturgus, *Phil.* 6–8.

15. The absolute primacy attributed to the Father is clear from the fragments of the *Thalia.* See especially S1–5, the contrast between Father and Son in S5–10, and the use of the term the "higher one" (*ho kreittōn*) in S25–30. For the fragments, see Williams, *Arius*, 101–3.

16. See especially the fragments of *Thalia*, S5–10, 25–30. Williams, *Arius*, 102–3.

17. Lionel R. Wickham, "The Syntagmation of Aetius the Anomean," *Journal of Theological Studies* 19, no. 2 (October 1, 1968): 532–69.

18. Eunomius, *Apol.* 7.

19. This puzzling phenomenon has been noted by Ayres and Radde-Gallwitz, but they do not provide an account of how these traditions developed and formed opposing theological trajectories. See Ayres and Radde-Gallwitz, "Doctrine of God," 874–75.

20. My approach in what follows is closely aligned with the project currently being undertaken by Samuel Fernández. Fernández wishes to re-narrate the fourth-century Trinitarian controversy (traditionally known as the "Arian" crisis) as a subsequent ("second-episode") development of the "Monarchian" crisis in the second and third centuries, thus offering an account of the historical development of patristic Trinitarian theology that bypasses the usual abrupt break in classical accounts

between the ante-Nicene and post-Nicene periods. For a glimpse of Fernández's approach, see Samuel Fernández, "¿Crisis arriana o crisis monarquiana en el siglo IV? Las críticas de Marcelo de Ancira a Asterio de Capadocia," in *Studia Patristica LXVI*, vol. 14: Clement of Alexandria/The Fourth-Century Debates (Leuven, Belgium: Peeters, 2013), 203–8. A more detailed account is found in Fernández's plenary lecture for the XVIII International Conference on Patristic Studies in Oxford, August 19–24, 2019, titled "Arian or Monarchian Crisis in the Fourth Century? Reevaluating the Evidence towards the Next Centenary of Nicaea (325–2025)."

21. See the heresiological catalogue found in *ComJn* 32.190–3 and the fragment of *ComTi* reported by Pamphilus in *Apol.* 33. For my detailed argument, see Ip, "'Arianism' *Ante-Litteram* in Origen's *Peri Archōn* 4.4.1."

22. In my view, the ambiguity concerning the kind of Father-Son distinction Origen proposes to counter Monarchianism (i.e., whether the alternative of all the key distinctions rejected by the Monarchians should be affirmed; see chapter 6 above), and with what terminologies such an anti-Monarchian distinction should be understood (i.e., whether anti-Monarchianism entails the affirmation of three *hypostaseis, idiotētes, ousiai, hypokeimena,* etc.), serves as one of the primary causes of confusion in post-Origenian theology. This is exemplified by the dispute between Dionysius of Rome and Dionysius of Alexandria. The two Dionysii could not agree on what constitutes a heretical understanding of Trinitarian distinctions. Dionysius of Alexandria thinks that the distinction καθ' ὑπόστασιν constitutes the only appropriate language to use to understand the Father-Son distinction vis-à-vis Monarchianism (more specifically, Sabellianism). See fr. 11 in Charles L. Feltoe, trans., *The Letters and Other Remains of Dionysius of Alexandria* (Cambridge: Cambridge University Press, 1904), 195–96. However, Dionysius of Rome believes that his Alexandrian namesake seems to imply tritheism (i.e., the affirmation of a distinction καθ' ὑπόστασιν between Father and Son is equivalent to affirming three gods). See the Roman bishop's letter in Feltoe, 176–82. For a detailed analysis of the controversy between the two Dionysii, see Simonetti, *Studi sulla cristologia del II e III secolo*, 273–97. In my view, Simonetti's account of post-Origenian theology remains the most convincing one available. See Manlio Simonetti, "The East after Origen," in *History of Theology*, vol. 1: *The Patristic Period*, ed. Angelo Di Berardino and Basil Studer OSB, trans. Matthew J. O'Connell, 192–204 (Collegeville, MN: Michael Glazier, 1996), for a brief summary in English.

23. For example, see Williams, *Arius*, 101–3, especially S1–4, 15–20, 25–30, and 40–41.

24. See Alexander of Alexandria in *Urk.* 4b.14 and Athanasius in *Syn.* 34–35.

25. One piece of evidence of this is found in Athanasius's discussion of the language of "image of God" in Col. 1:15 and Heb. 1:3. Athanasius makes no mention of the Origenian discussion of image as different from the source. A comparison of his *CAr.* II.33–34 and Origen's *PArch* I.2.6 and I.2.12–13 and his *ComMt* XV.10 will reveal this contrast clearly. I have further highlighted the discontinuity between

Athanasius and Origen in Pui-Him Ip, "Origen against Origen? The Paradoxical Legacy of Origen in Athanasius' Exegesis of Prov. 8:22 in Contra Arianos II," in *Perspectives on Origen in the History of His Reception*, ed. Alfons Fürst, Adamantiana 21 (Muenster: Aschendorff, 2021), 117–32.

26. This point perhaps helps explain why Arius felt the need to clarify that his theology does not lead to this position. See *Urk.* 1.3, 6.3.

27. Arius: *Urk.* 1, 6; Athanasius: *Decr.* 11, *CAr.* I.28, *Syn.* 52; Eusebius: *DE* IV.3, V.1, *ET* I.6.1–5, II.14.3–8; Hilary of Poitiers: *De Trin.* V.31, VII.11.

28. I put the terms "Arian" and "Eusebian" in quotation marks because I recognize that these terms are to some extent caricatures or imaginary realities created through, primarily, Athanasius's polemics. On this see David M. Gwynn, *The Eusebians: The Polemic of Athanasius of Alexandria and the Construction of the 'Arian Controversy'* (Oxford: Oxford University Press, 2007). On "Eusebian" theology more generally, see Mark DelCogliano, "Eusebian Theologies of the Son as the Image of God before 341," *Journal of Early Christian Studies* 14, no. 4 (2006): 459–84.

29. In *Eun.* (Basil), I.7 Basil seems to contradict Origen's discussion in *ComJn* 1.119: "Though our Lord is one in substance, and one substance, simple and not composite, he calls himself by different names at different times, using designations that differ from one another for the different conceptualizations." Origen instead (as we have seen in chapter 6) thinks that the different names (*epinoiai*) make the Son multiple and not simple, thus differentiating him from the Father. Basil affirms the simplicity of the Son also in *Eun.* I.23. Moreover, what is simple for Basil is the divine substance/nature (*Eun.* II.29, 32). Similarly, for Augustine it is the nature of the Trinity that is simple. See *Civ. Dei* XI.10.

30. The importance of this point for Origen has been masterfully set out in Hermanin de Reichenfeld, *The Spirit, the World and the Trinity*, 39–59. De Reichenfeld calls this distinction an "ontological subordination of priority" to differentiate it from the distinction between God and creation based on an "ontological subordination of superiority." See also John Behr, "'One God Father Almighty,'" *Modern Theology* 34, no. 3 (July 1, 2018): 320–30.

31. Anatolios, *Retrieving Nicaea*, 104.

32. John Henry Newman, *An Essay on the Development of Christian Doctrine*, 6th ed. (Notre Dame, IN: University of Notre Dame Press, 1989).

33. This evolution has been ably documented by Benjamin J. King, *Newman and the Alexandrian Fathers: Shaping Doctrine in Nineteenth-Century England* (Oxford: Oxford University Press, 2009), 181–217.

BIBLIOGRAPHY

PRIMARY SOURCES

For each work, I have provided the abbreviation used throughout the book (followed by the author's name in parentheses in cases in which more than one work has the same title), as well as the edition(s) and translation(s) used or consulted (if any), in the following order: (1) primary edition of the work in the original language consulted and cited, (2) primary edition of the English translation consulted and cited (if available), and (3) other editions consulted or quoted.

Collections of Multiple Authors

Long, A. A., and D. N. Sedley. *The Hellenistic Philosophers.* Vol. 1: *Translations of the Principal Sources with Philosophical Commentary.* Cambridge: Cambridge University Press, 1987.

Urk. — *Urkunden* (documents of the "Arian controversies")

Opitz, Hans-Georg. *Athanasius Werke* III/1: *Urkunden zur Geschichte des arianischen Streites,* 318–28. *Lieferung* 1–2. Berlin: Walter de Gruyter, 1934–35.

Alcinous

Did. — *Didaskalikos* (*The Handbook of Platonism*)

Whittaker, John. *Alcinoos, Enseignement des Doctrines de Platon.* Paris: Les Belles Lettres, 1990.

Dillon, John. *Alcinous: The Handbook of Platonism.* Oxford: Clarendon, 1993.

Aristotle

Met. — *Metaphysica* (*Metaphysics*)

Ross, W. D. *Aristotle's Metaphysics: A Revised Text with Introduction and Commentary.* Oxford: Clarendon, 1924.

Barnes, Jonathan. *The Complete Works of Aristotle.* Vol. 2, 1552–1728. Princeton, NJ: Princeton University Press, 1984.

Phys. — *Physica* (*Physics*)

Ross, W. D. *Aristotle's Physics: A Revised Text with Introduction and Commentary.* Oxford: Clarendon, 1936.

Barnes, Jonathan. *The Complete Works of Aristotle.* Vol. 1, 315–446. Princeton, NJ: Princeton University Press, 1984.

Athanasius of Alexandria

CAr. — *Orationes contra Arianos* (*Orations against the Arians*)

Metzler, Karin, and Kyriakos Savvidis. *Athanasius Werke* I/1: *Die dogmatischen Schriften*, 109–381. *Lieferung* 1–2. Berlin: Walter de Gruyter, 1998–2000.

Anatolios, Khaled. *Athanasius*, 71–141. London: Routledge, 2004.

Rusch, William G. *The Trinitarian Controversy*, 63–130. Philadelphia: Fortress, 1980.

Decr. — *De decretis Nicaenae synodi* (*On the Decrees of Nicaea*)

Opitz, Hans-Georg. *Athanasius Werke* II/1: *Die Apologien*, 1–45. Berlin: Walter de Gruyter, 1940.

Anatolios, Khaled. *Athanasius*, 142–71. London: Routledge, 2004.

Syn. — *De synodis* (*On the Councils of Ariminium and Seleucia*)

Opitz, Hans-Georg. *Athanasius Werke* II/1: *Die Apologien*, 231–78. Berlin: Walter de Gruyter, 1940.

Augustine of Hippo

Civ. Dei — *De civitate dei* (*The City of God*)

Dombart, B., and A. Kalb. *Augustinus: De civitate dei.* Libri XI–XXII. CCSL 48. Turnhout, Belgium: Brepols, 1955.

Trin. (Augustine) — *De Trinitate* (*On the Trinity*)

Mountain, W. J. and F. Glorie. *Augustinus: De Trinitate libri XV.* Libri I–XII. CCSL 50. Turnhout, Belgium: Brepols, 1968.

Hill, Edmund. *Saint Augustine: The Trinity.* New York: New City Press, 1991.

Basil of Caesarea

Eun. (Basil) — *Contra Eunomium* (*Against Eunomius*)

Sesboüé, Bernard, Georges-Matthieu de Durand, and Louis Doutreleau. *Basile de Césarée, Contre Eunome suivi de Eunome Apologie.* SC 299 and 305. Paris: Cerf, 1982–83.

DelCogliano, Mark, and Andrew Radde-Gallwitz. *Basil of Caesarea: Against Eunomius*. FoC 122. Washington DC: Catholic University of America Press, 2011.

Clement of Alexandria

Str. *Stromata* (*Miscellaneous*)

Stählin, Otto. *Clemens Alexandrinus* II: *Stromata* I–VI. GCS 15. Leipzig: Hinrichs, 1906.

Roberts, Alexander, and James Donaldson. *Ante-Nicene Fathers*. Vol. II: *Fathers of the Second Century*. Grand Rapids, MI: Eerdmans, 1986.

Dionysius of Alexandria

Feltoe, Charles Lett. *The Letters and Other Remains of Dionysius of Alexandria*. Cambridge: Cambridge University Press, 1904.

Epiphanius of Salamis

Pan. *Panarion*

Holl, Karl (rev. ed. Dummer, Jürgen). *Epiphanius II: Panarion haer.*, 34–64. GCS 31². Berlin: Akademie, 1980.

Williams, Frank. *The Panarion of Epiphanius of Salamis*. Books II and III: *De Fide*. Nag Hammadi and Manichaean Studies 79. Leiden: Brill, 2013.

Eunomius of Cyzicus

Apol. (Eunomius) *Apologia* (*Apology*)

Vaggione, Richard Paul. *Eunomius: The Extant Works*. Oxford Early Christian Texts. Oxford: Clarendon, 1987.

Eusebius of Caesarea

CM *Contra Marcellum* (*Against Marcellus*)

Klostermann, Erich, and Günther Christian Hansen. *Eusebius Werke IV: Gegen Marcell. Über die kirchliche Theologie: Die Fragmente Marcells* 3, 1–58. GCS 14. Berlin: Akademie, 1991.

Spoerl, Kelley McCarthy, and Markus Vinzent. *Eusebius of Caesarea: Against Marcellus and On Ecclesiastical Theology*. FoC 135. Washington, DC: Catholic University of America Press, 2017.

DE *Demonstratio evangelica* (*Demonstration of the Gospel*)

Heikel, Ivar A. *Eusebius Werke VI: Die Demonstratio evangelica*. GCS 23. Leipzig: J. C. Hinrichs, 1913.

Ferrar, W. J. *Eusebius: The Proof of the Gospel*. London: S.P.C.K., 1920.

ET — *De ecclesiastica theologia* (*Ecclesiastical Theology*)

Klostermann, Erich, and Günther Christian Hansen. *Eusebius Werke IV: Gegen Marcell. Über die kirchliche Theologie: Die Fragmente Marcells* 3, 59–182. GCS 14. Berlin: Akademie, 1991.

Spoerl, Kelley McCarthy, and Vinzent, Markus. *Eusebius of Caesarea: Against Marcellus and On Ecclesiastical Theology*. FoC 135. Washington, DC: Catholic University of America Press, 2017.

HE — *Historia ecclesiastica* (*Ecclesiastical History*)

Schwartz, Eduard. *Eusebius Werke II. Die Kirchengeschichte*. GCS 9/1–3. Berlin: J. C. Hinrichs, 1903–1909.

Deferrari, Roy J. *Eusebius Pamphili: Ecclesiastical History*, Books 6–10. FoC 29. Washington DC: Catholic University of America Press, 1955.

Gregory of Nyssa

Eun. (Gregory) — *Contra Eunomium II* (*Against Eunomius II*)

Karfíková, Lenka, Scot Douglass, and Johannes Zachhuber. *Gregory of Nyssa: Contra Eunomium II ; An English Version with Supporting Studies*. Proceedings of the Tenth International Colloquium on Gregory of Nyssa (Olomouc, Czech Republis, September 15–18, 2004). Supplements to *Vigiliae Christianae*, vol. 82, 59–201. Leiden: Brill, 2007.

Gregory Thaumaturgus

Paner. — *The Panergyric to Origen*

Crouzel, Henri. *Remerciement a Origène suivi de la lettre d'Origène a Grègoire*. SC 148. Paris: Cerf, 1969.

Phil. — *Epistola ad Philagrium* (*To Philagrius*)

PG 46: 1101–7.

Slusser, Michael. *St. Gregory Thaumaturgus: Life and Works*. FoC 98. Washington, DC: Catholic University of America Press, 1998.

Hilary of Poitiers

Trin. (Hilary) — *De Trinitate* (*On the Trinity*)

Doignon, J., G. M. de Durand, C. Morel, and G. Pelland. *Hilaire de Poitiers: La Trinité*. 3 vols. SC 443, 448, and 462. Paris: Cerf, 1999–2001.

Schaff, Philip, and Henry Wace. *Nicene and Post-Nicene*. Second series. Vol. 9: *Hilary of Poitiers: On the Trinity, on the Synods, John of Damascus: Exposition of the Orthodox Faith*. Edinburgh: Hendrickson, 1995.

Hippolytus

CN — *Contra Noetum* (*Against Noetus*)

Butterworth, Robert. *Hippolytus of Rome: Contra Noetum*. Heythrop Monographs 2. London: Heythrop College, 1977.

(Pseudo-) Hippolytus

Ref. — *Refutatio omnium haeresium* (*Against All Heresies*)

Wendland, Paul. *Hippolytus Refutatio omnium haeresium*. GCS 26. Leipzig: J. C. Hinrichs, 1916.

Legge, F. *Philosophumena; or, the Refutation of All Heresies*. Vol. II. London: S.P.C.K., 1921.

Irenaeus of Lyons

Haer. — *Adversus haereses* (*Against Heresies*)

Rousseau, Adelin, and Louis Doutreleau. *Irénée de Lyon: Contre les hérésies*. Livres I and II. SC 264 and 294. Paris: Cerf, 1979 and 1982.

Unger, Dominic J. *St. Irenaeus of Lyons: Against the Heresies*. Book 1. ACW 55. New York: Paulist Press, 1992.

Unger, Dominic J., and John Dillon. *St. Irenaeus of Lyons: Against the Heresies*. Book 2. ACW 65. New York: Paulist Press, 2012.

Jerome

CRuf. — *Contra Rufinum* (*Against Rufinus*)

Lardet, Pierre. *Saint Jérôme: Apologie contre Rufin*. SC 303. Paris: Cerf, 1983.

Fremantle, W. H. *Theodoret, Jerome, Gennadius, & Rufinus: Historical Writings*. Nicene and Post-Nicene Fathers, second series. Vol. 3. Edited by Philip Schaff and Henry Wace. Buffalo, NY: Christian Literature Publishing, 1892.

Justin Martyr

Dial. — *Dialogus cum Tryphone* (*Dialogue with Trypho*)

Marcovich, Miroslav. *Iustini Martyris Apologiae pro Christianis, Iustini Martyris Dialogus cum Tryphone*. Patristische Texte und Studien 38/47. Berlin: Walter de Gruyter, 2011.

Falls, Thomas B., and Thomas P. Halton. *St. Justin Martyr: Dialogue with Trypho*. FoC 3. Washington DC: Catholic University of America, 2003.

Novatian of Rome

Trin. (Novatian) *De Trinitate* (*On the Trinity*)

Diercks, G. F. *Novatiani Opera*. CCSL 4. Turnhout: Brepols, 1972.

Papandrea, James Leonard. *The Trinitarian Theology of Novatian of Rome: A Study in Third-Century Orthodoxy*. Lewiston, NY: Edwin Mellen, 2008.

Numenius of Apamea

des Places, Édouard. *Numénius: Fragments*. Paris: Les Belles Lettres, 1973.

Petty, Robert. *Fragments of Numenius of Apamea*. Platonic Texts and Translations 7. Westbury, UK: Prometheus Trust, 2012.

Origen of Alexandria

CCels. *Contra Celsum* (*Against Celsus*)

Borret, Marcel. *Origène: Contre Celse*. SC 132, 136, 147, and 150. Paris: Cerf, 1967–1969.

Chadwick, Henry. *Origen: Contra Celsum*. Cambridge: Cambridge University Press, 1953.

ComEp *Commentarii in Ephesios* (*Commentaries on Ephesians*)

Gregg, J. "The Commentary of Origen upon the Epistle to the Ephesians." *Journal of Theological Studies*, o.s. 3 (1901): 233–44, 398–420, and 554–76.

Heine, Ronald E. *The Commentaries of Origen and Jerome on St Paul's Epistle to the Ephesians*. Oxford: Oxford University Press, 2002.

ComJn *Commetarii in Iohannem* (*Commentaries on John*)

Blanc, Cécile. *Origène: Commentaire sur saint Jean*. SC 120, 157, 222, 290, and 385. Paris: Cerf, 1966–92.

Heine, Ronald E. *Origen: Commentary on the Gospel according to John, Books 1–10*. FoC 80. Washington, DC: Catholic University of America Press, 1989.

———. *Origen: Commentary on the Gospel according to John, Books 13–32*. FoC 89. Washington, DC: Catholic University of America Press, 1993.

ComMt — *Commentarii in Matthaeum* (*Commentaries on Matthew*)

Benz, Ernst, and Erich Klostermann. *Origenes Werke X: Origenes Matthäuserklärung I; Die griechisch erhaltenen Tomoi.* GCS 40. Leipzig: Teubner, 1935.

Heine, Ronald E. *The Commentaries of Origen on the Gospel of Matthew.* 2 vols. Oxford: Oxford University Press, 2018.

ComRm — *Commentarii in Epistulam ad Romanos* (*Commentaries on the Epistle of Romans*)

Hammond Bammel, C. P. *Der Römerbriefkommentar des Origenes Kritische Ausgabe der Übersetyung Rufins.* Buch 7–10. Freiburg im Breisgau: Herder, 1998.

Scheck, Thomas P. *Origen: Commentary on the Epistle to the Romans, Books 6–10.* FoC 104. Washington, DC: Catholic University of America Press, 2002.

ComTt — *Commentarius in Titum* (*Commentary on the Epistle of Titus*; see Pamphilus)

DialHe — *Dialogue with Heraclides*

Scherer, J. *Entretien d'Origene avec Heraclide.* SC 67. Paris: Cerf, 1960.

Chadwick, Henry, and J.E.L. Oulton. *Alexandrian Christianity,* 437–55. Philadelphia: Westminster John Knox Press, 1977.

Hom1S — *Homilia in I. Sam.* (*Homily on 1 Samuel*)

Nautin, Pierre, and Marie-Thérèse Nautin. *Homélies sur Samuel.* SC 328. Paris: Cerf, 1986.

Fürst, Alfons. *Die Homilien zum Ersten Buch Samuel. Origenes Werke* Band 7. Berlin: Walter de Gruyter, 2014.

HomEz — *Homiliae in Ezechielem* (*Homilies on Ezekiel*)

Borret, Marcel. *Homélies sur Ezéchiel.* SC 352. Paris: Cerf, 1989.

Scheck, Thomas P. *Origen: Homilies 1–14 on Ezekiel.* ACW 62. New York: Paulist Press, 2010.

HomJe — *Homiliae in Ieremiam* (*Homilies on Jeremiah*)

Klostermann, E. *Origenes Werke: Jeremiahomilien Klageliederkommentar Erklärung der Samuel- und Königsbücher.* GCS 6. Leipzig: Hinrichs, 1901.

Smith, John Clark. *Origen: Homilies on Jeremiah; Homilies on 1 Kings 28.* FoC 97. Washington, DC: Catholic University of America Press, 1998.

HomLv — *Homiliae in Leviticum* (*Homilies on Leviticus*)

Borret, Marcel. *Homélies sur Levétique.* SC 286 and 287. Paris: Cerf, 1981.

Barkley, Gary Wayne. *Origen: Homilies on Leviticus, 1–16.* FoC 83. Washington, DC: Catholic University of America Press, 2005.

PArch — *Peri Archōn* (*On First Principles*)

Main edition used:

Behr, John. *Origen: On First Principles.* 2 vols. Oxford Early Christian Texts. Oxford: Oxford University Press, 2017.

Fernández, Samuel. *Orígenes: Sobre Los Principios.* Madrid: Editorial Ciudad Nueva, 2015.

Consulted:

Crouzel, Henri, and Manlio Simonetti. *Traité des principes.* SC 252, 253, 268, and 269. Paris: Cerf, 1978–1980.

Görgemanns, Herwig, and Heinrich Karpp. *Origenes vier Bücher von den Prinzipien.* Texte zur Forschung 24. Darmstadt: Wissenschaftliche Buchgesellschaft, 1976.

Koetschau, Paul. *Origenes Werk V: De principiis.* GCS 22. Leipzig: J. C. Hinrichs, 1913.

Butterworth, G. W. *Origen: On First Principles.* Gloucester, UK: Peter Smith, 1973.

PEuch — *Peri Euchēs* (*On Prayer*)

Koetschau, Paul. *Origenes Werke II: Buch V–VIII gegen Celsus; Die Schrift vom Gebet.* GCS 3. Leipzig: J. C. Hinrichs, 1899: 297–403.

Chadwick, Henry, and J. E. L. Oulton. *Alexandrian Christianity,* 238–329. Philadelphia: Westminster John Knox Press, 1977.

Philoc. — *Philocalia*

Harl, Marguerite. *Philocalie 1–20; Sur les Ecritures.* SC 302. Paris: Cerf, 1983.

Lewis, George. *The Philocalia of Origen.* Edinburgh: T&T Clark, 1911.

SelGn — *Selecta in Genesim* (*Fragments on Genesis*)

PG 12: 92–145.

Pamphilus

Apol. (Pamphilus) — *Apologia pro Origene* (*Apology for Origen*)

Amacker, René, and Éric Junod. *Pamphile et Eusèbe de Césarée: Apologie pour Origène; suivi, de Rufin d'Aquilée sur la falsification des livres d'Origène.* SC 464–65. Paris: Cerf, 2002.

Scheck, Thomas P. *St. Pamphilus: Apology for Origen; Rufinus: On the Falsification of the Books of Origen.* FoC 120. Washington, DC: Catholic University of America Press, 2010.

Philo of Alexandria

Deus — *Quod Deus sit Immutabilis* (*On the Unchangeability of God*)

Colson, F. H., and G. H. Whitaker. *Philo.* Vol. III. LCL 247. Cambridge, MA: Harvard University Press, 1930.

Yonge, C. D. *The Works of Philo: Complete and Unabridged.* Edinburgh: Hendrickson, 1993.

Gig. — *De Gigantibus* (*On the Giants*)

Colson, F. H., and G. H. Whitaker. *Philo.* Vol. II. LCL 227. Cambridge, MA: Harvard University Press, 1929.

Leg. All. — *Legum Allegoriae* (*Allegories of the Laws*)

Colson, F. H., and G. H. Whitaker. *Philo.* Vol. I. LCL 226. Cambridge, MA: Harvard University Press, 1929.

Yonge, C. D. *The Works of Philo: Complete and Unabridged.* Edinburgh: Hendrickson, 1993,

Somn. — *De Somniis* (*On Dreams*)

Colson, F. H., and G. H. Whitaker. *Philo.* Vol. V. LCL 275. Cambridge, MA: Harvard University Press, 1934.

Plato

Parm. — *Parmenides*

Fowler, Harold North. *Plato: Cratylus. Parmenides. Greater Hippias. Lesser Hippias.* LCL 167. Cambridge, MA: Harvard University Press, 1926.

Phae. — *Phaedo*

Fowler, Harold North. *Plato: Euthyphro. Apology. Crito. Phaedo. Phaedrus.* LCL 36. Cambridge, MA: Harvard University Press, 1914.

Cooper, John M. and D. S. Hutchinson. *Plato: Complete Works,* 50–100. Indianapolis: Hackett, 1997.

Rep. — *Republic*

Emlyn-Jones, Christopher, and William Preddy. *Plato: Republic.* Vol. 1, Books 1–45. LCL 237. Cambridge, MA: Harvard University Press, 2013.

Cooper, John M., and D. S. Hutchinson. *Plato: Complete Works,* 972–1223. Indianapolis: Hackett, 1997.

Adam, James, ed. *The Republic of Plato, Edited with Critical Notes, Commentary and Appendices.* Vol. 1. Cambridge: Cambridge University Press, 1902.

Tim. — *Timaeus*

Bury, R. G. *Plato: Timaeus. Critias. Cleitophon. Menexenus. Epistles.* LCL 234. Cambridge, MA: Harvard University Press, 1929.

Cooper, John M., and D. S. Hutchinson. *Plato: Complete Works*, 1224–91. Indianapolis: Hackett, 1997.

Tatian

Orat. *Oratio ad Graecos* (*Oration against the Greeks*)
Whittaker, Molly. *Tatian: Oratio ad Graecos and Fragments*. Oxford: Oxford University Press, 1982.

Tertullian

APrax. *Adversus Praxean Liber* (*Against Praxeas*)
Evans, Ernest. *Tertullian's Treatise against Praxeas*. London: S.P.C.K, 1948.

SECONDARY SOURCES

Adam, James, ed. *The Republic of Plato*, edited with critical notes, commentary and appendices. Vol. 1. Cambridge: Cambridge University Press, 1902.

Amstutz, Joseph. *ΑΠΛΟΤΗΣ: Eine Begriffsgeschichtliche Studie zum jüdisch-christlichen Griechisch*. Bonn: Peter Hanstein, 1968.

Anatolios, Khaled. *Retrieving Nicaea: The Development and Meaning of Trinitarian Doctrine*. Grand Rapids, MI: Baker Academic, 2011.

Ayres, Lewis. "Irenaeus vs. the Valentinians: Toward a Rethinking of Patristic Exegetical Origins." *Journal of Early Christian Studies* 25, no. 2 (Summer 2015): 153–87.

———. *Nicaea and Its Legacy: An Approach to Fourth-Century Trinitarian Theology*. Oxford: Oxford University Press, 2006.

Ayres, Lewis, and Andrew Radde-Gallwitz. "Doctrine of God." In *The Oxford Handbook of Early Christian Studies*, edited by Susan Ashbrook Harvey and David G. Hunter, 864–85. Oxford: Oxford University Press, 2010.

Bardy, Gustave. "Monarchianisme." In *Dictionnaire de Théologie Catholique*, edited by Alfred Vacant, E. Mangenot, and Emile Amann, 10: 2193–2209. Paris: Letouzey et Ané, 1929.

Barnes, Michel René. "Irenaeus's Trinitarian Theology." *Nova et Vetera* 7 (2009): 67–106.

———. *The Power of God: Δύναμις in Gregory of Nyssa's Trinitarian Theology*. Washington, DC: Catholic University of America Press, 2001.

———. "'Shining in the Light of Your Glory': Finding the Simple Reading of Scripture." *Modern Theology* 35, no. 3 (2019): 418–27.

Barrett, Jordan P. *Divine Simplicity: A Biblical and Trinitarian Account*. Minneapolis: Fortress, 2017.

Barth, Karl. *Church Dogmatics*. Translated by G. W. Bromiley and Thomas F. Torrance. Vol. 2, part 1. Edinburgh: T&T Clark, 1957.

Bates, Matthew W. *The Birth of the Trinity*. Oxford: Oxford University Press, 2016.

Beatrice, Pier Franco. "The Word 'Homoousios' from Hellenism to Christianity." *Church History* 71, no. 2 (June 2002): 243–72.

Behr, John. "'One God Father Almighty.'" *Modern Theology* 34, no. 3 (July 1, 2018): 320–30.

———. "Synchronic and Diachronic Harmony: St. Irenaeus on Divine Simplicity." *Modern Theology* 35, no. 3 (2019): 428–41.

Benitez, Rick. "Plato and the Secularisation of Greek Theology." In *Theologies of Ancient Greek Religion*, edited by Esther Eidinow, Julia Kindt, and Robin Osborne, 301–16. Cambridge: Cambridge University Press, 2016.

Berchman, Robert M. *From Philo to Origen: Middle Platonism in Transition*. Brown Judaic Studies 69. Chico, CA: Scholars Press, 1984.

Blanc, Cécile, ed. *Origène: Commentaire sur saint Jean*. Paris: Cerf, 1982.

Boys-Stones, George R. *Platonist Philosophy 80 BC to AD 250: An Introduction and Collection of Sources in Translation*. Cambridge: Cambridge University Press, 2018.

Braun, René. *Deus Christianorum: Recherches sur le vocabulaire doctrinal de Tertullien*. 2nd ed. Paris: Études augustiniennes, 1977.

Brent, Allen. Review of *Der Paradoxe Eine: Antignostischer Monarchianismus im Zweiten Jahrhundert*, by Reinhard M. Hübner (with Markus Vinzent). *Journal of Ecclesiastical History* 53, no. 1 (2002): 114–17.

Briggman, Anthony. *God and Christ in Irenaeus*. Oxford: Oxford University Press, 2018.

Bruns, Christoph. *Trinität und Kosmos: Zur Gotteslehre des Origenes*. Münster: Aschendorff, 2013.

Calabi, Francesca. *God's Acting, Man's Acting: Tradition and Philosophy in Philo of Alexandria*. Leiden: Brill, 2008.

Chadwick, Henry, and J.E.L. Oulton, eds. *Alexandrian Christianity*. Philadelphia: Westminster John Knox Press, 2006.

Clark, Elizabeth A. *The Origenist Controversy: The Cultural Construction of an Early Christian Debate*. Princeton, NJ: Princeton University Press, 1992.

Cross, Richard. "Divine Simplicity and the Doctrine of the Trinity: Gregory of Nyssa and Augustine." In *Philosophical Theology and the Christian Tradition: Russian and Western Perspectives*, edited by David Bradshaw, 53–65. Washington, DC: Council for Research in Values and Philosophy, 2012.

Crouzel, Henri. *Théologie de l'image de Dieu chez Origène*. Paris: Aubier, 1956.

DelCogliano, Mark. *Basil of Caesarea's Anti-Eunomian Theory of Names: Christian Theology and Late-Antique Philosophy in the Fourth Century Trinitarian Controversy*. Leiden: Brill, 2010.

———. "Eusebian Theologies of the Son as the Image of God before 341." *Journal of Early Christian Studies* 14, no. 4 (2006): 459–84.

———. "The Interpretation of John 10:30 in the Third Century: Anti-Monarchian Polemics and the Rise of Grammatical Reading Techniques." *Journal of Theological Interpretation* 6 (2012): 117–38.

Dillon, John M., trans. *Alcinous: The Handbook of Platonism*. Oxford: Clarendon, 1993.

Dolezal, James E. *God without Parts: Divine Simplicity and the Metaphysics of God's Absoluteness*. Eugene, OR: Pickwick, 2011.

———. "Trinity, Simplicity and the Status of God's Personal Relations." *International Journal of Systematic Theology* 16, no. 1 (January 1, 2014): 79–98.

Dorner, Isaak A. *A System of Christian Doctrine*. Translated by Alfred Cave and John S. Banks. Vol. 1. Edinburgh: T&T Clark, 1883.

Dörrie, Heinrich, Matthias Baltes, Friedhelm Mann, Christian Pietsch, and Marie-Luise Lakmann. *Der Platonismus in der Antike: Grundlagen, System, Entwicklung; Die philosophische Lehre des Platonismus: Theologia Platonica. Bausteine 182–205: Text, Übersetzung, Kommentar*. Vol. 7.1. Stuttgart–Bad Cannstatt: Frommann-Holzboog, 2008.

Duby, Steven J. *Divine Simplicity: A Dogmatic Account*. London: Bloomsbury, 2015.

Edwards, Mark J. "Did Origen Apply the Word *Homoousios* to the Son?" *Journal of Theological Studies* 49, no. 2 (October 1, 1998): 658–70.

———. *Origen against Plato*. Routledge, 2017.

———. Review of *Der Paradoxe Eine: Antignostischer Monarchianismus im Zweiten Jahrhundert*, by Reinhard M. Hübner (with Markus Vinzent). *Journal of Theological Studies* 52, no. 1 (2001): 354–56.

———. Review of *Trinität und Kosmos: Zur Gotteslehre des Origenes*, by Christoph Brüns. *Journal of Ecclesiastical History* 66, no. 2 (April 2015): 390–91.

Evans, Ernest, ed. *Tertullian's Treatise against Praxeas: The Text Edited, with an Introduction, Translation, and Commentary*. London: S.P.C.K, 1948.

Feltoe, Charles L., trans. *The Letters and Other Remains of Dionysius of Alexandria*. Cambridge: Cambridge University Press, 1904.

Fernández, Samuel. "Arian or Monarchian Crisis in the Fourth Century? Reevaluating the Evidence towards the Next Centenary of Nicaea (325–2025)." Plenary lecture for the XVIII International Conference on Patristic Studies, Oxford, August 19–24, 2019.

———. "¿Crisis arriana o crisis monarquiana en el siglo IV? Las críticas de Marcelo de Ancira a Asterio de Capadocia." In *Studia Patristica LXVI*, edited by Markus Vinzent, 203–8. Leuven, Belgium: Peeters, 2013.

———. "La generación del Logos como solución al problema monarquiano, según Orígenes." In *Multifariam: Homenaje a los profesores Anneliese Meis, Antonio Bentué y Sergio Silva*, edited by Samuel Fernández, J. Noemi, and R.

Polanco, 193–229. Santiago, Chile: Pontificia Universidad Católica de Chile, 2010.

———. "Verso la teologia Trinitaria di Origene: Metafora e linguaggio teologico." In *Origeniana Decima: Origen as Writer*, edited by Sylwia Kaczmarek and Henryk Pietras, 457–73. Leuven, Belgium: Peeters, 2011.

———, ed. *Orígenes: Sobre los principios* (Madrid: Editorial Ciudad Nueva, 2015)

Festugière, André-Jean. *La Révélation d'Hermès Trismégiste IV: Le Dieu inconnu et la gnose*. Paris: Lecoffre, 1944.

Franks, Christopher A. "The Simplicity of the Living God: Aquinas, Barth, and Some Philosophers." *Modern Theology* 21, no. 2 (2005): 275–300.

Gavrilyuk, Paul L. "Plotinus on Divine Simplicity." *Modern Theology* 35, no. 3 (2019): 442–51.

Gerson, Lloyd P. "From Plato's Good to Platonic God." *International Journal of the Platonic Tradition* 2, no. 2 (January 1, 2008): 93–112.

———. *God and Greek Philosophy: Studies in the Early History of Natural Theology*. London: Routledge, 1990.

Grant, Robert M. *Gods and the One God*. Philadelphia: Westminster John Knox Press, 1988.

Gwynn, David M. *The Eusebians: The Polemic of Athanasius of Alexandria and the Construction of the "Arian Controversy."* Oxford: Oxford University Press, 2007.

Hadot, Ilsetraut. *Arts libéraux et philosophie dans la pensée antique*. Paris: Études augustiniennes, 1984.

Hadot, Pierre. "Les divisions des parties de la philosophie dans l'Antiquité." *Museum Helveticum* 36, no. 4 (1979): 201–23.

Hägg, Henny Fiskå. *Clement of Alexandria and the Beginnings of Christian Apophaticism: Knowing the Unknowable*. Oxford: Oxford University Press, 2006.

Hanson, R. P. C. "Did Origen Apply the Word 'Homoousios' to the Son?" In *Épektasis: Mélanges patristiques offerts au cardinal Daniélou*, edited by C. Kannengiesser and J. Fontaine, 293–303. Paris: Beauchesne, 1975.

———. "Did Origen Teach That the Son Is *ek tēs ousias* of the Father?" In *Origeniana Quarta*, edited by Lothar Lies, 201–2. Innsbruck: Tyrolia, 1987.

———. *The Search for the Christian Doctrine of God: The Arian Controversy*, 318–381. Grand Rapids, MI: Baker Academic, 2006.

Harnack, Adolf von. *History of Dogma*. Translated by Neil Buchanan. Vol. 3. Boston: Little, Brown, 1907.

Hasker, William. *Metaphysics and the Tri-Personal God*. Oxford: Oxford University Press, 2013.

Heine, Ronald E. "Origen on the Christological Significance of Psalm 45 (44)." *Consensus* 23, no. 1 (1997): 21–37.

———. *Origen: Scholarship in the Service of the Church*. Oxford: Oxford University Press, 2010.

———. "Stoic Logic as Handmaid to Exegesis and Theology in Origen's Commentary on the Gospel of John." *Journal of Theological Studies* 44, no. 1 (1993): 90–117.

———. "The Christology of Callistus." *Journal of Theological Studies* 49, no. 1 (1998): 56–91.

———, ed. *Origen: Commentary on the Gospel According to John, Books 13–32*. Washington, DC: Catholic University of America Press, 1993.

———, trans. "The Christology of Callistus." *Journal of Theological Studies* 49, no. 1 (1998): 56–91.

———. *Origen: Homilies on Genesis and Exodus*. Washington, DC: Catholic University of America Press, 2002.

Hermanin de Reichenfeld, Giovanni. *The Spirit, the World and the Trinity: Origen's and Augustine's Understanding of the Gospel of John*. Leuven, Belgium: Brepols, 2021.

Hinlicky, Paul R. *Divine Simplicity: Christ the Crisis of Metaphysics*. Grand Rapids, MI: Baker Academic, 2016.

Holmes, Stephen R. "'Something Much Too Plain to Say': Towards a Defence of the Doctrine of Divine Simplicity." *Neue Zeitschrift für Systematische Theologie und Religionsphilosophie* 43, no. 1 (2008): 137–54.

Hübner, Reinhard M (with Markus Vinzent). *Der Paradox Eine: Antignostischer Monarchianismus im zweiten Jahrhundert*. Leiden: Brill, 1999.

Inwood, Brad. *Stoics Reader: Selected Writings and Testimonia*. Trans. Lloyd P. Gerson. Indianapolis: Hackett, 2008.

Ip, Pui Him. "'Arianism' *Ante-Litteram* in Origen's *Peri Archōn* 4.4.1." *Journal of Theological Studies* 72, no. 1 (2021): 247–78.

———. "Athenagoras of Athens and the Genesis of Divine Simplicity in Christian Theology." In *Studia Patristica C*, edited by Hugh A. G. Houghton, Megan L. Davies, and Markus Vinzent, 61–70. Leuven, Belgium: Peeters, 2020.

———. "Origen against Origen? The Paradoxical Legacy of Origen in Athanasius' Exegesis of Prov. 8.22 in Contra Arianos II." In *Perspectives on Origen in the History of His Reception*, edited by Alfons Fürst, 117–32. Adamantiana 21. Muenster: Aschendorff, 2021.

———. "Re-imagining Divine Simplicity in Trinitarian Theology." *International Journal of Systematic Theology* 18, no. 3 (2016): 274–89.

Jacobson, Howard. "A Philonic Rejection of Plato." *Mnemosyne* 57, no. 4 (January 1, 2004): 488.

Jenson, Robert W. *Systematic Theology: The Triune God.* 2 vols. Vol. 1. Oxford: Oxford University Press, 1997.

Kalvesmaki, Joel. "Formation of the Early Christian Theology of Arithmetic Number Symbolism in the Late Second and Early Third Century." PhD dissertation, Catholic University of America, Washington, DC, 2006.

———. *The Theology of Arithmetic: Number Symbolism in Platonism and Early Christianity.* Washington, DC: Harvard University Press, 2013.

Karamanolis, George E. *The Philosophy of Early Christianity.* London: Routledge, 2014.

King, Benjamin J. *Newman and the Alexandrian Fathers: Shaping Doctrine in Nineteenth-Century England.* Oxford: Oxford University Press, 2009.

Kinzig, Wolfram. Review of *Der Paradoxe Eine: Antignostischer Monarchianismus im Zweiten Jahrhundert*, by Reinhard M. Hübner (with Markus Vinzent). *Theologische Literaturzeitung* 131, no. 9 (2006): 1015–18.

Kleve, Knut. "Albinus on God and the One." *Symbolae Osloenses* 47, no. 1 (January 1, 1972): 66–69.

Koslicki, Kathrin. *The Structure of Objects.* Oxford: Oxford University Press, 2008.

Lamberton, Robert. *Homer the Theologian: Neoplatonist Allegorical Reading and the Growth of the Epic Tradition.* Berkeley: University of California Press, 1989.

Lampe, G.W.H., ed. *A Patristic Greek Lexicon.* Oxford: Clarendon, 1961.

Lashier, Jackson. "Irenaeus as Logos Theologian." *Vigiliae Christianae* 66, no. 4 (January 1, 2012): 341–61.

———. *Irenaeus on the Trinity.* Leiden: Brill, 2014.

Le Boulluec, Alain. *La notion d'hérésie dans la littérature grecque, IIe-IIIe siècles.* Vol. II: *Clément d'Alexandrie et Origène*. Paris: Études augustiniennes, 1985.

Lienhard, Joseph T. *Contra Marcellum: Marcellus of Ancyra and Fourth-Century Theology.* Washington, DC: Catholic University of America Press, 1999.

Logan, Alastair H. B. "Origen and Alexandrian Wisdom Christology." In *Origeniana Tertia*, edited by Richard Hanson and Henri Crouzel, 123–29. Rome: Edizione dell'Ateneo, 1985.

———. "Origen and the Development of Trinitarian Theology." In *Origeniana Quarta*, edited by Lothar Lies, 424–29. Innsbruck: Tyrolia, 1987.

Long, A. A., and D. N. Sedley, eds. *The Hellenistic Philosophers.* Vol. 1: *Translations of the Principal Sources with Philosophical Commentary.* Cambridge: Cambridge University Press, 1987.

Long, D. Stephen. *The Perfectly Simple Triune God: Aquinas and His Legacy.* Minneapolis: Fortress, 2016.

Louis, Pierre, and John Whittaker, trans., *Alcinoos: Enseignement des doctrines de Platon.* Paris: Belles Lettres, 1990.

Maas, Wilhelm. *Unveränderlichkeit Gottes: Zum Verhältnis von griech-philosophischer und christlicher Gotteslehre.* Munich: Ferdinand Schöningh, 1974.

Mansfeld, Jaap. "Compatible Alternatives: Middle Platonist Theology and the Xenophanes Reception." In *Knowledge of God in the Graeco-Roman World*, edited by R. van den Broek, Tjitze Baarda, and Jaap Mansfeld, 92–117. Leiden: Brill, 1988.

———. "Three Notes on Albinus." In *Studies in Later Greek Philosophy and Gnosticism*. London: Variorum Reprints, 1989.

Martens, Peter W. *Origen and Scripture: The Contours of the Exegetical Life*. Oxford: Oxford University Press, 2014.

Meinwald, Constance C. *Plato*. London: Routledge, 2016.

Morales, Xavier. "'Modalism'—Critical Assessment of a Modern Interpretative Paradigm." In *Studia Patristica* CXXIII, edited by Markus Vinzent, 217–47. Leuven, Belgium: Peeters, 2021.

Mortley, Raoul. "The Fundamentals of the Via Negativa." *American Journal of Philology* 103, no. 4 (1982): 429–39.

Mullins, R. T. "Simply Impossible: A Case against Divine Simplicity." *Journal of Reformed Theology* 7, no. 2 (January 1, 2013): 181–203.

Nautin, Pierre. *Lettres et écrivains chrétiens des IIe et IIIe siècles*. Collana patristica e del pensiero cristiano 2. Paris: Cerf, 1961.

———. *Origène: Sa vie et son oeuvre*. Paris: Beauchesne, 1977.

Neuschäfer, Bernhard. *Origenes als Philologe*. 2 vols. Basel: Reinhardt, 1987.

Newman, John Henry. *An Essay on the Development of Christian Doctrine*. 6th ed. Notre Dame, IN: University of Notre Dame Press, 1989.

———. *The Arians of the Fourth Century*. Edited by Rowan D. Williams. Notre Dame, IN: Gracewing, 2001.

Nikiprowetzky, V. "L'exégèse de Philon d'Alexandrie dans le *De gigantibus* et le *Quod Deus*." In *Two Treatises of Philo of Alexandria: A Commentary on De Gigantibus and Quod Deus Sit Immutabilis*, edited by David Winston and John M. Dillon, 5–75. Chico, CA: Scholars Press, 1983.

Orbe, Antonio. *Hacia la primera teología de la procesión del Verbo*. 2 vols. Rome: Aedes Universitatis Gregorianae, 1958.

———. "Origenes y los Monarquianos." *Gregorianum* 72, no. 1 (1991): 39–72.

Ortlund, Gavin. "Divine Simplicity in Historical Perspective: Resourcing a Contemporary Discussion." *International Journal of Systematic Theology* 16, no. 4 (2014): 436–53.

Osborn, Eric F. *The Emergence of Christian Theology*. Cambridge: Cambridge University Press, 1993.

———. *Irenaeus of Lyons*. Cambridge: Cambridge University Press, 2001.

Pannenberg, Wolfhart. "The Appropriation of the Philosophical Concept of God as a Dogmatic Problem of Early Christian Theology." In *Basic Questions in Theology*, vol. 2, 119–83. Minneapolis: Fortress, 1971.

———. *Systematic Theology*. Translated by Geoffrey W. Bromiley. Vol. 1. Grand Rapids, MI: Eerdmans, 2010.

Perrone, Lorenzo, ed. *Origenes: Die neuen Psalmenhomilien; Eine kritische Edition des Codex Monacensis Graecus 314*. Translated by Lorenzo Perrone. Berlin: Walter de Gruyter, 2015.

Platter, Jonathan M. *Divine Simplicity and the Triune Identity*. Berlin: Walter de Gruyter, 2021.

Radde-Gallwitz, Andrew. *Basil of Caesarea, Gregory of Nyssa, and the Transformation of Divine Simplicity*. Oxford: Oxford University Press, 2009.

———. "Gregory of Nyssa and Divine Simplicity: A Conceptualist Reading." *Modern Theology* 35, no. 3 (July 2019): 452–66.

Ramelli, Ilaria L. E. "Origen and the Platonic Tradition." *Religions* 8, no. 2 (February 2017): 1–20.

———. "Origen, Greek Philosophy, and the Birth of the Trinitarian Meaning of Hypostasis." *Harvard Theological Review* 105, no. 3 (2012): 302–50.

———. "Origen's Anti-Subordinationism and Its Heritage in the Nicene and Cappadocian Line." *Vigiliae Christianae* 65, no. 1 (2011): 21–49.

Riel, Gerd van. *Plato's Gods*. Farnham, UK: Ashgate, 2013.

Sagnard, François M. M. *La gnose Valentinienne et le témoignage de saint Irénée*. Études de philosophie médiévale 36. Paris, 1947.

Salles, Ricardo, ed. *God and Cosmos in Stoicism*. Oxford: Oxford University Press, 2009.

Scott, Alan. *Origen and the Life of the Stars: A History of an Idea*. Oxford: Oxford University Press, 1991.

Sedley, David. "Plato's Theology." In *The Oxford Handbook of Plato*, edited by Gail Fine. 2nd ed., 627–44. Oxford: Oxford University Press, 2019.

Sheridan, Mark. *Language for God in Patristic Tradition: Wrestling with Biblical Anthropomorphism*. Downers Grove, IL: InterVarsity Press, 2015.

Simonetti, Manlio. *La crisi ariana nel IV secolo*. Rome: Institutum Patristicum Augustinianum, 1975.

———. "The East after Origen." In *History of Theology*, vol. 1: *The Patristic Period*, edited by Angelo Di Berardino and Basil Studer OSB, translated by Matthew J. O'Connell, 192–204. Collegeville, MN: Michael Glazier, 1996.

———. *Studi sulla cristologia del II e III secolo*. Rome: Institutum Patristicum Augustinianum, 1993.

Slusser, Michael. "The Exegetical Roots of Trinitarian Theology." *Theological Studies* 29 (1988): 461–76.

———. Review of *Der Paradoxe Eine: Antignostischer Monarchianismus im Zweiten Jahrhundert*, by Reinhard M. Hübner (with Markus Vinzent). *Journal of Early Christian Studies* 9, no. 3 (2001): 407–8.

Stead, G. C. "Divine Simplicity as a Problem for Orthodoxy." In *The Making of Orthodoxy: Essays in Honour of Henry Chadwick*, edited by Rowan D. Williams, 255–69. Cambridge: Cambridge University Press, 1989.

———. *Divine Substance*. Oxford: Clarendon, 1977.

———. *Philosophy in Christian Antiquity*. Cambridge: Cambridge University Press, 1994.

Stroumsa, G. "The Incorporeality of God." *Religion* 13, no. 4 (1983): 345–58.

Thomassen, Einar. *The Spiritual Seed: The Church of the "Valentinians."* Leiden: Brill, 2008.

Tzamalikos, P. *Anaxagoras, Origen and Neoplatonism: The Legacy of Anaxagoras to Classical and Late Antiquity.* 2 vols. Arbeiten zur Kirchengeschichte 128. Berlin: Walter de Gruyter, 2016.

———. *Origen: Cosmology and Ontology of Time*. Leiden: Brill, 2006.

Vaggione, Richard Paul. *Eunomius of Cyzicus and the Nicene Revolution.* Oxford: Oxford University Press, 2001.

Vinzent, Markus. "From Zephyrinus to Damasus: What Did Roman Bishops Believe?" In *Studia Patristica LXIII*, vol. 11, 273–86. Leuven, Belgium: Peeters, 2013.

Waers, Stephen E. "Wisdom Christology and Monarchianism in Origen's Commentary on John." *Greek Orthodox Theological Review* 60, nos. 3–4 (2015): 93–113.

White, Michael J. "Stoic Natural Philosophy (Physics and Cosmology)." In *The Cambridge Companion to the Stoics*, edited by Brad Inwood, 124–52. Cambridge: Cambridge University Press, 1999.

White, Thomas Joseph. "Divine Simplicity and the Holy Trinity." *International Journal of Systematic Theology* 18, no. 1 (January 1, 2016): 66–93.

Wickham, Lionel R. "The Syntagmation of Aetius the Anomean." *Journal of Theological Studies* 19, no. 2 (October 1, 1968): 532–69.

Widdicombe, Peter. *The Fatherhood of God from Origen to Athanasius.* Oxford: Oxford University Press, 2001.

Williams, Rowan D. *Arius: Heresy and Tradition.* Revised edition. Grand Rapids, MI: Eerdmans, 2002.

———. "Christological Exegesis of Psalm 45." In *Meditations of the Heart: The Psalms in Early Christian Thought and Practice; Essays in Honour of Andrew Louth*, edited by A. Andreopoulos, Carol Harrison, and Augustine Casiday, 17–32. Turnhout, Belgium: Brepols, 2011.

———. "Damnosa Haereditas: Pamphilus' Apology and the Reputation of Origen." In *Logos: Festschrift für Luise Abramowski zum 8 Juli 1993*, edited by Christoph Markschies, Hanns Christof Brennecke, and Ernst Ludwig Grasmück, 151–69. Berlin: Walter de Gruyter, 1993.

———. "Newman's Arians and the Question of Method in Doctrinal History." In *Newman after a Hundred Years*, edited by I. T. Ker and Alan G. Hill, 263–85. Oxford: Clarendon, 1990.

———. "On Not Misreading Origen." *Modern Theology*, "Re-thinking Origen." Special issue, forthcoming, 2022.

Winston, David, and John M. Dillon, eds. *Two Treatises of Philo of Alexandria: A Commentary on De Gigantibus and Quod Deus Sit Immutabilis.* Chico, CA: Scholars Press, 1983.

Wolfson, Harry Austryn. *Philo: Foundations of Religious Philosophy in Judaism, Christianity, and Islam*. 2 vols. Cambridge, MA: Harvard University Press, 1962.

Zambon, Marco. “Middle Platonism.” In *A Companion to Ancient Philosophy*, edited by Mary Louise Gill and Pierre Pellegrin, 561–76. Oxford: Wiley-Blackwell, 2009.

SCRIPTURE INDEX

GENERAL INDEX

PUI HIM IP is tutorial course director and research associate at the Faraday Institute for Science and Religion, Cambridge, and affiliated lecturer in the Faculty of Divinity, University of Cambridge. He has taught patristics at the University of Oxford and King's College London, and science and religion at the University of Cambridge.

ROWAN WILLIAMS was the 104th Archbishop of Canterbury from 2002 to 2012. He became Master of Magdalene College at Cambridge University in 2013, retiring in 2020.

Milton Keynes UK
Ingram Content Group UK Ltd.
UKHW020049150824
446702UK00017B/196